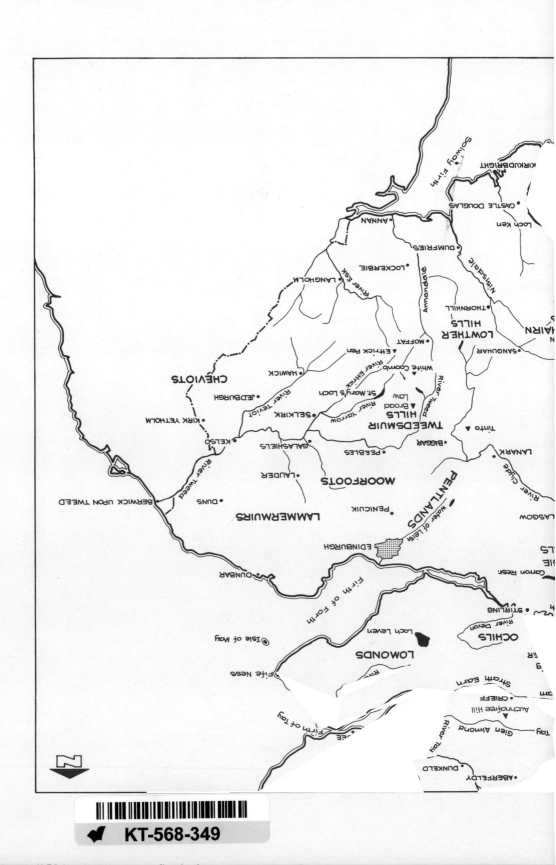

THE
CORBETTS
AND
OTHER SCOTTISH HILLS

SCOTTISH MOUNTAINEERING CLUB
HILLWALKERS GUIDE
VOLUME TWO

Edited by
Scott Johnstone
Hamish Brown
Donald Bennet

First published in Great Britain by the Scottish Mountaineering Trust in 1990

Copyright © by the Scottish Mountaineering Trust

British Library Cataloguing in Publication Data
The Corbetts and other Scottish hills.
　　1. Scotland. Hill walking
　　I. Johnstone, G. Scott (George Scott) *1922-*
　　II. Bennet, Donald J. (Donald John) *1928-*
　　III. Brown, Hamish M. *1934-*
　　796.522

　　ISBN 0-907521-29-0

Illustrations
　　　Front cover:　　Cranstackie　　　*H.M.Brown*
　　　Rear cover:　　The Cobbler　　*D.Scott*
　　　Title page:　　Suilven from Canisp　　　*A.O'Brien*
　　　Page opposite:　Approach to Streap　　*C.Townsend*

Maps drawn by Jim Renny
Book design by Donald Bennet
Production by Peter Hodgkiss
Typeset by Westec, North Connel
Colour separations and graphic work by Par Graphics, Kirkcaldy
Printed by Pillans and Wilson, Edinburgh
Bound by Hunter and Foulis, Edinburgh

Distributed by Cordee, 3a DeMontfort Street, Leicester, LE1 7HD

CONTENTS

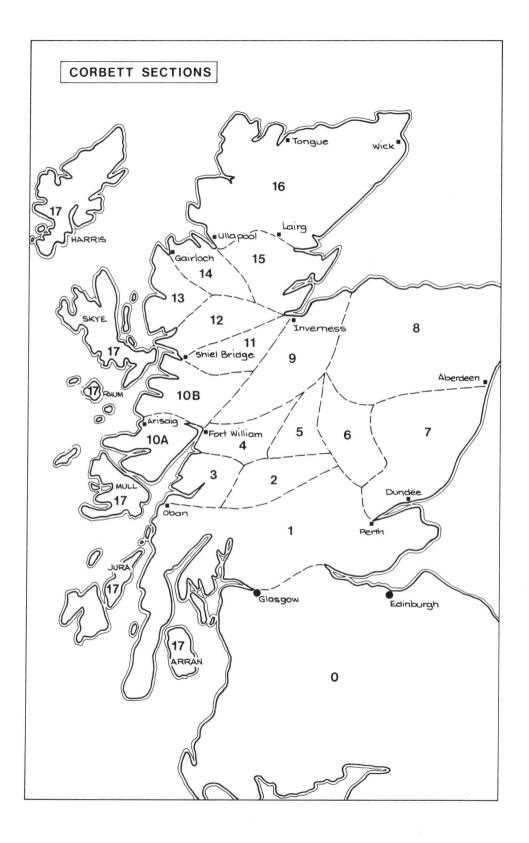

THE CLIMBER AND THE MOUNTAIN ENVIRONMENT

With increasing numbers of walkers and climbers going to the Scottish hills, it is important that all of us who do so should recognise our responsibilities to those who live and work among the hills and glens, to our fellow climbers and to the mountain environment in which we find our pleasure and recreation.

The Scottish Mountaineering Club and Trust, who jointly produce this and other guidebooks, wish to impress on all who avail themselves of the information in these books that it is essential at all times to consider the sporting and proprietory rights of landowners and farmers. The description of a climbing, walking or skiing route in any of these books does not imply that a right of way exists, and it is the responsibility of all climbers to ascertain the position before setting out. In cases of doubt it is always best to enquire locally.

During the stalking and shooting seasons in particular, much harm can be done in deer forests and on grouse moors by people walking through them. Normally the deer stalking season is from 1st July to 20th October, when stag shooting ends. Hinds may continue to be culled until 15th February. The grouse shooting season is from 12th August until 10th December. These are not merely sporting activities, but are essential for the economy of many Highland estates. During these seasons, therefore, especial care should be taken to consult the local landowner, factor or keeper before taking to the hills.

Climbers and hillwalkers are recommended to consult the book *HEADING FOR THE SCOTTISH HILLS*, published by the Scottish Mountaineering Trust on behalf of the Mountaineering Council of Scotland and the Scottish Landowners Federation, which gives the names and addresses of factors and keepers who may be contacted for information regarding access to the hills.

It is also important to avoid disturbance to sheep, particularly during the lambing season between March and May. Dogs should not be taken onto the hills at this time, and at all times should be kept under close control.

Always try to follow a path or track through cultivated land and forests, and avoid causing damage to fences, dykes and gates by climbing over them carelessly. Do not leave litter anywhere, but take it down from the hill in your rucksack.

The number of walkers and climbers on the hills is leading to increased, and in some cases very unsightly erosion of footpaths and hillsides. Some of the revenue from the sale of this and other SMC guidebooks is used by the Trust to assist financially the work being carried out to repair and maintain hill paths in Scotland. However, it is important for all of us to recognise our responsibility to minimise the erosive effect of our passage over the hills so that the enjoyment of future climbers shall not be spoiled by landscape damage caused by ourselves.

As a general rule, where a path exists walkers should follow it and even where it is wet and muddy should avoid walking along its edges, the effect of which is to extend erosion sideways. Do not take short-cuts at the corners of zig-zag paths. Remember that the worst effects of erosion are likely to be caused during or soon after prolonged wet weather when the ground is soft and waterlogged. A route on a stony or rocky hillside is likely to cause less erosion than on a grassy one at such times.

The proliferation of cairns on the hills detracts from the feeling of wildness, and may be confusing rather than helpful as regards route-finding. The indiscriminate building of cairns on the hills is therefore to be discouraged.

Climbers are reminded that they should not drive along private estate roads without permission, and when parking their cars should avoid blocking access to private roads and land, and should avoid causing any hazard to other road users.

Finally, the Scottish Mountaineering Club and the Scottish Mountaineering Trust can accept no liability for damage to property nor for personal injury resulting from the use of any route described in their publications.

The Scottish Mountaineering Trust will donate £1 from the proceeds of the sale of each copy of this guidebook to grant aid for repair and maintenance of mountain footpaths in Scotland.

Two Torridonian Corbetts, Beinn Damh (left) and An Ruadh-stac (right) with Maol Chean-dearg between them   *M. Moran*

INTRODUCTION

Although the publication of this guidebook will inevitably change this situation, there can be little doubt that at the time of writing the name Corbett is not nearly as well known among those who climb the Scottish hills and mountains as is the name Munro. John Rooke Corbett was a district valuer based in Bristol and a keen member of the Scottish Mountaineering Club in the years between the two World Wars. He was a distinguished student at Cambridge University and an original member of the Rucksack Club. Corbett was a regular attender at SMC meets, a committee member and joint editor of the second edition of the *Northern Highlands* guidebook. He completed the Munros and Tops in 1930, only the second person to do so, and more remarkably he climbed all Scotland's 2000ft hills.

Out of this extensive experience and knowledge came Corbett's eponymous tables in which he listed all those hills of height between 2500ft (762m) and 3000ft (914.4m) with a drop of at least 500ft (152.4m) between each listed hill and any adjacent higher one. In this way the separation between the Corbetts is more clearly defined than is the case with the Munros, and the fairly large height drop between Corbetts ensures that they are quite distinct hills, unlike the Munros where the criterion for separation does not involve a rigidly fixed drop between adjacent summits. When Corbett died, his list was passed to the SMC by his sister. As has been the case with the Munros, the list of Corbetts has changed over the years as a result of changes in hill heights measured by the Ordnance Survey. The present list differs from the original one by 19 additions and 15 deletions, and contains 221 Corbetts.

Corbett's list, along with Percy Donald's list of 2000ft hills in Southern Scotland, has been added to Munro's tables to create the book which we have at present. The current (1984) edition of *Munro's Tables* contains an anomaly in that the geographical boundaries between the sections of the list of Munros on the one hand and the list of Corbetts on the other are not the same. This anomaly will be removed, and in the next edition of *Munro's Tables* the Corbetts will be listed in the same geographical areas as the Munros. This change is incorporated in this Corbetts guidebook, and one additional section has been introduced, namely Section 0 - Galloway and the Borders - which does not feature in the list of the Munros. In addition, a new sub-section has been introduced in this book: Section 10A for Morvern, Sunart, Ardgour and Moidart, an area of the Western Highlands which has no Munros and which, if added to the existing Section 10, would cover a disproportionately large area of the Highlands. The area of Section 10 of the Munros becomes Section 10B in this book.

The geographical division between Sections 5 and 6 goes through the Gaick Pass between the neighbouring hills of An Dun and Maol Creag an Loch, which can most logically be climbed together. These two hills are described together in Section 6.

The gateway to Ardgour, looking across Loch Linnhe at Corran ferry   *D.J. Bennet*

There remains the problem of Corrieyairick Hill and Gairbeinn, both 896m high, but the drop between them is less than the required 152.4m. Evidently they should not both be regarded as Corbetts, but no one (not even the Ordnance Survey) seems to know which is the higher, so both are included.

So much for the quantitative aspects of the Corbetts and Corbett's tables. Let us turn now to the qualitative aspects of these hills. Corbetts's list includes so many fine and favourite hills that any hillwalker with much experience of the Highlands and Islands is certain to have climbed many of them, even if he has not set out systematically to climb all the Corbetts. The Munros may well form the mountain heartland of most of the Highlands, but the lower Corbetts have their place in the geography of our hills. In some areas, for example the Cairngorms, they are the outliers of the main mountains; in others they fill the gaps between them; thirdly (and most impressively) they are the principal peaks in those parts of the Highlands where there are few if any Munros.

Any hillwalker who, with somewhat blinkered vision, concentrates his (or her) efforts entirely on the Munros will be in danger of missing many of the best of Scottish mountains. Height alone is no criterion and there are in the ranks of the Corbetts many peaks of great character, interest and beauty that are the equal of all but a few Munros. The dedicated Munroist will in his travels acquire a detailed knowledge of many parts of the Highlands, but not all. There will be gaps in his knowledge which an exploration of the Corbetts will fill, and this provides another very good reason for climbing these hills. Many a remote and unfrequented Corbett commands from its summit views into equally remote and unknown corners of the Highlands. This exploration can and should be extended still further by climbing the lower hills which are included in this book, hills chosen for inclusion by reason of their character and interest.

It would be wrong to think of the Corbetts as lesser hills, giving shorter and easier expeditions than the Munros. Many of them, particularly those which rise from near sea-level in the Western and Northern Highlands and the islands and some of the remote hills of the Grampians, give climbs that are long and demanding. Baosbheinn, Beinn Dearg Mhor and Foinaven are just three examples of Corbetts whose traverses are major hillwalking days. The separateness of the Corbetts resulting from the 500ft drop criterion means that there are few instances where three or four or more can be combined in long traverses such as are possible with the Munros. There is only one example in this book where a traverse of more than three Corbetts is described.

In no part of the mainland do the Corbetts contribute more to the mountainous character of the land than in the Western and Northern Highlands. In Ardgour and Moidart, for example, where there are no Munros, peaks such as Garbh Bheinn, Sgurr Dhomhnuill, Sgurr Ghiubhsachain and Rois-Bheinn dominate the wild landscape. Just to their north, Streap, Sgurr na h-Aide and Ben Aden yield nothing except a few metres of height to the big peaks of western Lochaber and Knoydart

In Applecross, Coulin and Torridon the Corbetts may be rather overshadowed by the three great mountains - Beinn Alligin, Liathach and Beinn Eighe, but Beinn Bhan, Fuar Tholl, Beinn Dearg and Baosbheinn

Leum Uilleim from Loch Ossian   *H.M. Brown*

are splendid peaks which exhibit as well as their big-ger neighbours the classic features of Torridonian mountain architecture. Beinn Lair to the north of Loch Maree has on its north face an array of buttresses and gullies almost equal to the two greatest mountain cliffs in Scotland - the north face of Ben Nevis and Sron na Ciche in Skye. In the far north-west the Corbetts are the dominant mountains. Cul Mor, Quinag, Foinaven and Ben Loyal are just a few of the very fine peaks in that area, which also includes some of the best of the 'lower hills' - Ben Mor Coigach, Stac Pollaidh and Suilven.

The Corbetts also contribute much to the mountain scenery of the islands. Arran, Jura, Rhum and Harris owe their mountainous character to a few Corbetts and many more lower hills of outstanding interest. The ridges of Arran and Rhum, although not on the same scale as the Black Cuillin of Skye, have a distinc-tive quality that fully compensates for their smaller scale. Surprisingly, Skye has only two Corbetts, but some of its lower hills give superb high-level walks. Most of the larger islands of the Outer Hebrides have their hills, some of them of very modest height. How-ever, the quality of an island hill is not judged by its height, rather by its situation bounded by the limitless horizons of the sea.

In the southern part of Scotland the Corbetts are the highest hills in Galloway and the Borders. Merrick, Corserine, White Coomb and Broad Law may overtop their neighbours, but there are other hills such as Tinto, the Eildon Hills and the Pentlands that inspire great affection among hillwalkers in that part of the country.

In the Southern Highlands there are many fine hills

in the list of Corbetts, but none can match The Cobbler. The outline of its three rocky peaks makes it one of the best-known mountains of the Highlands, and it is cer-tainly one of the most frequently climbed. Nearby in the Arrochar Alps there are two or three other fine little mountains such as The Brack and Beinn an Lochain (once a Munro). Further east Ben Ledi is one of the most distinctive outposts of the Highlands.

Going further north into the Central Highlands, the Corbetts are a less distinctive part of the landscape. There are some good ones on both sides of Glen Etive and in Appin, but in Lochaber and Badenoch, which may be considered to be the heart of the Highlands, there are no Corbetts of particular interest. To the east, in the Grampians, Ben Vrackie is a well-known and prominent hill. Elsewhere the Corbetts form part of the vast undulating plateau that is characteristic of the country that stretches north-east from Blair Atholl to-wards Braemar, and in Deeside and around the Cairngorms they form a discontinuous ring of outly-ing hills among which Morven and Ben Rinnes are especially prominent.

The layout of this book will be familiar to those who know *The Munros*, the first guide in this two-volume series. The scope and purpose are the same, namely to provide a concise and practical guide in which each article describes a natural day's expedition which may be either a single Corbett or the traverse of two or three. Most routes are described as starting and finish-ing at convenient points on public roads as it is recognised that most hillwalkers use cars to reach their chosen hills. However, this should not be inter-preted as a discouragement to bothy- and tent-based exploration, which brings its greater rewards. The

Looking towards the Luss hills (left) and Loch Long from Beinn Narnain   G.S. Johnstone

length and difficulty of each day may vary considerably, and as noted above the Corbetts should not be regarded as 'lesser Munros'. Some of the days described in this book are quite long, but they have been chosen as providing routes which may be the easiest or the natural choice, or following well-defined natural features or paths, or being of particular scenic interest. Many variations and alternatives may exist, but lack of space precludes a complete description of them.

The descriptions apply to summer ascents, but most of them can be applied in winter as well, bearing in mind the hazards of snow and ice, the shorter hours of daylight and the need for additional equipment. In winter, however, some of the routes described may become quite intimidating and dangerous, and the Torridonian peaks in particular present difficulties which may be beyond the competence of some hillwalkers. To keep within one's capabilities is the basic principle of safe winter hillwalking in Scotland.

The maps in this book are intended to illustrate the text and serve as aids to route planning. They cannot take the place of a proper map in the field. The recommended maps for hillwalking are the Ordnance Survey's Second Series Landranger 1:50,000 maps. It is worthwhile ensuring that one uses these most up-to-date maps, as they show features such as recently planted forests and bulldozed tracks which may not appear on earlier ones. Hill heights quoted in this book are taken from the Second Series 1:50,000 maps except in a few cases where 1:25,000 maps are used for greater accuracy.

In the text, to distinguish between heights and distances, the abbreviation m (eg 150m) is used to denote a height, and the word metre (eg 200 metres) is used to denote a distance. Distances and heights are rounded up to the nearest ½km and 10m respectively, and times for ascents are calculated on the basis of 4½km per hour for distance walked, plus 10m per minute for climbing uphill. Times are rounded up to the nearest 10 minutes, but no allowance is made for stops nor the extra time required by rough or difficult ground. (The above times are a close metric approximation to Naismith's time-honoured formula). Times quoted are for ascents only, so extra must be added for stops and the descent. Where two or more hills are traversed in succession, the times at each summit are cumulative from the day's starting point.

A useful publication for those dependent on public transport in the Highlands is the booklet *Getting Around the Highlands and Islands*, published by the Highlands and Islands Development Board. This booklet lists all bus, train, ferry and air services in the Highlands. The Post Office also publishes a useful timetable of Postbus services in the Highlands.

In order to distinguish between the Corbetts and the Lower Hills, the latter are denoted by asterisks in the contents list at the beginning of each section, and are also listed separately in the Index.

There are a few instances where the names of Corbetts are either non-existent or unsatisfactory on the Ordnance Survey maps. In an attempt to remedy this, the editors have introduced names which are appropriate and which in due course may come to be accepted. The following examples may be mentioned:-

1. The high ridge on the north side of Glen Kinglas in the Arrochar Alps has the name Binnein an

On the north side of Beinn Eighe, Meall a'Ghiubhais (left) and Ruadh-stac Beag (right)   *D. Rubens*

Fhidhleir given to its 811m west top, but no name for its 817m highest point 1½km to the east. The name Stob Coire Creagach is proposed for this point, Coire Creagach being the corrie to its north-east overlooking upper Glen Kinglas.

2. The highest point of the hill on the south side of Loch Voil is un-named, although it has the trig point (771m). Apparently it is known locally as the surveyors' peak, and is given the name Stob Fear-tomhais which is the Gaelic translation of this.

3. The flat-topped hill to the east of Loch an Duin at the Gaick Pass does not appear to have a name, although the craggy hillside above the loch is called Creag an Loch. The name Maol Creag an Loch is proposed for the hill itself.

4. At the head of the Cona Glen in north Ardgour the 770m Corbett hitherto called Druim Tarsuinn may not be correctly named. The name Druim Tarsuinn probably refers to the ridge extending north-west beyond the Bealach an Sgriodain. The Corbett might be more correctly referred to as the west peak of Meall Mor, but this is also doubtful. No local explanation has been found, and the name Stob a'Bhealach an Sgriodain has been proposed for the Corbett in view of its proximity to the pass of that name.

Finally, one other change in name may be noted. At the head of Glen Dessarry the prominent pointed peak is called Sgurr na h-Aide on the 1:50,000 map, a name which has hitherto been assumed to apply to the whole hill. However, the latest 1:25,000 map shows this name as applying to the lower west top with the higher east top called Bidean a'Chabair, and this name is now used to refer to the Corbett.

The Merrick hills from Craignaw   P. McCracken

SECTION 0

Galloway and the Borders

Shalloch on Minnoch from Craiglee   I. Brown

Shalloch on Minnoch; 768m; (OS Sheet 77; 405907)

Shalloch on Minnoch and Kirriereoch Hill (which was formerly also a Corbett) form part of the range of hills which lies east of the hilly road between Straiton and Bargrennan in the Galloway Forest Park. This road reaches 433m at its highest point to the north-west of Shalloch on Minnoch and this makes a tempting starting point, but if both hills are to be combined it is better to leave a car at the Bell Memorial car park just north of the junction of the roads from Barr and Straiton at (353907). Extensive forests cover the western slopes of these hills.

From the car park follow the burn down to Laglanny to join a forest road to the derelict farm of Shalloch on Minnoch, WSW of the hill of the same name. Continue up the Shalloch Burn, which can be crossed on girders about 500 metres beyond the farm. Follow a fire-break slanting up a tributary burn which leads out of the forest to the grassy W ridge of Shalloch on Minnoch. (6km; 530m; 2h 20min).

Leave the summit in a SE direction and descend SSE to the Nick of Carclach and climb to Tarfessock (696m). A long ill-defined ridge continues SSE, pitted with lochans and decorated with dark grey and pinkish outcrops and light grey erratics. After crossing a fence, steep uphill work on grass and scree leads to Kirriereoch Hill (786m). The small summit cairn is 150 metres S of a ruined wall.

Merrick is 2km S, but is better left for another day as most walkers will find the route back from Kirriereoch Hill long enough. This descends the

W ridge along the wall, a turning NW towards a conspicuous fire-break by the Pillow Burn leading down through the forest. Alternatively, go up the Cross Burn for 200 metres to a wigwam-shaped bothy, cross the burn and take a path NW through the trees which soon joins a forest road going W about 400 metres N of the Pillow Burn. Both routes join up to pass between Kirriereoch farm and Kirriereoch Loch to reach the public road 4½km S of the starting point.

The Ministry of Defence has leased buildings at Shalloch on Minnoch and Kirriemore, and holds frequent military exercises in the Galloway Forest Park. Despite official assurances that walkers will not be turned back from the hills, this has occasionally happened. If you are stopped, you may wish to point out this assurance.

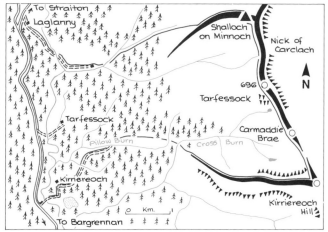

Corserine from Dungeon Hill   *J. Cleare/Mountain Camera*

Corserine; 814m; (OS Sheet 77; 498871)

Corserine is the central and highest point of a long, high, curving ridge which runs in a southerly direction from Loch Doon to Clatteringshaws Loch. The southern half of the range is known as the Rhinns of Kells, and the whole ridge has come to be known as the Kells Range.

The traverse of the whole 13km long ridge is a fine expedition as it seldom falls below 600m and gives excellent views. However the traverse ends a long way from the start, so some suitable transport arrangement is necessary. A public road along the W bank of Loch Doon ends at Craigmalloch, but cars are permitted to the bridge over the Carrick Lane and possibly as far as the Gala Lane at the S end of the loch. Access to the Kells Range from there is along a forest road on the E side of Loch Doon and Gala Lane, with fire-breaks leading E to the hills from it.

The first of the higher hills is Coran of Portmark (622m). From there the ridge runs S over Bow (611m), Meaul (698m) and Carlin's Craig (807m) to Corserine at the meeting of four ridges. A longish descent follows, then up over Millfire (716m) and Milldown (734m) to Meikle Millyea (746m). From there the ridge drops W of S over Little Millyea and Darrou to a forest road on the N side of the River Dee which leads down to the A712 road at Clatteringshaws Loch. A bridge over the river leads to Craigencallie which can be reached by car from the A712.

The shortest ascent of Corserine is from the E by a road which leaves the A713 at Polharrow Bridge and goes to a car park near Forest Lodge. From there follow the road along the S side of the Polharrow Burn past Fore Bush and along the S side of Loch Harrow. Continue by a forest ride to the foot of a break at the W end of the loch which goes up through the trees and leads onto North Gairy Top. A gradual ascent along a long ridge leads to the trig point on the expansive grassy summit of Corserine. (6km; 690m; 2h 30min).

The return can be made along the ridge to the SSE over Millfire and Milldown to Meikle Millyea. From there descend the NE ridge, turning E to reach the lower slopes. Continue E along the edge of the forest to a stile and fire-break leading N for about 300 metres to reach the forest road past Burnhead back to the car park.

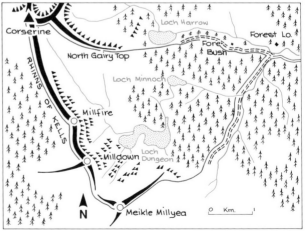

Merrick from the south-east   R.D.Walton

Merrick; 843m; (OS Sheet 77; 428855)

The Merrick is the highest point of the range containing Shalloch on Minnoch and Kirriereoch Hill, and it is also the highest hill in the Southern Uplands.

The quickest and easiest route to the hill is also one of the finest, and starts from the end of the public road in Glen Trool at the upper of two car parks. A well-used path goes from there up the W bank of the Buchan Burn, with grand views of its cataracts and over the oakwoods and conifers fringing Loch Trool to the surrounding hills. The path starts above the burn but joins it where it leaves its hanging valley. It then swings away higher and enters the forest with an alternative route descending around the forest to the burn again. Both routes meet at Culsharg bothy (415821). A path leads NW from there through the forest, then N to a wall running to the top of Benyellary (719m).

Continue along the wall in a N then NE direction to a col. When the slope broadens out leave the wall and ascend the grassy hillside by the path. The upper slopes leading to the summit of Merrick are studded with granite boulders left by the Ice Ages. (6km; 770m; 2h 40min). On a clear day it is possible to see the Scottish Highlands, Ireland's Mourne Mountains and England's Lake District.

An interesting return route descends E then SE to pass between Loch Enoch and the Buchan Burn. The rock face known as The Grey Man is nearby at (437846), while an island in Loch Enoch carries its own little loch. The Rig of Loch Enoch gives a good ridge-walk back SSE over Buchan Hill to Glen Trool.

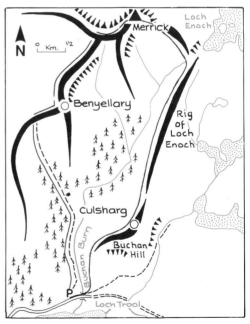

Lamachan Hill from Curleywee   *P. McCracken*

Lamachan Hill; 716m; (OS Sheet 77; 435770)

The high ground between Newton Stewart and the Loch Trool - Loch Dee gap is dominated by the ridge joining Larg Hill (675m), Lamachan Hill and Curleywee (674m). The A712 and A714 roads form rather distant boundaries to the east and west, converging towards Newton Stewart. Forestry plantations surround the range on all sides, making access difficult for those without up-to-date large scale maps.

The car park on the north side of Loch Trool at (416804) is a good starting point for traversing the three hills as the forests can be avoided from there. Walk down to Buchan and continue E along the dirt road. Just before Glenhead cross the Glenhead Burn by a bridge and go SE along the S bank of the burn between the forest and the boundary wall on part of the Southern Upland Way. Turn S along the Way up the Shiel Burn to a forest road and follow this towards Loch Dee. Near the summit of the road climb SE into the corrie and gain the N ridge of White Hill which leads SW to Curleywee. (2h 30min).

Steep slopes W of Curleywee lead down to the Nick of Curleywee and a rough ridge to Bennanbrack. From there turn SW again along grassy slopes to the summit of Lamachan Hill. (8km; 800m; 3h 20min). Larg Hill, which lies about 2km SW, can be included in the traverse, following a ruined fence down to the narrow col and a stone wall from there to the top. (4h

from the start).

It is necessary to return across the col and climb a short distance towards Lamachan Hill before contouring N to Cambrick Hill. From there the descent to Glen Trool goes down the Shiel Burn. The Southern Upland Way is reached just beyond the first ranks of trees in the Glentrool Forest.

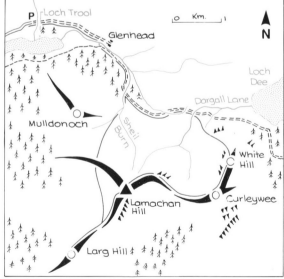

On the path to Cairnsmore of Fleet   *K.M. Andrew*

Cairnsmore of Fleet; 711m; (OS Sheet 83; 502671)

Cairnsmore of Fleet is a long ridge running in a north-west to south-east direction 9km east of Newton Stewart. The ridge is steep and bouldery on the east, but the granite bedrock is mostly hidden on the gently sloping grassy western face. The popular route to the hill uses an excellent and easily graded path up the west side.

To reach this route leave the A75 road 5km SE of Newton Stewart at Muirfad (457630). Follow the side road to the E to a three-way junction under the former railway viaduct. Take the middle road through the centre of the viaduct into Cairnsmore Estate. Cars are allowed along the estate road for about 1½km. Ignore a branch road going left to Cairnsmore House, then go left around estate buildings and left again to a parking area by a track leading into a field (472641).

Cross the field diagonally, going NE, and go through another gate and over a stile into Glenure Forest. The path is easily followed as it climbs steadily through the trees and onto the moors N of Crammery Hill. It continues NE up the open slopes and then turns N along the ridge to the summit cairn,

passing a memorial to the many airmen killed on this hill in several crashes.

The south top is 2km away, and is easily reached in 30 minutes along the fairly level and generally firm grassy ridge. By retracing your steps for 1km, an easy horizontal traverse leads back to the path for the descent.

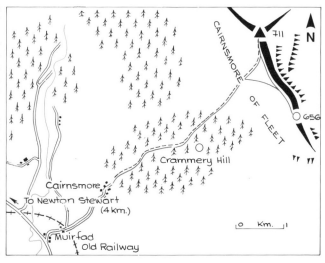

Criffel from Caerlaverock in the Nith estuary   *I. Brown*

Criffel; 569m; (OS Sheet 84; 957619)

Criffel is an isolated granite hill rising to the north of the Solway Firth on the west side of the estuary of the River Nith. It lies 4km south of New Abbey, and is bounded on the east and south by the A710 road from New Abbey to Southwick. On the west side of Criffel there are a few lesser ridges, but that side of the hill has little attraction for walkers as the approaches are long and tedious through coarse grass, heather and forests. Forestry developments have added to the defences on the north side of Criffel also, so the east side of the hill offers the best line of approach.

Start at Ardwall 1km W of the A710 road, where cars can be left just before the farm (971635). The route to Criffel is signposted and goes through a gate heading SSE for 100 metres, then turns WSW to another gate leading into the forest which cloaks the E side of the hill.

A well-marked path leads directly up a fire-break on the S side of the burn which flows down to Loch Kindar. This route is taken to a stile above the forest from where the path turns more towards the S and heads straight up to the large summit cairn which is associated with the Earl of Douglas. (3km; 530m; 1h 40min).

Before descending, the N ridge can be followed for 1½km to Knockendoch for a good view of New Abbey to add to the summit views which on a good day include the Isle of Man and the Lake District hills as well as the expanse of the Solway Firth.

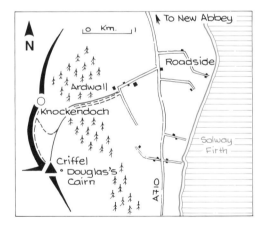

Cairnsmore of Carsphairn from Craiglee   I. Brown

Cairnsmore of Carsphairn; 797m; (OS Sheet 77; 594980)

Cairnsmore of Carsphairn lies 6km north-east of the village of Carsphairn, which is the mid-point of the A713 road between Ayr and Castle Douglas. The B729 road from Carsphairn to Moniaive crosses south of the hill and sends off a minor branch road north up the Water of Ken. Approaches to the hill can be made from from Craigengillan on this minor road, Knockgray on the B729 or Green Well of Scotland on the A713.

The approach from Green Well of Scotland is very direct and easy along a vehicular track starting just E of the A713 bridge over the Water of Deugh. Follow this track through a gate by the roadside bungalow and NE up the Deugh past a large cattle shed. After the Benloch Burn the track climbs across the W slopes of Willieanna and Dunool to a stone wall on the lip of a corrie with Dunool (541m), Black Shoulder (688m) and Cairnsmore of Carsphairn forming the high points of its boundary ridge. The stone wall is followed across the Polsue Burn and NE up the steepening slope which leads directly to the Cairnsmore. A trig point stands at the top of the wall only a few metres from the large summit cairn. (5½km; 600m; 2h 20min).

To descend along the ridge follow the high ground S to Black Shoulder, just over 1km from Cairnsmore. Continue down alongside a wall to a little lochan to the SW, then go over Dunool and Willieanna. The track back to Green Well can be regained on the W side of either of these hills.

The approach from Knockgray follows a shorter track which leaves a boggy stretch of ground at the head of the valley to be crossed.

Craigengillan is the start of another track into the hills, but Beninner (710m) has to be crossed on this route with a 40m loss of height before the SE ridge of Cairnsmore is reached.

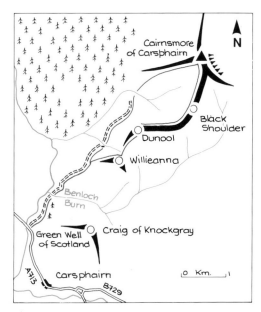

The Hart Fell hills above Moffat   G.S. Johnstone

Hart Fell; 808m; (OS Sheet 78; 113135)

The hills between Moffat and the Talla Reservoir are mostly steep-sided and rounded on top. So far they are relatively free from forestry. The walking is mostly over grass with wet ground in the valleys. It is sheep country, and the fences along the crests of most of the ridges are invaluable aids to navigation in bad weather, especially where changes in direction occur at strategic points.   Hart Fell has the advantage over its neighbours of fine views over Annandale and Nithsdale to the Solway Firth. The nearest starting point to Moffat for climbing the hill is at Moffat Well (092072), 2½km up the Birnock Water. The 8km long ridge from there over Greygill Head (474m) and Swatte Fell (728m) takes 3 hours, and has few advantages over the SW ridge above Hartfell Spa.

That route starts from a parking place 6km up the Ericstane road, at the pedestrian signpost to Hartfell Spa (076104). It is worth following the path to the spa which is a spring within a beehive-shaped shelter set in a highly eroded gully. Above it the ridge is gained by a steep scramble, and leads with fine views to the top. (5km; 640m; 2h 20min).

In good weather it is well worth continuing NW across a deep col to Whitehope Knowe and round the headwaters of the River Annan, crossing Chalk Rig Edge and Great Hill to reach the Devil's Beef Tub. From there a well-marked path descends to Corehead and thence back via Ericstane to the car in 2 hours from the top.

Another way up Hart Fell is from Capplegill (144097) on the Moffat Water. This route starts up the very steep grass slope on the NW side of the A708 road and then follows the edge of the cliffs above the Blackhope Burn, again with fine views.

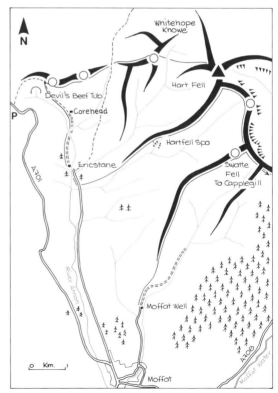

White Coomb from Loch Skeen   *J. Cleare/Mountain Camera*

White Coomb; 822m; (OS Sheet 79; 163151)

White Coomb lies near the middle of the eastern side of the highly dissected upland area between Peebles and Moffat. It has the same rounded character as all the neighbouring hills, but its northern slope falls away in crags above the Midlaw Burn and Loch Skeen. The extensive summit views range from the Eildon Hills to Criffel, the Solway Firth and a silhouette of the high Cumbrian fells.

The most direct route to the hill starts from the National Trust for Scotland car park below the Grey Mare's Tail waterfall on the A708 road. The first view of the hill is from the top of the falls where the footpath levels off. If the stream can be crossed there, one can follow the remains of a wall straight up to Upper Tarnberry. This wall avoids the peat and continues to the summit with only a short break at a rock outcrop near the top; there is a small path beside it for most of the way, but it misses the summit cairn by about 100 metres where it takes a sharp turn to the WNW. (2km; 610m; 1h 40min).

Another route from the same starting point is to continue up the footpath beside the Tail Burn above the Grey Mare's Tail nearly to Loch Skeen. Cross the burn where two streams meet and aim across the peat for the lower slopes of the E shoulder of White Coomb.

The suggested descent is W then N along the high ground over Firthhope Rig (801m) and Donald's Cleugh Head, then down E along the spur on the SW side of Loch Skeen to rejoin the path down the Tail Burn.

A different approach to White Coomb is from the Megget Stone (OS Sheet 72; 151203) on the minor road from Tweedsmuir to St. Mary's Loch. This takes 4 hours and includes

the tops of Nickies Knowe (760m), Lochcraig Head (800m) and Firthhope Rig, returning by Molls Cleugh Dod (784m). If Great Hill (774m) is also included in this round, it takes in five tops over 2500ft. In mist it is comforting to know that there is a fence or wall along all the crests, and a wall from Lochcraig Head to Firthybrig Head.

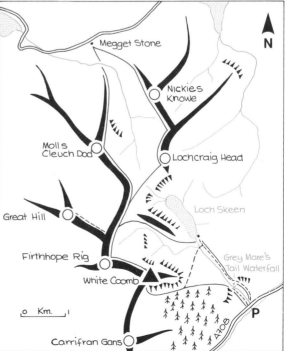

Broad Law from the Tweed valley   *H.M. Brown*

Broad Law; 840m; (OS Sheet 72; 146235).

This Corbett lies in the heart of the hills between Peebles and Moffat. In general they are all rounded, grassy and highly dissected into ridges and spurs so that walking along their crests is dry, with good views.

The usual starting point for the ascent of Broad Law is the Megget Stone (151203) at the highest point of the minor road from Tweedsmuir in the Tweed Valley to St. Mary's Loch. A fence leads up the crest of the broad ridge over the minor humps of Fans Law and Cairn Law to the long gentle rise to Broad Law. The wide crest of the hills continues NE to Cramalt Craig and from there to Dollar Law which overlooks the head of the Manor Valley.

An alternative route of ascent is from Peebles up the Manor Valley to Manorhead farm, from where a steep ridge leads up to Dun Law. From there the way continues over Cramalt Craig to Broad Law. If Dollar Law is included in the return, 4 hours will be needed for the round trip.

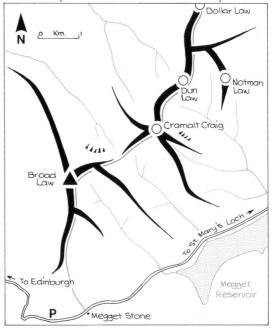

The Lowther Hills from Daer Water   H.M. Brown

Lowther Hill; 725m; (OS Sheet 78; 890107)
Green Lowther; 732m; (OS Sheet 78; 091121)

The Lowther Hills are a group of rolling Border hills stretching south-east from the old lead-mining village of Wanlockhead which, at a height of 468m, claims to be the highest village in Scotland. The hills straddle the Dalveen Pass and extend 15km to Queensberry over a succession of rounded 600m tops. The two highest hills of the group, Green Lowther and Lowther Hill, are perhaps the least scenically attractive because of the large radar installations on their summits, but for all that they form a dominant pair with a long high-level ridge connecting them. To the south-west of Lowther Hill is the deep valley of the Enterkin Pass (533m), a historic and formerly important route through the hills which is now a right of way.

The easiest route up Lowther Hill is from Wanlockhead and is part of the Southern Upland Way. It starts from the road above the village Visitor Centre and is waymarked. Although it follows in part the road up to the summit installations, it is quite a pleasant walk. (2km; 260m; 1h).

For a more interesting route, however, follow the road uphill to the point where the Enterkin Pass path leaves it at a sharp bend (not very obvious), and follow this path S to the col at the head of the pass. Then climb to the summit of East Mount Lowther, curiously named as it is to the SW of Lowther Hill. (3½km; 160m; 1h 10min). A mountain indicator covers an impressive panorama from the Lake District to the Highlands, with Lowther Hill itself appearing very fine.

Return to the col and climb up towards Lowther Hill, whose actual summit is defended by a perimeter fence and a "NO ENTRY" sign. (5½km; 350m;

1h 50min). Go clockwise round the fence to join the continuation of the road which leads NE along the ridge to Green Lowther, 1½km distant. Despite the tarmac, this is a pleasant walk. (7km; 390m; 2h 10min).

Continued progress NE along the ridge is possible, but it takes one further away from one's starting point, and the direct return is across trackless grouse moor, where walkers are not likely to be welcome. It is better, therefore, to return to Wanlockhead by Lowther Hill and the Southern Upland Way.

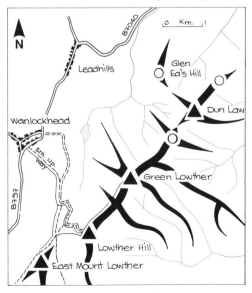

The Culter Hills from Culter Water   *D.J. Bennet*

Culter Fell; 748m; (OS Sheet 72; 052291)

The Culter Hills are bounded on the west by the A702 road and on the east by the A701. They are sprawling hills, gently rounded along their summits, but in many places steep-sided on their lower slopes and cut by deeply-etched valleys and streams. Culter Fell is the highest of this group.

From the map the natural ascent would seem to be from Culter Waterhead heading NE over Knock Hill. Sadly a bulldozed track up this route so disfigures the hillside that this way and the other possible one up Kings Beck starting lower down Culter Water cannot be recommended. The alternative ascent from the east, starting at Holms Waterhead, is to be preferred and has the added attraction that the summit is in view for virtually the whole ascent.

The road up the Holms Water from the A701 2km S of Broughton ends ½km beyond Glenkirk at a gate. From there tracks along the N side of the Holms Water can be followed to beyond Holms Waterhead where the right-hand track which climbs diagonally across the hillside ahead is followed. At a gate another right-hand track is followed, indistinct at first, W up Leishfoot Hill to the col between Moss Law and Culter Fell. From the col the boundary fence up the S ridge is followed to the summit of Culter Fell. (3km; 490m; 1h 30min).

From the summit there are various possibilities for the return to Glenkirk. One which gives a relatively short circuit is to continue N, then NE and on to Chapelgill Hill, whence descend SE to the valley. An alternative and much longer walk goes back S to Moss Law, SW across the head of the Holms Water to Coomb Hill, then NE to Glenlood Hill and finally NW down to the valley.

With their large populations of grouse and sheep, Culter Fell and its neighbouring hills should be avoided during the shooting and lambing seasons unless it is certain that no adverse effects will be caused.

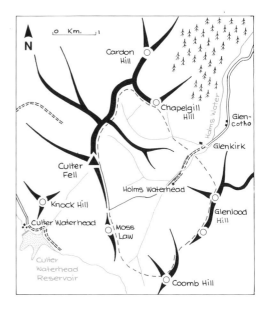

Tinto from Startup Hill above Lamington   *I. Brown*

Tinto; 707m; (OS Sheet 72; 953344)

Tinto is situated 10km south of Carstairs Junction and although strictly speaking it lies within the Midland Valley of Scotland, it is usually regarded as being the north-western outpost of the Border hills. It stands in complete isolation, with the River Clyde flowing round its base for many miles, and this makes Tinto the most prominent landmark in the upper reaches of the Clyde Valley, and also a splendid viewpoint in good weather.

The most popular ascent, although probably the least exciting, is from Fallburn to the NE of the hill, where there is a large car park. A broad track goes SW up the ridge of Totherin Hill to the summit which for some reason has one of the largest cairns on any Scottish hill. (5km; 460m; 1h 50min).

Another route starts to the E of the hill at a small parking space on the A73 road at (985353). The path is at first rather difficult to find, but it is quite obvious as one approaches the appropriately named Wee Hill. From there it leads SW then NW to Scaut Hill, before turning W to the summit of Tinto. (4km; 460m; 1h 40min).

A slightly more adventurous approach is from the S, starting at Millrig. A path goes up the W side of the West Burn and then zig-zags to the E of Pap Craig and over The Dimple to the summit. (3½km; 450m; 1h 30min). The ground is fairly steep, and care should be taken in mist if using this route as a means of descent.

It should be added that any traverse of Tinto combining two of the three routes described above

involves a walk of a few kilometres along the A73 road, which is usually busy with traffic.

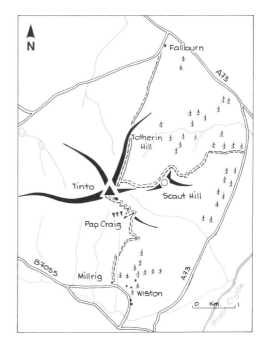

The Pentlands: Turnhouse Hill (left) to the Kips   W. Myles

The Pentland Hills: Scald Law; 579m; (OS Sheets 65 and 66; 192611)

The Pentlands are a well-rounded range of hills stretching from the southernmost suburbs of Edinburgh south-west to Carnwath. The best area for walking is in the northern half, and since no single hill constitutes an expedition by itself, the classic Pentland Round is described. It is possible to shorten this circular traverse at any one of a number of points, but unless suitable transport arrangements can be made, or the rather infrequent bus service along the A702 road used, it is necessary to return to the starting point on foot.

The classic round starts at Flotterstone (234631) where there is ample car parking. The road NW to Glencorse Reservoir is taken and after 400 metres a gate leads to a bridge which in turn leads by a rough track to the summit of Turnhouse Hill. To the S of this track is Rullion Green where the Covenanters were defeated by General Tam Dalyell in 1666.

A ridge leads SW to Carnethy Hill (576m) and so on to the highest of the Pentlands, Scald Law. Continuing the traverse over East and West Kip, a track is reached which crosses the Pentlands from south to north. Southwards this track leads to Nine Mile Burn, with its ancient hostelry, the Habbies' Howe Inn. Halfway down the track is the Font Stone, where even to this day infants are occasionally baptised. The area was at one time a monastic settlement where

the earliest coalmining is reputed to have taken place in Scotland. The track itself is of historic importance and was used in pre-Reformation times by monks carrying news from the religious centres in the

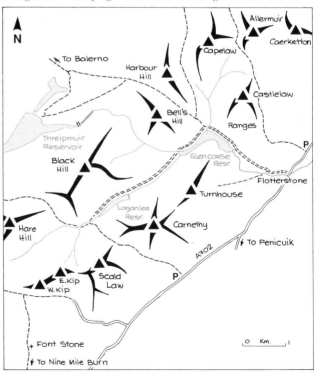

Borders such as Jedburgh and Melrose to those at Linlithgow and Stirling.

Following the track WNW, one comes to Hare Hill, and from there the circuit continues over a succession of grassy tops: Black Hill, Bell's Hill, Harbour Hill, Capelaw, Allermuir and finally Caerketton which is close to the artificial ski slopes at Lothianburn.

Finally, to descend, one can skirt to the S of Allermuir, go SW to Castlelaw, to the E of which a track leads to the A702 road ¾km N of the day's starting point. (24km; 1470m; 8h). On the S side of Castlelaw there is a military firing range, and red flags fly and sentries are posted when firing is in progress.

The Eildon Hills from Scott's View at Bemersyde　　　　　　　　*I. Brown*

The Eildon Hills; 422m; (OS Sheet 73; 548323)

Although of insignificant height and occupying an area of no more that two square kilometres, the Eildons are celebrated in song and verse as well as on canvas as are few other Scottish hills. They are situated immediately south of Melrose, and form three distinct peaks of roughly equal height which gives them a certain distinction over other Border hills.

They can be tackled from several points, but the most usual route starts in Melrose and goes S between the two northern hills. To save wear on the paths it is best to leave the track and make directly for the northern hill (404m) which boasts a fort dating from pre-historic times. A good path leads to the middle hill, the highest of the three. (There is a military firing range near the top of this hill, so if it is in use and red flags are flying, it is advisable to avoid the summit by following one of two paths lower down).

The continuation to the third of the Eildons (371m) goes S for 750 metres. This gives good views of the flat country to the S and E, and completes the round.

Although it can hardly be said that the Eildons are mountaineering hills, they are well worth a visit on a good day for the views to be had of the beautiful and historic Border landscape.

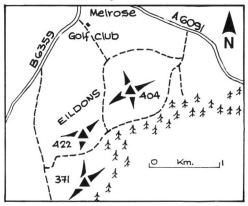

The Campsie Fells across Strath Blane   *D.J. Bennet*

SECTION 1

The Midland Valley to the River Tay

Dumgoyne from the east   *P. Hodgkiss*

Dumgoyne; 427m; (OS Sheet 64; 542827)
Earl's Seat; 578m; (OS Sheet 64; 570838)

The Campsie Fells are mostly a featureless expanse of high moorland giving rough walking across tussocky grass and boggy hollows. Earl's Seat is the highest point, but like much of the Campsies it is an unremarkable hill whose best feature is its northern escarpment which overlooks the Endrick valley. The most distinctive of the Campsies is Dumgoyne, an old volcanic plug standing in isolation from the rest of the plateau at its western end. Its distinctive position and shape make it the most popular of the Campsies for the hillwalker, and its ascent is probably the best short walk in these hills.

Start from the A81 road in Strath Blane at (540811) and walk up the private road past Craigbrock farm towards Cantywheery cottage. Just after crossing a bridge and before reaching this cottage (100 metres to its NW) go through a gate and follow a grassy track uphill towards a prominent little crag above Craigbrock Wood. Pass NW of this crag and reach the stream on the left. Cross the stream and a drystone dyke and contour WNW along sheep tracks below the rounded hill Dumfoyn. Cross another little stream and climb gradually up a sheep track across the S face of Dumgoyne below its crags to reach the SW shoulder. Finally turn NE and reach the top up an easy grass slope. By this route the crumbly crags on the S and E sides of Dumgoyne are avoided. (3km; 390m; 1h 20min).

The return to Strath Blane by the ascent route gives a very short day, barely an afternoon's stroll, and the walk can be readily extended to Earl's Seat if one wants more exercise. Descend NE from Dumgoyne down a short steep slope to a col at about 340m, and climb E onto the broad grassy ridge just N of the little knoll of Drumiekill Knowes. Continue NE along this

broad undulating ridge to the grassy knolls of Clachertyfarlie Knowes. Descend ENE across a boggy hollow and finally climb more steeply to the trig point of Earl's Seat. Even in the thickest of weather the top is easy to find at the meeting point of three fences. (6½km; 670m; 2h 40min).

To return to Strath Blane descend SW across the little streams and ditches that form the source of the Ballagan Burn and cross very rough boggy ground, climbing slightly to cross a fence at Graham's Cairn, (½km S of Clachertyfarlie Knowes). Continue down the Cauldhame Glen on the S side of the burn to rejoin the uphill route ½km above Cantywheery cottage.

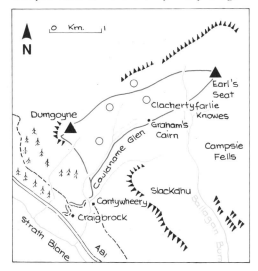

Beinn Chaorach (left) and Beinn Each from Beinn Dubh   P. Hodgkiss

Doune Hill; 734m; (OS Sheet 56; 290971); *hill of the black water*
Beinn Chaorach; 713m; (OS Sheet 56; 288924); *hill of the sheep*

The Luss hills, bounded by Loch Lomond, Loch Long and Glen Fruin, form a compact group of grassy rounded hills which give very pleasant hillwalking within easy reach of Glasgow. Access from the west above Loch Long is not recommended, as there are forest plantations, firing ranges and other military installations on that side of the hills. Glen Fruin is a possible starting point for the southern hills, but Luss village, which can be reached by bus from Glasgow, is the best place from which to reach most of these hills. There is a narrow public road for 3km up Glen Luss, but little parking space at the point near Glenmollochan farm where the public road ends. Further north, Glen Douglas gives access to the northern hills.

Although none of the Luss Hills have the status of Corbetts, there are four over 700m, and the whole group gives a wide selection of hillwalks from short half-days to much longer outings. These hills are principally used for sheep-farming, so particular care should be taken, especially in the spring lambing season, not to cause disturbance. Several notices at the roadside in Glen Luss warn against taking dogs on the hills.

Doune Hill can be reached over the summit of Beinn Eich (702m), the prominent conical hill seen from Luss village looking west. From the end of the public road in Glen Luss walk up to Edentaggart farm, and from there climb directly up the broad grassy ridge to Beinn Eich. Continue NE along a level ridge of grass and eroded peat over Beinn Lochain to the rounded summit of Doune Hill, crowned by a triangulation pillar. The descent may be varied by going

SE down to the head of Glen Mollochan and returning to Glen Luss along a track along the N side of the burn. (7km; 800m; 2h 40min).

The ridge on the N side of Glen Luss, consisting of Beinn Dubh and Mid Hill, can be approached directly from Luss village up the long easy-angled SE ridge of Beinn Dubh (643m). This ridge gives good views over Loch Lomond. The traverse continues to Mid Hill (655m), from where a return can be made to Glen Luss down the grassy ridge on the W side of Glen Striddle.

On the S side of Glen Luss there is a long ridge culminating at its W end in Beinn Chaorach (713m). The N side of this ridge overlooking Glen Luss has some quite steep grassy corries. Beinn Chaorach itself can be most easily climbed from Glen Fruin, starting up the private road on the E side of the Auchengaich Burn and climbing steep grassy slopes on the SW side of Beinn Tharsuinn (655m). From there a broad and fairly level ridge leads 1km NW to Beinn Chaorach. (3km; 600m; 1h 40min).

A longer traverse of this southern ridge can be made from Luss, starting along the private road to Auchengavin farm. Past the farm, walk SW through fields on the NW side of the Auchengavin Burn and climb either Coille-eughain Hill or Beinn Ruisg (593m) to reach Creag an Leinibh (658m) at the head of a steep little corrie. Continue along the grassy ridge W to Beinn Tharsuinn and Beinn Chaorach, from where the best descent is due E from a point about 250 metres N of the summit. This leads down a well-defined grassy ridge on the N side of the Shieling Burn to a footbridge over the Luss Water and a 5km walk down the glen to Luss village.

On Auchengaich Hill, looking towards Beinn a'Mhanaich   D.J. Bennet

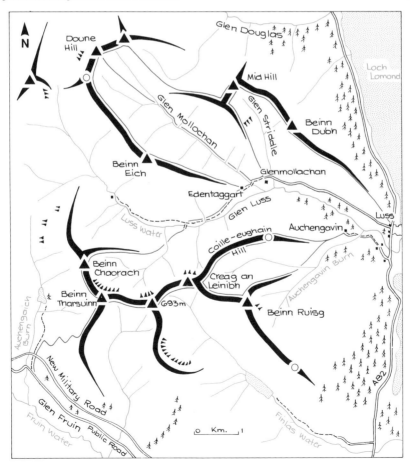

Clach Bheinn from Loch Eck   *D.J. Bennet*

Beinn Mhor; 741m; (OS Sheet 56; 108908); *big hill*
Clach Bheinn; 643m; (OS Sheet 56; 126886); *hill of the stone*

The district of Cowal is relatively unfrequented by hillwalkers despite the fact that it is remarkably rugged and hilly. Possibly the extensive afforestation in many of the glens which clothe the lower hillsides in dense blankets of spruce and fir is a deterrent to climbers.

The Cowal landscape is certainly dominated by forestry, and several villages, such as that in Glen Branter, have been built up round the forest industry. Loch Eck, a splendid narrow loch in the heart of the district, is surrounded by forested hillsides, and to the west of the loch is Beinn Mhor, the highest hill in Cowal. The west side of Loch Eck is a continuous series of wooded crags and corries, well seen from the A815 road between Strachur and Dunoon. To the south-east of Beinn Mhor is the lower, but impressive looking Clach Bheinn, which has some remarkable crags and huge pinnacle-shaped boulders on its north side.

The traverse of Beinn Mhor and Clach Bheinn is the best hillwalk in Cowal. Two approach routes are possible. The longer one, and scenically the finer, starts at the Benmore Gardens, and one has to walk 6km along the forest road on the west side of Loch Eck to reach Bernice before starting the climb. A shorter, but less scenically attractive route is from Glen Massan on the south side of Beinn Mhor. Anyone with time to spare should also visit the Benmore Gardens with their fine collection of rhododendrons and avenues of redwood trees.

The shorter route from Glen Massan starts at the end of the public road up the glen about ½km W of Stonefield. There is a small parking space for cars. Walk up the glen along a private road for 2km to Glenmassan farm, and after crossing the Allt Coire

Mheasan follow a narrow forest road N up the lower tree-covered slopes of Sron Mor, the SSW ridge of Beinn Mhor. When the road ends, continue along a narrower path which goes N and emerges above the trees onto the grassy flank of the ridge. This path, becoming no more than a faint track, leads almost to the crest of the ridge ½km SW of the summit of Beinn Mhor. The trig point is on a rocky knoll at the S end of a flat area of grass and small rocky outcrops. (6km; 670m; 2h 30min).

On a clear day most of the familiar hills of the Southern Highlands are visible. But the view that one gets of these hills, Ben Cruachan, Ben Lui, the Arrochar Alps and Ben Lomond, is rather different from the more familiar views from their more frequently climbed neighbours to the north.

To continue to Clach Bheinn, go SE across a wide grassy ridge towards the edge overlooking Coire an t-Sith. In places the ground is quite boggy. Continue S then SE and reach the col below Clach Bheinn. A short grassy slope with rock outcrops leads to the summit cairn. There is another cairned point, only slightly lower, about 100 metres to the NE.

To descend to Glen Massan return SW across the col and cross the flat top of Creachan Mor. Continue SE down a narrowing ridge to the first col and then bear S on a descending traverse of the steep hillside to reach an obvious gap in the forest at (121 871). Go down this gap to the glen.

The longer route starts at the Benmore Gardens and goes N for 6km along the forest road on the W side of Loch Eck to Bernice. (A bicycle could be used along this road). Take the road on the N side of the burn in the Bernice Glen for as far as it goes up the glen, and continue by a path through the forest up to the pass

Beinn Mhor from Clach Bheinn   *D.J. Bennet*

at the foot of the NE ridge of Beinn Mhor. Climb this quite steep ridge, with crags on one's left, to the flatter summit of the hill. (10km; 730m; 3h 30min).

From Clach Bheinn the descent to Loch Eck can be made down the SE ridge, or in a more circuitous way down the NE ridge to visit the Paper Cave where it is said that the Campbells hid their family deeds and documents in the troubled times of the 17th century.

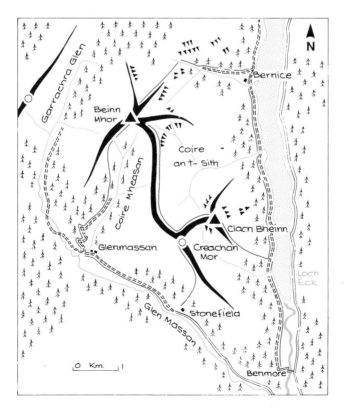

Ben Donich (left) and The Brack (right) above Lochgoilhead   *D. J Bennet*

Ben Donich; 847m; (OS Sheet 56; 218044); *brown hill*

Ben Donich occupies a commanding position in the angle between Glen Croe and Gleann Mor, 3km SSW of the Rest and be Thankful pass. Four ridges radiate from its summit, to north, south, east and west, and the hill is almost entirely surrounded by forest. On the whole it is a grassy hill, and the only distinct crags are in the corrie between the north and west ridges. The most direct route of ascent is up the N ridge, starting from the B828 road in Gleann Mor ½km SW of the Rest and be Thankful. A Forestry Commission road branches off and leads into the forest at the foot of the N ridge. Tree felling near this point may obstruct the ascent, but at the time of writing an easy way through the trees is found by following the forest road S for a few hundred metres to a fence, and then climbing uphill on the SW side of this fence to a gate at the tree-line. Once above the forest continue steeply up the grassy hillside to reach the N ridge at a little col.

From there the crest of the N ridge is followed.

A short distance higher the first of several rock fissures is reached, and one should be careful if there is snow on the ground as these fissures form miniature crevasses. Spectacular crags on the W side of the ridge give some interest to the climb, which ends over one or two grassy knolls before the trig point of the summit is reached. (3½km; 550m; 1h 40min).

An alternative but longer approach, which enables Ben Donich and The Brack to be climbed together, can be made from the Forestry Commission office at the foot of Glen Croe. Walk along the forest road up Glen Croe below the N face of The Brack for almost 4km to reach the start of a well marked path at (242047). This path leads S to the Bealach Dubh-lic (384), the col between the N ridge of The Brack and the E ridge of Ben Donich. From the bealach both hills can be easily climbed. The E ridge of Ben Donich is easy-angled, broad and featureless - not a very interesting route. (7km; 830m; 3h).

The Brack; 787m; (OS Sheet 56; 245031); possibly *speckled hill*

The Brack is a very rugged hill overlooking Ardgartan near the head of loch Long. The north face above Glen Croe is particularly steep and rocky, with an impressively dark and gloomy crag high up under the summit. The long broad east ridge, Cruach Fhiarach, extends towards Ardgartan, but its flanks are extensively forested all round, and no ascent routes exist on that part of the hill.

The most direct ascent is up the north side of the hill above Glen Croe, starting at the Forrestry Commission office at the foot of that glen (270037). Walk up Glen Croe along the forest road on the S side of the Croe Water for 2km to a point a few hundred metres

beyond a double bend in the road. A stream draining the NE corrie of The Brack tumbles down through the forest there, and a few metres E of the bridge over this stream an inconspicuous path strikes very steeply uphill. Follow this path up along a clearing by the stream, cross a fence and reach the open hillside above the forest. Continue up the path, which is not very distinct and higher up crosses to the W side of the stream and leads steeply upwards to a large pointed boulder at the foot of the north face crags.

Keep on directly upwards, with the crags on one's right, and climb a steep, wide grassy gully without difficulty to reach the N ridge of The Brack. There is a trace of a path all the way. Finally, turn S and climb the last hundred metres of the N ridge to the trig point on the summit.

An easier alternative to the steep climb up the grassy gully is to bear SE from the pointed boulder up a shallow grassy corrie, keeping well below the upper crags and boulders, to reach the E ridge at a col. Turn right there and climb the upper part of the E ridge to the summit. (3½km; 750m; 2h).

The return route can be varied by descending the SW ridge of The Brack. It is broad and hummocky, and calls for accurate navigation in mist. Pass below the 579m knoll on its E side and reach the path from Lochgoilhead to Ardgartan near the point where it enters the forest. Follow this path E into the forest and continue down the Coilessan Glen by the forest road, crossing and recrossing the burn before the final 3km along a tarred road back to the Forestry Commission office in Glen Croe.

The Brack from Glen Croe   D.J. Bennet

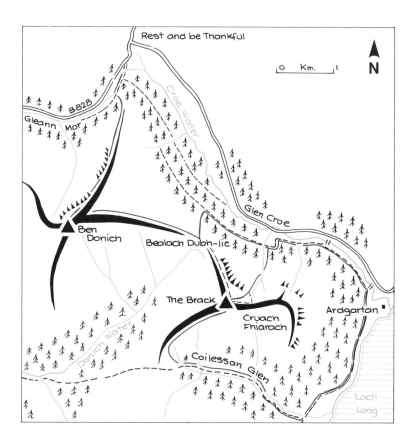

Beinn Bheula from Ben Donich across the head of Loch Goil   W.R. Morrison

Beinn Bheula: 779m; (OS Sheet 56; 155983); *hill of the ford*

To the west of Lochgoilhead there is an area of steep craggy hills with dense coniferous forests along their lower slopes. Beinn Bheula is the highest of these hills. Its east face, which is well seen from Lochgoilhead, is quite rocky, a succession of little crags and escarpments rising one above another from the forested glen of the Lettermay Burn to the level summit ridge. The west side of Beinn Bheula is much less attractive scenically, and although the hill can be easily climbed on that side from Invernoaden, the north-eastern approach from Loch Goil is more interesting.

Start at a group of houses at Lettermay and walk up the Forestry Commission road which begins S of these houses. In 1½km the road divides; take the right-hand branch slightly downhill to a footbridge over the Lettermay Burn. On the N side of the burn strike NW uphill through the forest for just over 100 metres to reach a fire-break. Follow the path SW along this clearing on a gradually rising traverse which in just over 1km leads out of the forest beside the stream flowing from the Curra Lochain.

Cross the stream and climb SW up grassy slopes with rocky knolls here and there. The terrain can be confusing in mist. The route follows the line of the very indistinct NE ridge of Beinn Bheula, up which there is a trace of a path in places. Beyond a little knoll make a rising traverse leftwards up a grassy gully in the crags to reach the crest of the hill a few hundred metres N of the summit. The final climb to the triangulation point is along a smooth grassy ridge, in contrast to the rough slopes below. (5km; 730m;

2h 20min).

A traverse of the hill can be made by continuing S along the broad grassy ridge to the twin humps of Creag Sgoilte. From there descend SSW at first, avoiding crags and a steep drop due S, and then bear SE once on flatter ground. A broad col is reached, and at it the faint traces of a path are found, marked by posts at intervals. Follow this line of posts NE down to the outflow of Lochain nan Cnaimh and take the path (now much more obvious) down into the forest. This path leads along a fire-break by a gradually descending traverse to reach the upper end of a forest road, which in turn leads down to Lettermay.

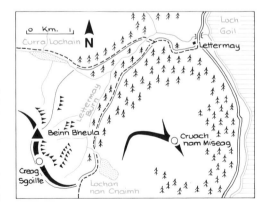

The Cobbler from the Narnain Boulders   P. Hodgkiss

The Cobbler (Ben Arthur); 884m; (OS Sheet 56; 259059)

The three jagged rock peaks of The Cobbler give it the most distinctive character and appearance of any mountain in the southern half of the Highlands. It is The Cobbler, more than any other 'little mountain' in Scotland, which justifies the claim of the Corbetts to be taken as seriously as the Munros, and it is not surprising that The Cobbler has for long (possibly since the West Highland Railway reached Arrochar) been one of Scotland's most popular and best-known peaks. Yet, despite its formidable appearance as seen from Arrochar or high up in its eastern corrie, the ascent to the foot of the rock which forms its summit is easy. The last few metres to the topmost point are a different matter, and the true summit is reserved for those with a little rock climbing ability and a good head for heights. The normal ascent route starts from the A83 road near the head of Loch Long at the start of the road to Succoth. On the NW side of the main road a wide path leads into the forest. Follow this path uphill through the trees to reach a forest road at 100m. Continue upwards along a 'staircase' of old concrete blocks, the remains of an old rail track from the days of the construction of the Loch Sloy hydro-electric scheme.

At the top of the track take a path traversing horizontally SW to reach the Allt a'Bhalachain at a small dam. Continue up the NE side of this burn along a well-defined path past the Narnain Boulders to a crossing of the burn. Climb up the path into the corrie below the three peaks and reach the col between the Centre and North peaks, the last part of the ascent being quite steep.

From the col a short diversion NE leads, with a little easy scrambling, to the spectacular North Peak. The route to the summit of The Cobbler goes SW from the col by a path up the broad grassy ridge to the foot of the summit rock. To reach the top of the summit rock, crawl through a hole formed by two huge blocks, scramble along an exposed ledge on the S side and climb a few metres up to the airy summit. (4½km; 890m; 2h 30min).

Two alternative routes from Glen Croe are possible. Firstly, for those staying at Ardgartan Youth Hostel or camp site, a convenient path starts from the A83 road at the foot of Glen Croe and climbs up to reach the long SE ridge which is followed to the foot of the S peak. From there traverse N into the corrie to join the path of the previous route.

The shortest route, but the least rewarding scenically, starts about 4km up Glen Croe at (243060). Climb up the SE bank of the stream and the tributary which has its source just below the col between the North and Centre peaks. This route leads to easy ground just N of the summit, and takes little more than 1h 30min from the road.

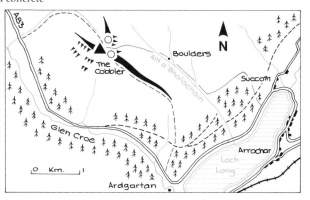

Beinn an Lochain; 901m;
(OS Sheet 56; 218079); *hill of the little loch*

Beinn an Lochain is a prominent hill at the head of Glen Croe which at one time appeared in the list of Munros, but more recent and more accurate measurements of its height by the Ordnance Survey have placed it firmly in the list of Corbetts. Its east face rises steeply for 650m above Loch Restil in a succession of crags, mostly grass-covered and of no climbing interest. The summit overlooks the equally steep north face which has some impressive cliffs above Glen Kinglas. Between these two faces the north-east ridge rises in a succession of steps, and is a fine feature of the hill. The south top (834m) is about 600 metres due south of the summit, and from it the southern perimeter of the hill drops in long steep grassy slopes, interspersed with little crags, to Gleann Mor.

The best route of ascent, though not necessarily the shortest, is the north-east ridge, which is steep and narrow enough in places to give the impression of real mountaineering. The foot of the ridge near Butterbridge is planted with rows of trees, so a better starting point is about ½km NNE of the N end of Loch Restil. Cars can be parked not far from that point beside the A83 road.

Cross the burn flowing from Loch Restil and head NW for a few hundred metres over rough ground to reach a wide grassy gully which leads easily onto the NE ridge. There is a fairly well-defined, but narrow path up this ridge, which at about 600m becomes fairly level over two little bumps (637m) and then steepens suddenly.

Looking up the NE ridge of Beinn an Lochain   *D. Green*

The path makes a rising traverse rightwards across steep grass to avoid crags on the crest of the ridge, which is regained at another level section (764m). Continue to the foot of the last rise, where the path is just on the left side of the crest, avoiding the steep rocks at the edge of the N face. The climb ends suddenly at the summit cairn. (2km; 660m; 1h 40min).

The ascent from the Rest and be Thankful due W up steep slopes with many little crags leads directly to the S top, from where an easy walk N along a level ridge past two or three tiny lochans leads to the summit. This is not as interesting a route as the NE ridge, but can be combined with it to give a good traverse of the hill. (2km; 650m; 1h 40min).

Beinn Luibhean; 858m; (OS Sheet 56; 243079); *hill of the little plant*

This hill is very much a satellite of Beinn Ime, being only 1½km from it and separated by a high col, the Bealach a'Mhargaidh (c. 680m). The ascent of Beinn Luibhean can easily be combined with Beinn Ime, and possibly also Beinn Chorranach, to give a short but pleasant traverse above Glen Kinglas.

The western perimeter of Beinn Luibhean is continuously steep, and does not invite an ascent on that side, and a forestry plantation NW of the summit prevents access from that direction. Possibly the best route is from the A83 road 2km N of the Rest and be Thankful, starting about 200 metres S of the bridge over the Kinglas Water near a ruined cottage.

Walk past the ruin and continue by a well-defined path up the SW side of the burn which flows down from the Bealach a'Mhargaidh. Higher up beyond the trees the path becomes less distinct, and the grassy corrie steepens below the level expanse of the bealach. Once this flat ground is reached, bear W and climb the E ridge of Beinn Luibhean past many little rock outcrops to the cairn on top of a small crag. (3km; 660m; 1h 50min).

A slightly shorter, but continuously steep ascent can be made from a parking place beside the A83 road in Glen Croe 2km due S of the summit of Beinn Luibhean.

Stob Coire Creagach from the Rest and be Thankful   *D.J. Bennet*

Stob Coire Creagach (Binnein an Fhidhleir); 817m; (OS Sheet 56; 231109); *peak of the craggy corrie (fiddler's peak)*

The north side of Glen Kinglas is dominated throughout its entire length of over 10km from its head down to Loch Fyne by a long high ridge, whose southern slopes drop in a single sweep from the summits to the glen. There are several tops on this ridge, and the western one has the name Binnein an Fhidhleir (811m); but this is not the highest point which is 1½km further E, due N of Butterbridge and unnamed on any map. The name Stob Coire Creagach is proposed for this highest point, Coire Cregach being the name on the OS 1:25,000 map given to the corrie overlooking Glen Kinglas further NE.

Any ascent of this hill from Glen Kinglas (which is the only practicable starting point) is bound to take the form of a short but relentlessly steep climb of over 600m. This is particularly true if one choses to start from any point W of Butterbridge. The slopes overlooking upper Glen Kinglas are more varied, being quite craggy.

The shortest and probably most painless ascent to the highest point starts just W of the bridge taking the A83 road over the Kinglas Water. Strike due N up the steep grassy hillside and at about 400m reach a discontinuous line of crags. A grassy gully leads obviously through these, and above it the angle eases. Bear NW and continue up the grassy hillside to the final steepening where a few more little crags, easy to avoid, guard the summit. (1½km; 630m; 1h 30min).

Anyone wanting more exercise can either go W to Binnein an Fhidhleir and enjoy the view out to Loch Fyne, or NE along the knobbly ridge above Coire Creagach. The latter leads in 3km to the end of the hill from where one can descend into the head of Glen Kinglas and return by the track down the glen.

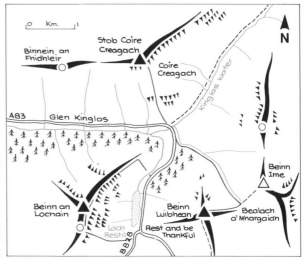

On the broad ridge between Troisgeach and Meall an Fhudair   *D. Green*

Meall an Fhudair; 764m; (OS Sheet 56; 271192); *gunpowder hill*

Meall an Fhudair and its lower (and more popular) neighbour Troisgeach (734m) form a large and rather shapeless mass of high ground between Glen Fyne and the foot of Glen Falloch. It is not a hill of well-defined ridges and corries, but rather a great featureless lump; its eastern end has quite steep slopes with little rock outcrops everywhere, and the summit area is a very broad knolly ridge holding numerous small lochans.

This hill, and in particular its eastern summit of Troisgeach, is a popular short climb which gives good views down Loch Lomond and northwards to Ben Lui and its neighbours. Once the highest point of Meall an Fhudair is reached a fine view opens out to the south-west down Glen Fyne and west to Beinn Bhuidhe.

The ascent starts at the foot of Glen Falloch opposite Glen Falloch farm, and follows a hydro-electric road which zig-zags up the lower hillside of Troisgeach Bheag to the junction with a higher road which contours round the hillside. Leave this road behind and climb due W up the broad ridge to reach Troisgeach. The ridge onwards to Meall an Fhudair goes WNW at first to the intermediate top of Meall nan Caora (722m), and then WSW across very rough country dotted with lochans. However, it is perfectly feasible to take a more direct line, going about half a kilometre towards Meall nan Caora and then heading W across the southern flank of that top. The rough and rather featureless nature of the ground above 650m makes accurate navigation essential in thick weather. (6km; 800m; 2h 40min).

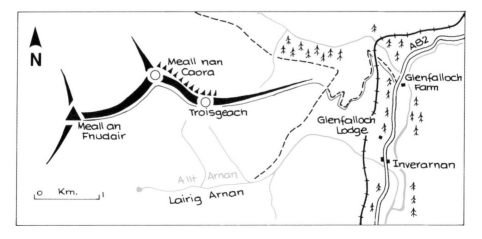

Beinn Chuirn from Dailrigh in Strath Fillan   *H.M. Brown*

Beinn Chuirn; 880m; (OS Sheet 50; 281292); *cairn hill*

When seen from the east, looking up the Cononish Glen, Beinn Chuirn looks rather like a small version of Ben Lui; both hills have similar east-facing corries, but Beinn Chuirn is very much overshadowed by its big neighbour. On its north side it drops in steep slopes to Glen Lochy, with a narrow strip of forestry plantations along its lowest edge beside the River Lochy.

Two routes of ascent are recommended; taken together they make a good traverse. The shorter one starts in Glen Lochy 2km NW of the summit of Beinn Chuirn. The longer one starts at Tyndrum and goes for 3½km along a private road to Cononish farm before climbing the SE ridge of the hill. The slopes of Beinn Chuirn above Cononish are at present being explored for gold, and bulldozed tracks across the hillside and other workings are creating an unsightly mess. These workings may become permanent and even more unsightly, or like so many gold prospecting operations they may come to nothing, except to leave a permanent scar on the hillside.

The Glen Lochy route starts a short distance W or Arrivain. Cross the River Lochy at a railway bridge and climb up the E bank of the Allt Garbh Choirean for about ½km. Once above the trees bear ESE on the N side of the northernmost stream in the corrie (a tributary of the Allt Garbh Choirean) and climb a grassy spur which steepens near its top,

(but is not as craggy as the First Series 1:50,000 OS map indicates). This spur leads to a little lochan 400 metres NW of the summit. (2km; 660m; 1h 40min).

The Tyndrum route starts at the Lower Station and follows the private road for 3½km to Cononish. Continue along the track W from the farm for a few hundred metres and climb W up the grassy hillside, keeping well S of the prominent Eas Anie waterfall. Once above the steepest part of the slope gradually bear NW, cross level ground above the Eas Anie and continue NW up the broad SE ridge of Beinn Chuirn. Near the top the ridge becomes level for a short distance past the top of a steep gully on the E face, and then continues easily for about 200 metres up to the summit cairn. The remains of an old fence cross the summit a few metres N of the cairn. (6km; 700m; 2h 30min).

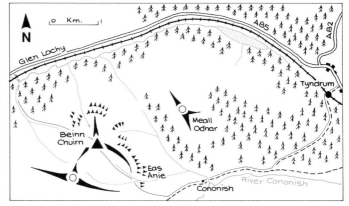

Looking west along Loch Katrine to Beinn a'Choin   *G.S. Johnstone*

Beinn a'Choin; 770m; (OS Sheet 56; 354130); *hill of the dog*

Beinn a'Choin is the highest of a group of hills enclosed within a triangle formed by Loch Lomond to the west, Loch Arklet to the south and the trench of Glen Gyle and Loch Katrine which runs from northwest to south-east. When ascended as a circuit in conjunction with its satellites Maol Mor and Stob an Fhainne these grassy hills give a pleasant round, providing fresh perspectives of the surrounding Munros and lochs of the Southern Highlands.

The ascent starts from Corriearklet farm which, along with the hill ground, belongs to Strathclyde Regional Council's water department. The unclassified public road running past the farm is narrow and pro-

vides no convenient, satisfactory parking places. Instead drive up the private road to the farm and ask permission to park there.

To start, pass through the farm and climb NE onto the ridge of Maol Mor, then head NNW to the summit which is marked by a triangulation pillar. Continue NW along the broad hummocky ridge to the Bealach a'Mhaim then up the final slopes, crossing a fence 200 metres before reaching the small summit cairn of Beinn a'Choin. (6km; 730m; 2h 40min).

The fence goes directly from the summit to Stob an Fhainne and is a useful guide in poor visibility. From this last summit descend SE back to the farm.

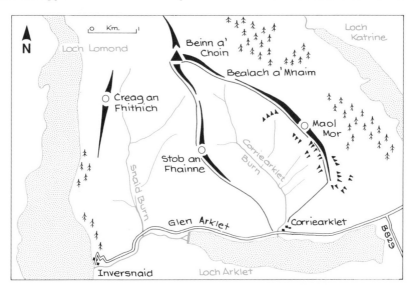

Ben Venue from Loch Achray   *G.S. Johnstone*

Ben Venue; 729m; (OS Sheet 57; 474064); *hill of the caves* or *hill of the stirks*

Ben Venue is a rugged little mountain overlooking The Trossachs and Loch Katrine. Its north-east face above the Achray Water is quite steep, with crags and trees on the lower slopes, which give an impression of impregnability; however, this impression is misleading. The eastern side of the hill is densely forested in Gleann Riabhach.

A traverse of the hill from south to north is recommended, provided an obliging driver is available at the end of the day. This walk goes from Ledard near the west end of Loch Ard to the Loch Achray Hotel.

From Ledard on the B829 road 7km W of Aberfoyle take the track N for 3km through the forest and then NE·under the shoulder of Beinn Bhreac, Ben Venue's worthy neighbour. The path continues NE, and although one branch drops SE towards Gleann Riabhach, continue NE along quite a good path which zig-zags up steeper ground to the summit of Ben Venue. (5km; 690m; 2h 20min). On a fine day there is a splendid panorama NW beyond the head of Loch Katrine.

The traverse continues SE for a few hundred metres along a path to the lower SE top of the hill (727m) which as the trig point. Two descent routes are possible. The easier one goes S down easy slopes to reach the path at the upper edge of the trees in Gleann Riabhach. This path, which is often very muddy, continues down the glen and leads to a forest road, which in turn leads to the Loch Achray Hotel.

An alternative, and probably rather more attractive descent route goes down the corrie on the NE side of

Ben Venue, following rather a faint path beside a stream. Lower down the slope becomes more precipitous and one descends steeply through birch woods to reach another path near the Loch Katrine sluices. Follow this path E and in 1½km reach the Loch Achray Hotel.

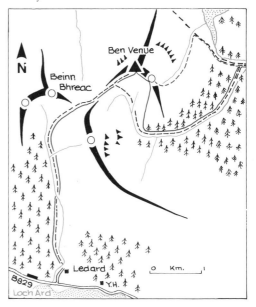

Stob a'Choin from the north-west   P. Hodgkiss

Stob a'Choin; 865m; (OS Sheet 56; 417160); *dog peak*

Situated 3km south-west of Inverlochlarig, Stob a'Choin is the highest point of the range of hills lying between the glacial trenches of Loch Katrine and Glen Gyle to the south and Loch Voil and the River Larig to the north.

This fine hill, with its steep northern flanks and wedge-shaped summit, increasingly dominates the view as one approaches up the narrow public road from Balquhidder. In character and appearance it closely resembles the Crianlarich hills to the north and the walking reflects this with the same mix of steep grassy lower slopes and knobbly ridges.

The public road ends at the Inverlochlarig Tourist Information Centre car park which lies ¾km E of the farm. From the car park follow the road through Inverlochlarig and its steadings westwards up the main valley until a footbridge (427174) gives dry access to the south side of the River Larig.

Follow the river upstream for ½km to a sheepfold, then climb due S to approximately 450m, where a diagonal SW ascent below a line of broken crags leads to a platform on the steep N ridge of Stob a'Choin at 630m. This ridge leads directly to the N top, which although it has a cairn and the finer views, is 4m lower than its twin, the

S top. This at 869m (not 865m as on the OS map) is the true summit. (4½km; 740m; 2h 20min).

If conditions are favourable, a traverse eastwards over Meall Reamhar and Craig nan Saighead before dropping down to the footbridge is recommended as an alternative descent route. (Note that new plantings bar the direct access to the forestry road near Blaircreich).

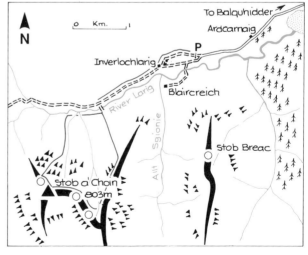

In the view south-west from Balquhidder, Stob Fear-tomhais is hidden behind its outlier Creag Mhor   D.J. Bennet

Stob Fear-tomhais; 771m; (OS Sheet 57; 474163); *surveyor's peak*

This hill is not named on the Ordnance Survey map, but is shown as 771m high. It is sometimes referred to as Ceann na Baintighearna, but this name applies to the northern top, about 1½km away and 70m lower. Locally it is known as 'the surveyor's peak' because of the triangulation pillar at its summit, and the name Stob Fear-tomhais is the Gaelic translation of this local name. It is the highest of the hills immediately south of Loch Voil and Loch Doine, but is infrequently climbed. The ascent from Ballimore farm, 3km south of Balquhidder up Glen Buckie, gives a pleasant short day in a quiet back-water close to the tourist honeypots of Strathyre and the Trossachs.

The road from Balquhidder up Glen Buckie is narrow, and provides few parking places, the best one for the climb being outside Ballimore farm. Cross the bridge over the Calair Burn and go SW along the right of way to Brig o' Turk. Follow the path for 1½km until it swings S, and at that point bear W and cross the Allt a'Ghlinne Dhuibh (no bridge). Then climb the broad, undulating E ridge of Stob Fear-tomhais over a few little knolls to the triangulation pillar which gives the hill its name. (6km; 560m; 2h 20min).

Note that the road on the N side of the Calair Burn passes through a private deer farm, which should be avoided.

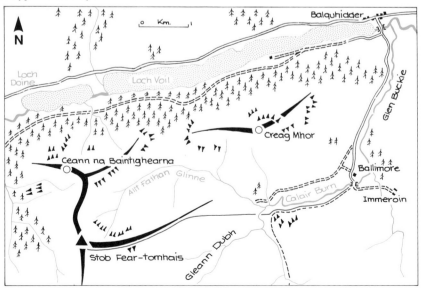

Ben Ledi from Callander   *J. Crumley*

Ben Ledi; *879m; (OS Sheet 57; 563098); hill of the gentle slope* or *God's hill*

Ben Ledi stands to the north - east of the Trossachs, and is a very prominent hill. Like Ben Lomond to its west and Ben Vorlich to its north-east, it is clearly visible from Central Scotland across the flat plain of the rivers Forth and Teith, the three mountains being the southern outposts of the Highlands. The east side of Ben Ledi rises above the Pass of Leny and Loch Lubnaig, and this flank of the mountain is extensively forested.

Although it is possible to climb Ben Ledi from the W or up the SE ridge from Coilantogle farm, the most popular routes are on the forested E side. Leave the A84 road ½km NW of the Pass of Leny and just after crossing the bridge over the River Leny reach a Forestry Commission car park.

From the car park follow a well-defined (and often rather muddy) path W uphill through the forest. Above the tree-line the path bears SW, making a rising traverse below crags to reach the grassy crest of the SE ridge. The ascent continues up the broad undulating crest of this ridge to the summit of Ben Ledi. (4½km; 760m; 2h 20min).

An interesting round can be made by continuing NW then N along the ridge to the broad col holding Lochan nan Corp. From there descend E into the Stank Glen and follow forest roads and paths either on the N or S side of the stream to reach the foot of the glen, from where it is 1km back to the car park.

The traverse to Benvane (see below) can be continued from Lochan nan Corp along the broad ridge over several knolls, including Stuc Dhubh, and this makes a fine traverse. However, the problem remains of returning to the day's starting point; a friendly driver will be needed if a walk of several kilometres along the track on the west side of Loch Lubnaig is to be avoided.

Benvane; 821m; (OS Sheet 57; 535137); *white hill*

Benvane is the highest point on the ridge which runs for 8km NNW from the summit of Ben Ledi towards Balquhidder on the W side of Loch Lubnaig. As noted above, the two hills can be combined in a single fine traverse. Like Ben Ledi, Benvane is forested along most of its eastern slopes.

Apart from its SE ridge, which is climbed if one is coming from Ben Ledi, two other routes of ascent are possible, both quite short.

From Strathyre one can drive S on the minor road to Kipp and start the ascent from there. Continue S along the forest road and go right to follow another road W up to the col between Benvane and Beinn an t-Sithein. 200 metres after this road turns N at the col there is a path through a short break in the wood which leads to a stile over the deer fence into new plantations. Continue NW beside the plantation to a gate in the new fence from where there is an easy ascent WSW up the open grassy hillside to a point 1½km N of the summit of Benvane. An old fence runs along the ridge to the summit. (5½km; 670m; 2h 30min).

From Balquhidder go S up Glen Buckie for 3km to a car park near Ballimore farm. Cross the bridge over the Calair Burn and go a short distance SW along the right of way to Brig o'Turk, then climb easy slopes S onto the long N ridge of Benvane, avoiding occasional peat hags. This ridge leads directly to the summit. (4km; 620m; 2h).

Looking across the north end of Loch Lubnaig to Benvane   H.M. Brown

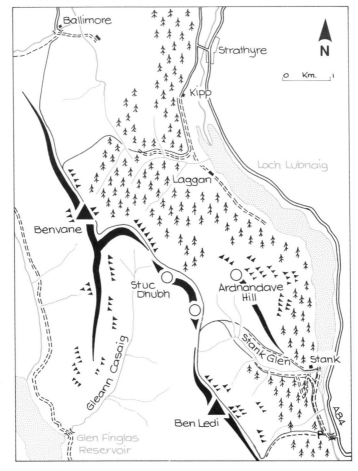

Meall an t-Seallaidh from Glen Buckie   *D.J. Bennet*

Meall an t-Seallaidh; 852m; (OS Sheet 51; 542234); *hill of the sight*
Creag MacRanaich; 809m; (OS Sheet 51; 546256); *MacRanaich's crag*

These two hills lie on a surprisingly impressive line of cliffs around the broad head of Glen Kendrum. They can be taken separately in which case they give quite entertaining short days out, or they can be traversed together provided suitable retrieval arrangements can be arranged from widely separate points.

Meall an t-Seallaidh, the less distinguished of the two, is best approached by way of the right of way up the Kirkton Glen, which starts beside the Auld Kirk at Balquhidder, where Rob Roy McGregor is buried. Parking here is rather restricted but there is some along the roadside to the S. (The church car park is of course for its own functions). The path joins a forestry access road and recent clearing may give rise to a bit of map consultation. The path breaks out of the forest near Lochan an Eireannaich (worth a visit) and the route then doubles back to the ridge between Cam Chreag and the summit over rough, but easy-angled, ground. There are two tops a few yards apart of which the most northerly (cairn) seems just to be the higher (5½km; 700m; 2h 50min). There are wide unobstructed views from the top which no doubt give rise to the mountain's name.

Creag MacRanaich is a hill of some character which, were it about 100m higher, would be among the better southern Munros. It can be approached from the S in two ways. One route starts from Leitters (575209) and, by using the track of the dismantled railway line, gains the track going NW up Glen Kendrum. The other is to combine its ascent with that of Meall an t-Seallaidh. The disadvantage of both of

these approaches is the restricted parking (virtually non-existent in the first case).

The route chosen therefore starts at the farm of Ledcharrie on the A85 road (506282), where there is ample parking. A track (start of the right of way) runs S for 750 metres to reach the dismantled railway line which is followed ENE to where it joins the Gleann Dubh track, the start of which is found 20 metres E of the bridge at (528284). This track is followed SSE until it peters out. In good visibility a prominent V-shaped nick can be seen on the ridge to the SE, and the summit lies behind this feature. In poor visibility a bearing should be calculated to the summit since the upper area of this ridge is both complex and broken. For example, although the map shows a lochan, there are in fact two, almost equal in size and each with a hillock to its SE side. (7km; 650m; 2h 50min). The return to the railway bridge is best made by first going N down the ridge and then NW when the ground is less broken and steep.

To connect the two mountains in one expedition involves the traverse of rather complicated ground at the head of Gleann Dubh, not to be undertaken in misty weather, but very pleasant in good visibility. Coming from Creag MacRanaich, avoid the crags on the SW side of this hill and reach the tributary of the Gleann Dubh burn. This can be followed SW to reach the ridge which leads rockily from point 813m to Meall an t-Seallaidh. Alternatively, a shorter route can be taken up a gully to the N of Cam Chreag. The route can just as readily be taken in reverse.

Creag MacRanaich from Edinchip   *G.S. Johnstone*

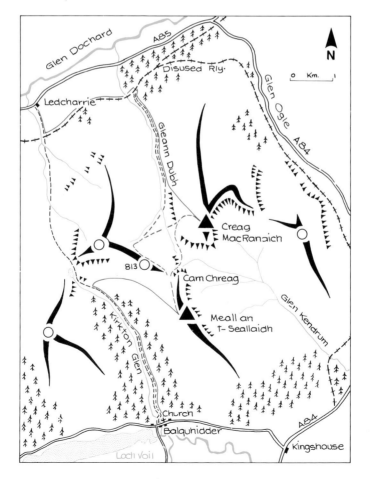

Beinn Each from Arivurichardich   H.M. Brown

Beinn Each; 813m; (OS Sheet 57; 602158); *horse hill*

Beinn Each stands on the southern edge of the Highlands. It is a major summit on the twisting and hummocky south-west ridge of the popular Stuc a'Chroin.

The nearest point of access is the southern end of Glen Ample (584136). From a lay-by on the side of the A84, follow the right of way which climbs steeply through trees behind Ardchullarie More to join a forest track leading N through Glen Ample. After 1½km leave the track and climb steeply up the N side of the burn which comes down in a series of small waterfalls from below Beinn Each's summit. Follow the N branch to its source. Continue N for a further 200 metres then turn NE and follow a line of fence posts to the summit. (3km; 690m; 1h 50min).

Stuc a'Chroin (617174) lies 2½km to the NE along a knobbly ridge. From Beinn Each descend steeply N to Bealach nan Cabar. Continue NE over a lower top to Bealach Glas, and climb E then NE to the summit. The route follows the line of an old fence which winds its way through many little outcrops. (5½km; 1030m; 2h 50min).

A large sign on the Glen Ample right of way gives notice of the restrictions during the stalking season.

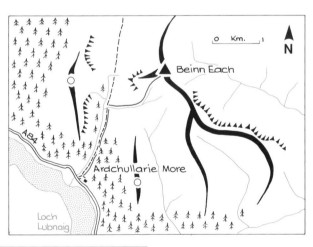

Meall na Fearna; 809m; (OS Sheets 51 and 57; 651186); *alder hill*

Meall na Fearna stands on the western edge of a tract of rugged hill country lying to the east of Ben Vorlich between Glen Artney and Strath Earn. For the most part it is a grassy hill with heather and peat bog which is home for many grouse, hare and deer. From both north and south the summit is hidden by smaller outlying tops. The high undulating ground above 600m may cause route finding problems in misty weather.

The shortest approach is from the N. Park on the grass verge at Ardvorlich on the S side of Loch Earn. Go through the E gate of Ardvorlich House and follow the private road which soon becomes a rough track S into Glen Vorlich. After 1km, at a bifurcation, take the grassy E branch and follow it for 3½km to the Glen Vorlich - Gleann an Dubh Choirein bealach. In its upper reaches the Glen Vorlich path is intermittent and boggy. The route continues steeply NE onto an

Meall na Fearna from the south-west   *H.M. Brown*

unnamed outlying top and then turns SE via a shallow col of peat hags to the summit marked by a handful of stones (6½km; 660m; 2h 30min).

There is a longer southern approach from Glen Artney. From the car park by Glenartney Church go SW along the road to Glenartney Lodge. Continue NNW on a good track along Srath a'Ghlinne. Leave the track after 3½km. It is possible to cycle to this point. Strike W up the N side of the burn which leads onto point 742m. Descend to a col of peat hags and continue up the final grassy slope to Meall na Fearna (8½km; 650m; 3h).

Both routes have restrictions during the stalking season.

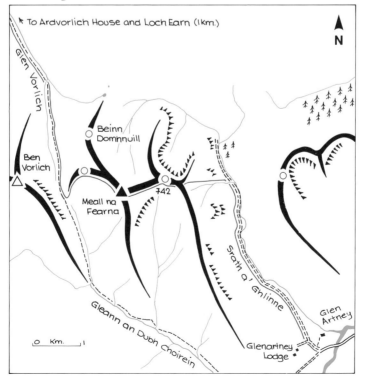

Looking across Loch Tay from the lower slopes of Ben Lawers to Creag Uchdag   G.S. Johnstone

Creag Uchdag; 879m; (OS Sheet 51; 708323); *crag of the hollows*
Creagan na Beinne; 888m; (OS Sheet 51 and 52; 744369); *hill of the rocks/crags*
Auchnafree Hill; 789m; (OS Sheet 52; 808308); *hill of the deer forest field*

Between Loch Tay, Strath Earn and the Sma' Glen there is some surprisingly hilly country with one Munro (Ben Chonzie), these three Corbetts, and several other sprawling summits of near-Corbett height. While Auchnafree Hill can be climbed along with Ben Chonzie, the Corbetts themselves are well scattered with deep glens separating them. Historically the glens have been important through routes and various cross-country combinations are described into which one could fit the Corbetts. The hills are generally big convex domes, deeply cut by corries and often with rough peaty plateaux. As many tracks bulldozed from the glens up onto the heights are not shown on the First Series OS maps, the more recent Landranger series is recommended.

Glen Almond and Glen Lednock give lengthy valley access from east and south, with shorter Glen Turret between. On the Loch Tay side the glens are much shorter. Glen Almond has a private road up most of its length, but is a pedestrian (and cycle) right of way through to Ardtalnaig on Loch Tay. Glen Turret has a private surfaced water authority road up to the dam and an estate road thereafter almost up to Lochan Uaine. (The public are allowed to motor up to the dam, despite the notice at the start of the road). The public road in Glen Lednock ends at the dam but it is easy to walk along the north side of the reservoir to pick up the old right of way (cut by the raised water level) which leads to the old ferry inn of Ardeonaig on Loch Tay. From Invergeldie, 2km below the Loch Lednock dam, another right of way goes over to the head of Glen Almond at Dunan and down to Ardtalnaig. There is also an interesting path from Glen Quaich (4km from Amulree) through Glen

Lochan to Auchnafree in Glen Almond.

Combining Corbetts with good cross-country routes is recommended; there are many possibilities, one or two of which may be mentioned. Motor to Invergeldie and by Loch Lednock, take in Creag Uchdag on the way to Ardeonaig for the night. The next day walk to Ardtalnaig and traverse Creagan na Beinne to Dunan, then on over to Invergeldie again. Auchnafree Hill can be traversed using Glen Almond and Glen Turret. As the whole area is sheep country with plenty of grouse moors too, and some stalking, dogs are not welcome and the sporting season is best avoided. There are also huge numbers of mountain hares, particularly on Auchnafree Hill and Ben Chonzie. The Strath Earn side also has an unusual number of waterfalls: Monzie, Keltie, Barvick, Turret, The Deil's Cauldron and Sput Rolla below the Lednock dam.

Creag Uchdag from the south is reached by setting off from the car park at the Lednock dam and walking along the north shore. A steady rising traverse thereafter leads to the knobbly heights (3½km; 530m; 1h 50min). From the N the path can be followed up the Finglen to the watershed, then E for the summit. Minor crags, on both routes, can easily be avoided. (6km; 760m; 2h 50min).

Creagan na Beinne is easiest from the N, Ardtalnaig, side. It is worth walking through Gleann a'Chilleine to Dunan (notable moraine bumps) and ascending the Corbett by its S ridge, descending by the N ridge and either down to Tullichglass or by the stalking path beyond an intermediate bump towards Beinn Bhreac. (10km; 760m; 3h 20min). Waterfall fanatics could descend to the NNE and visit the Acharn

Falls.

Auchnafree Hill is almost equally easy from three directions: Glen Turret, Glen Almond and Glen Lochan. Glen Turret is very attractive, starting in rich farm land and ending in utter solitude. It is worth walking up to the dam rather than motoring. The Falls of Turret are worth a diversion. At (806286) a track (not on any map) zig-zags up to the slot of the burn below Ton Eich; use this, then go up the prow of Ton Eich and round to Auchnafree's large cairn. (From dam 6km; 390m; 2h. Add an hour if walking up from the Distillery). Descend westwards to enjoy the fastness of the upper Turret.

From Newton Bridge there is an equally good walk up Glen Almond to Auchnafree. A new track twists up onto Crom Chreag from which Auchnafree Hill is easily reached (11km; 560m; 3h 30min). The same ascent would also be made if coming through Glen Lochan from Glen Quaich (9km; 660m; 3h 20min). Glen Almond can be regained by descending any of the deep corries which are such a feature of its southern flanks. The Allt Coire Chultrain is perhaps most interesting. The crest eastwards is very broken and boggy in places but offers a high-level return route to Newton Bridge.

Looking NW from Knock of Crieff to Glen Turret   *D.J. Bennet*

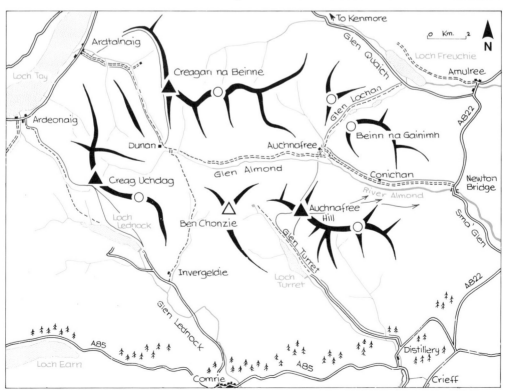

A typical Ochils landscape; Ben Ever from the south   J. Renny

Ben Cleuch; 721m; (OS Sheet 58; 903007)
Dumyat; 418m; (OS Sheet 57; 835977)

The Ochil Hills cover a large area in Central Scotland from Auchtermuchty to Bridge of Allan, a distance of some 40km from east to west and 10km from south to north. They are very prominent hills, especially when seen from the south on which side they form a steep and imposing front overlooking the River Forth. The principal area of higher hills is to the west of the A823 road through Glen Devon. A wide selection of hillwalking routes is possible from various starting points such as the hillfoot towns of Dollar, Tillicoultry, Alva and Menstrie which are linked by a good bus service.

The route described here starts at the quarry in the NW corner of Tillicoultry. From there go up the picturesque Mill Glen and N up the ridge to The Law and then NW to the summit of Ben Cleuch. (4km; 670m; 2h). To continue the walk westwards go NW at first across featureless ground to Ben Buck, then to Blairdenon Hill (631m), whose summit can be found in bad visibility as the meeting point of three fences.

From there to Dumyat the way is over very featureless terrain, following a bearing SW for 4½km across the head of the Old Wharry Burn and past Loss Hill to reach the Lossburn Reservoir. At the W end of the

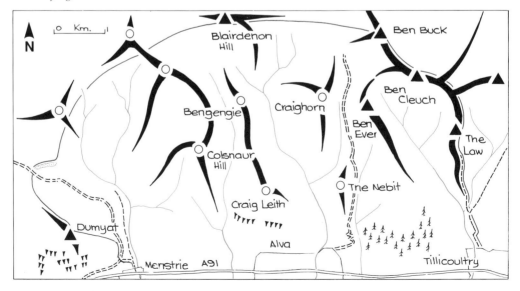

reservoir there is a track which leads to the summit of Dumyat, 1½km SE, and 10km from Ben Cleuch.

When clear, the view from Dumyat is spectacular across the winding River Forth and beyond Stirling Castle to ranges of hills near and far. As on most of the Ochils, the southern slopes of Dumyat are steep and craggy, and do not give good routes of descent. The best way down is E or NE for 1km to reach the track from Lossburn Reservoir down to Menstrie.

West Lomond from Bishop Hill   G.S. Johnstone

West Lomond; 522m; (OS Sheets 58 and 59; 197067)
East Lomond; 424m; (OS Sheets 58 and 59; 244062)

The Lomonds Hills of Fife are a prominent group of hills as befits their name, Lomond meaning beacon. They are well seen in distant views from south of the Forth to north of the Tay, landmarks in the west of Fife. Their attraction is that although they are of no great height, they command splendid views of their surroundings, the undulating agricultural land of Fife and Kinross, dotted with small towns and villages. They form part of the Fife Regional Park, which has its ranger service and attracts many visitors to walk on the hills.

Although it is possible to make some quite long walks on the Lomonds, for example starting at Scotlandwell at their western end and climbing Bishop Hill first, the most popular starting point is at the car park at (228062) on the road which crosses the hills from Leslie to Falkland.

From that point a track goes WNW for 3km past Miller's Loch to reach West Lomond. (3km; 230m; 1h 10min). The final steep slope has a zig-zag path which is suffering from severe erosion and is at present barred. There are alternative routes to the N and S.

Another even shorter walk leads E from the car park along a track and path to East Lomond, which is suffering from the same erosion problem as West Lomond. (2km; 140m; 50min).

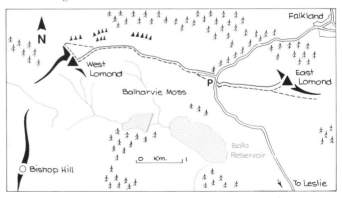

Glen Lyon   D.J. Bennet

SECTION 2

The River Tay to Rannoch Moor

Farragon Hill, with Ben Lawers beyond, from Ben Vrackie   G.S. Johnstone

Farragon Hill; 783m; (OS Sheet 52; 841553)
Meall Tairneachan; 787m; (OS Sheet 52; 807544)

The Farragon Hills are the highest points on the expanse of high moorland stretching westwards from Pitlochry towards Schiehallion. In the age of North Sea oil this area has acquired an added commercial importance as the source of the mineral barytes, and there are two or three mines high up on these hills with tracks across the hillsides.

The two hills can be traversed from east to west, or vice versa, but this is only possible if suitable transport arrangements have been made. Such a traverse is described. Alternatively, it will be necessary to return to one's starting point, which increases the distance to be covered.

Start about 4km NE of Aberfeldy from the minor road on the N side of the River Tay near Edradynate. Follow one of the tracks which lead NW to the S end of Loch Derculich; continue towards the crest of the ridge NW of the loch and climb W to Farragon Hill. (7km; 700m; 2h 50min).

The summit is quite craggy, and in poor visibility the descent requires care. There is, however, a gap in the crags on the SW side which gives an easy way down. Continue WSW for about ½km, then leave the ridge and bear W across a rather boggy corrie to reach the end of a mine track at (827550). This track leads WSW to a barytes mine, but it is badly drained and often wet and muddy, so it may be better to avoid it. Once past the mine a good track leads W and the summit of Meall Tairneachan is a short distance S of its highest point. (12km; 900m; 4h 10min).

To complete the traverse, continue for 3½km NW down the track which eventually leads through recently planted forest to reach the B846 road just N of Loch Kinardochy.

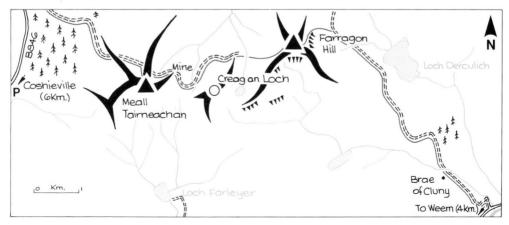

Beinn Dearg from the south   *G.S. Johnstone*

Beinn Dearg; 830m; (OS Sheet 51; 609497); *red hill*
Cam Chreag; 862m; (OS Sheet 51; 536491); *crooked crag*

These two rounded hills rise on the north side of Glen Lyon above Bridge of Balgie and the policies of Meggernie Castle. The right of way across the Lairig Ghallabhaich from Glen Lyon to Loch Rannoch passes between them. The Landranger (Second Series) Ordnance Survey map is advisable for these hills, as it shows some bulldozed tracks and recent afforestation not shown on earlier maps. Both hills can be climbed from Innerwick, but it is better to tackle them separately rather than attempt a high level traverse between them as the intervening ground is rough and there is a lot of descent and ascent. The approaches from the north are much longer, only the Lairig Ghallabhaich right of way giving access through the extensive Rannoch Forest.

Going to Cam Chreag, take the track from the car park on the W side of the Allt Ghallabhaich through the trees and across the Allt a' Choire Uidhre. Further W the track crosses back to the S bank of this stream and continues for 2½km to end at a hut below the E face of Cam Chreag. The crags on the this face are nowhere very big, and the ascent can best be made about ½km SE of the summit to reach the long level shoulder of the hill. (6km; 660m; 2h 30min).

The descent can be varied by going S down heathery slopes to reach the Glen Lyon road just above

Gallin, 4½km W of Innerwick. The walk along the road in this part of the glen is very pleasant.

For Beinn Dearg head up the east bank of the Allt Ghallabhaich, keeping by the river until the forest is reached. The pull up through the forest is quite steep and one can either continue along the right of way and turn E ½km after leaving the forest, or alternatively climb the zig-zag forest track to the edge of the trees and climb E from there up the long W flank of Beinn Dearg, which is a great dome. It is a finer hill than Cam Chreag, with good views to the Ben Lawers range. (4½km; 630m; 2h 10min).

On the descent it is rewarding to walk out along the level shoulder of Creag Ard, from where there is a good view eastwards down the length of lower Glen Lyon. From Creag Ard the return to Innerwick goes W then SW to avoid the steepest slopes and forest plantings.

A longer circuit of Beinn Dearg and Creag Ard together with Carn Gorm can be made starting and finishing at Camusvrachan.

If it is intended to climb Beinn Dearg and Cam Chreag in a single day, it is not necessary to return to Innerwick provided the streams at the confluence of the Allt a' Choire Uidhre and the Allt Ghallabhaich can be crossed.

Looking up Glen Lyon to Creag Ard, the southern shoulder of Beinn Dearg   G.S. Johnstone

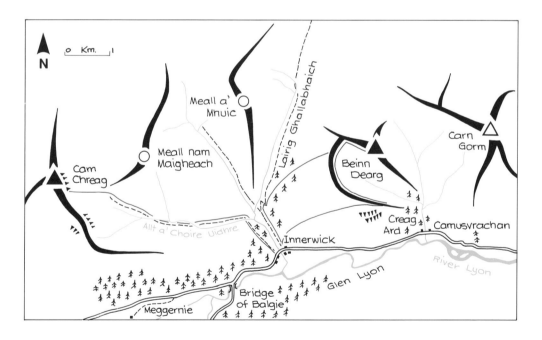

Looking east from Beinn Achaladair to Ben Lawers and the Glen Lyon hills   D.J. Bennet

Meall nan Subh; 806m; (OS Sheet 51; 461397); *hill of the soo (raspberry)*

The Landranger (Second Series) Ordnance Survey map gives at last a clear indication of the character of this hill; a mass of rough bumps and crags. The skirting bogs and braes one has to discover for oneself. This contorted landscape gives the hill some character, and its position, close to the road between Glen Lyon and Glen Lochay, means that it can be climbed as a coda to larger scores in those glens.

This road crosses the pass between Meall nan Subh and its massive neighbour Beinn Heasgarnich, and there is a gate just south of its highest point at (452386) which may be locked. However, one can usually drive as far as the gate, if not from one glen to the other, so the ascent of this hill can be started at a height of 500m which makes it one of the easiest in this book.

Park at any convenient point near the gate and leave the road near its highest point. There are several rocky spurs, each one a temptation to rest awhile, and it is worth wending over to the most northerly bump (459398) which is the best viewpoint and gives a reward out of all proportion to the effort needed to reach it. Beinn Heasgarnich shows its great proportions, and there is a grand view down the length of Glen Lyon.

The highest point is about 200 metres to the SE, but in thick weather it might be difficult to decide which of the three or four bumps on the flat summit is the true top. (1½km; 310m; 1h). Descend more or less by the route of ascent. Far from having no features of interest, this small hill well rewards its modest ascent.

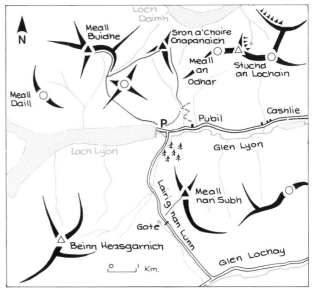

Sron a' Choire Chnapanich; 837m; (OS Sheet 51; 456453); *nose of the lumpy corrie*
Meall Buidhe; 907m; (OS Sheet 51; 427450); *yellow hill*

The name of Sron a' Choire Chnapanich is not shown on the Second Series Landranger map, but it well describes the nose which juts out above Loch an Daimh. This hill's real status was only challenged in the SMC Journal in 1984, for even the First Series 1:50,000 map showed it as a mere 686m contour separated from its neighbours by about 200ft of height. In fact, the drop is far greater, more nearly 200m, and the Second Series map finally in 1987 showed the hill as it really is.

Meall Buidhe to its west is rather lost in the jumble of hills on the north side of Loch Lyon, and is not particularly popular. The best view of it is from the empty heart of Rannoch Moor.

Both these hills are usually climbed from Glen Lyon. The head of this glen is a remote dead-end, and sees few visitors. Cars can be parked under the NE corner of the Loch Lyon dam, and the climb started from there.

A path of sorts has been beaten along the N shore of Loch Lyon, but after 1km the easiest option is to make a steep rising traverse NW to reach the col at about 700m between the headwaters of the Eas nan Aighean and the Feith Thalain. A fence leads N up the bold shoulder ahead, and above it a wide upland walk leads round W to Meall Buidhe. (5km; 570m; 2h 10min). The northern slopes drop down in a great brown sweep to Rannoch Moor, with the vast Rannoch Forest and the railway adding touches of human geometry to the landscape, in contrast with the convex slopes on the Loch Lyon side.

Return to the col from where the fence eventually leads on to the second Corbett, however rather than following it, it is easier to go down the Feith Thalain for 1km and then bear up E to reach another wide col 1km SW of Sron a' Choire Chnapanich.

The final slopes up the SW side of this hill give remarkably smooth walking on mossy turf and heather, shorn to the texture of coir matting. The summit has a tiny cairn on its grassy prow high above Loch an Daimh. (10km; 810m; 3h 40min).

Looking north-west from Meall Ghaordaidh to Sron a'Choire Chnapanich   K. Anderson

Descend the SSE ridge and continue in the same direction towards the Allt Phubuill, avoiding the expanse of peat bogs at the head of this burn. Reach a zig-zag track 1km N of Pubil, and follow it downhill for a short distance before crossing the Allt Phubuill and bearing SW across the lowest slopes of Meall Phubuill to reach the Loch Lyon dam.

Looking east from Meall Ghaordaidh over the south ridge of Beinn nan Oighreag to Ben Lawers   *D.J. Bennet*

Beinn nan Oighreag; 909m; (OS Sheet 51; 542412); *cloudberry hill*

In the 1930's it was suggested that Beinn nan Oighreag might just be a Munro, so it saw a flurry of activity unequalled until the present. Historically, this hill must have seen plenty of droving and other traffic on foot through the Lairig Breisleich, the most direct pass from Bridge of Balgie in Glen Lyon to Killin. Old descriptions described the pass as "a villainous bog, all peat hags and heathery hummocks". On the new Second Series map the summit has moved a few hundred metres south along the crest, and large clusters of shielings are shown in the glen leading south from the Lairig Breisleich. It is this glen which gives the most attractive route of ascent.

Less than 1km up Glen Lochay beyond the power station a track climbs on the N side of the glen through trees and zig-zags up to the start of a path which continues NW above the Allt Dhuin Croisg to reach the central group of shielings. Immediately above these shielings the S ridge of Beinn nan Oighreag rises at an easy angle and gives a straightforward ascent to the summit. (7km; 770m; 2h 50min).

If suitable transport can be arranged on the road from Loch Tay to Glen Lyon, it would be pleasant to descend the NE ridge, thus completing the traverse of the hill. It is also quite possible to combine the ascent of Beinn nan Oighreag with its neighbouring Munro, Meall Ghaordaidh, the col between them being about 640m. Otherwise, the simplest return to Glen Lochay is by the route of ascent.

It is also possible to climb Beinn nan Oighreag from the east, starting at 500m from the road between Loch Tay and Glen Lyon at a small hut near the point (582417) where the road turns north to follow the Allt Bail a' Mhuilinn down to Glen Lyon. Bear due west across the rounded ridge which is the lowest part of the north ridge of Beinn nan Eachan in the Tarmachan Hills, then descend to the unavoidable bogs at the summit of the Lairig Breisleich and climb directly up the east side of Beinn nan Oighreag. (4½km; 560m; 2h). A line of fence posts across the pass may be useful in misty conditions.

Meall nam Maigheach; 779m; (OS Sheet 51; 586436); *hill of the hare*

In previous editions of Munro's Tables, and on Ordnance Survey maps prior to the Second Series, this hill was shown as Meall Luaidhe *(hill of lead)*, quite a common name hereabouts and indicative of the mining of lead ores in the past. (V.A.Firsoff's book *In the Hills of Breadalbane* records this activity well). The reason for the name Gleann Da-Eig *(glen of the two eggs)* for the glen on the east side of Meall nan Maigheach is not known, but that glen offers the most pleasing route up the hill, although few walkers actually take it. The possibility of a starting point at a height of 500m on the

Loch Tay to Glen Lyon road is irresistible. Beinn nan Oighreag (see above) can also be climbed from the same starting point, offering two easy Corbetts in one day.

The best starting point is at the roadside hut (582417) where the road turns north to follow the Allt Bail a' Mhuilinn. Parking elsewhere is not easy, and the obvious spot near the cairn at the watershed is not recommended. The natural line from there to the hill over Meall nan Eun runs into unfriendly terrain of peat hags and heather.

Start at the hut and bear N to reach a wall which leads up onto the summit. Avoid the direct line as it runs into another peaty area. (2km; 290m; 1h). In descent it is easy to follow the wall down to the road.

Those seeking an interesting walk rather than a short exercise in bog-dodging should start in Glen Lyon at Camusvrachan. Cross the River Lyon, go W to Roroyere and follow the stalker's path up the W side of the Allt Gleann Da-Eig. Once the north-facing crags of Creag an Eildreag are passed, climb up the fine eastern prow of this hill which so dominates the views from Glen Lyon and is, in its turn, a magnificent viewpoint up and down what many regard as the finest glen south of the Caledonian Canal. A grand walk of 3km leads SW to the rather undistinguished top of Meall nan Maigheach. (6½km; 620m; 2h 30min). There is a bulldozed track in Gleann Da-Eig, and this can be used as an alternative route of return to Glen Lyon by first descending steeply E from the summit to reach it.

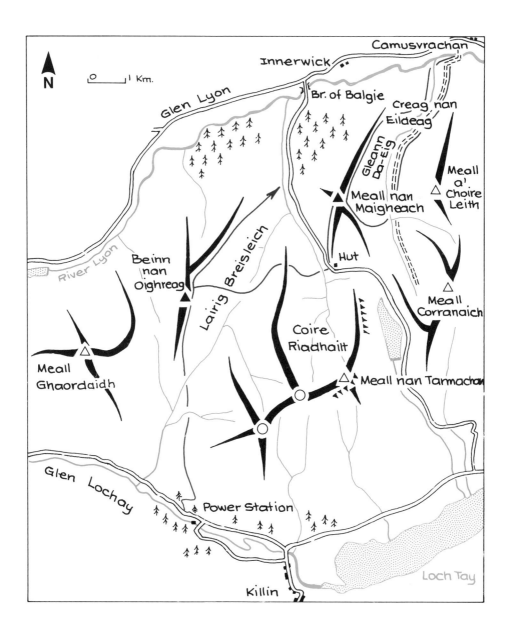

Beinn Odhar from Strath Fillan   D.J. Bennet

Beinn Odhar; 901m; (OS Sheet 50; 338339); *dun-coloured hill*
Beinn Chaorach; 818m; (OS Sheet 50; 359328); *sheep hill*
Cam Chreag; 885m; (OS Sheet 50; 375346); *crooked crag*
Beinn nam Fuaran; 806m; (OS Sheet 50; 361381); *hill of the well*
Beinn a' Chaisteil; 886m; (OS Sheet 50; 348364); *hill of the castle*

These steep-sided grassy hills lying to the north-west of Tyndrum are bounded on the south and west by the A82 road, and to the north by the Auch Gleann. To their east rise the two Munros of Ben Challum and Creag Mhor. They from a very compact group, so that despite a good deal of climbing and descent, it is quite possible to traverse all of them in a single day.

Possibly the best starting point for the traverse, certainly one which has adequate provision for car parking and a trouble-free approach to the hills, is on the A82 road just N of the Beinn Odhar summit at (329331). Just N of this point the West Highland Way makes use of a cattle-creep to cross under the West Highland Railway. From the E side of the railway climb steeply SE to gain the S ridge of Beinn Odhar which is followed up an old track to a long-since disused lead mine, beyond which a small lochan is passed before reaching the summit. (2½km; 600m; 1h 40min).

Descend SE for 400 metres to reach a lochan where one comes to an electric fence. Follow this ESE to the col between Beinn Odhar and Beinn Chaorach and up onto the ridge of the latter hill. The fence turns N about 200 metres N of the summit of Beinn Chaorach. (5km; 970m; 3h). Descend the smooth ridge NNE to the next col, where there is a small wind generator, presumably to provide power for the electric fence. From there bear NE then E up more broken hillside to the top of Cam Chreag. (7½km; 1220m; 3h 50min).

Descend the long NNW ridge of Cam Chreag

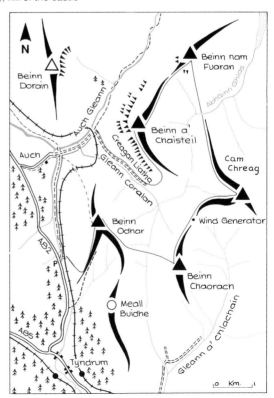

Beinn a'Chasteil   H.M. Brown

to the Abhainn Ghlas, cross this stream and climb due N to the summit of Beinn nam Fuaran. (11½km; 1630m; 5h 20min). Drop down steeply SW to a bealach of peat hags and follow the fence in the same direction to the summit of Beinn a' Chaisteil. (13½km; 1970m; 6h 20min).

The broken cliffs of Creagan Liatha prevent a direct descent to Glen Coralan, so head SE down the ridge for 1½km until a steep curving descent leads to a track in the glen which can be followed down to the Auch Gleann and the meeting with the West Highland Way

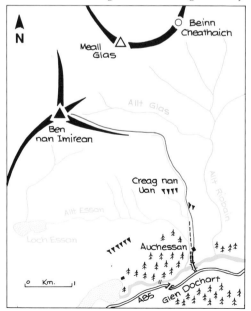

near Auch. Finally, walk S along the Way for almost 3km, climbing about 100m to return to the day's starting point.

It is possible to start and finish this traverse at the point where the private road to Auch branches off the A82 road at (317354), but there is only limited space for cars to park at the side of this very busy road. If this approach is adopted, walk down to Auch, cross the Allt Coire Chailein and then climb SE to cross the railway by a footbridge and continue steeply in the same direction to reach the N ridge of Beinn Odhar.

Beinn nan Imirean; 849m; (OS Sheet 51; 419309) *hill of the ridge.*

Beinn nan Imirean stands at the west end of the extensive tract of relatively uninteresting hills and moorland between Glen Dochart and Glen Lochay, and is itself a modest hill which appears as the outlier of Meall Glas. However, the drop between the two hills is more than enough to give Beinn nan Imirean its Corbett status. The shortest approach to it is from Glen Dochart across the low skirt of gentle-angled moorland of peat hags and winding streams northeast of Loch Iubhair.

There is limited space at the side of the A85 road to park cars near the private road to Auchessan. From there follow a track N up the E side of the unnamed stream which flows down past the E side of Creag nan Uan. Follow this stream towards its source over rough moorland and strike WNW to Meall Garbh and up the SE ridge of Beinn nan Imirean to its summit. (5km; 690m; 2h 20min).

Garbh Bheinn and Sgorr na Ciche from Loch Leven   H.M. Brown

SECTION 3

Northwest Argyll and Appin

Beinn a'Bhuiridh and the eastern ridges of Ben Cruachan from Beinn Eunaich   *D.J. Bennet*

Beinn a'Bhuiridh; 897m; (OS Sheet 50; 094283); *hill of roaring (of stags)*

Those who have made the complete circuit of Ben Cruachan's huge corrie holding the North of Scotland Hydro-Electric Board's pumped-storage reservoir will have discovered Beinn a'Bhuiridh to be a fine summit in its own right, jutting out southwards to command views along several glens and across Loch Awe. For those still to make an ascent of this hill, there is a variety of routes, or it could be an excuse for that full circuit round the Cruachan horseshoe.

The hill is perhaps best ascended as part of a traverse, for example up the Monadh Driseig ridge and down the path to the Falls of Cruachan, or alternatively up the Allt Coire Ghlais to the Larig Torran (the pass between Beinn a'Bhuiridh and Stob Garbh) and down by the road from the dam to Lochawe. As the A85 road is busy in summer, walking along it is no pleasure, and the route described below is one circuit which starts and finishes at the same point and thus requires no road walking. The Hydro-Electric Board's Visitor Centre in the Pass of Brander, St Conan's Kirk and Kilchurn Castle, as well as the delightful woodland and water scenery along the shore of Loch Awe, are additional attractions in the vicinity of Beinn a'Bhuiridh.

The start is at the junction of the A85 road and the old military road, now the B8077, where there is room for car parking along the edge of the B8077. Take the track, which was once part of an old mineral line to quarry workings, round to the Allt Coire Ghlais. Follow the burn up into the Cqire Glas, a wild place with bold crags to the S, but with an easy climb up to the Larig Torran.

Cattle used to be driven across this pass to graze in the corrie where the reservoir now is, and Wallace led his men this way. From the pass there is a steep pull of 270m up to the rock-knobbly summit of Beinn a'Bhuiridh and a view S which comes like a revelation. (6km; 840m; 2h 50min).

Descend the long E ridge over Monadh Driseig to return to the starting point; a treat given good evening light on the Ben Lui hills. The lowest slope at the foot of the ridge is steep and there are some crags, so it is advisable when setting out at the beginning of the day to look at this slope and note a suitable way down through the crags.

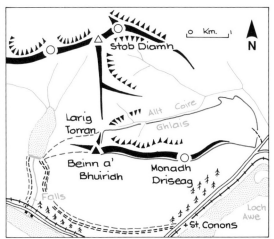

Looking up Glen Strae to Beinn Mhic-Mhonaidh   *H.M. Brown*

Beinn Mhic-Mhonaidh; 796m; (OS Sheet 50; 208349); *hill of the son of the moor*

Viewed up Glen Strae, this rather shy hill rises in a bold parabolic outline, but from the east its real stepped-ridge shape is apparent. Glen Strae might appear to give the natural approach, but there may be problems crossing the river. The ascent from Glen Orchy is shorter and more varied, despite the vast areas of conifers on that side of the hill.

About half way along the B8074 road through Glen Orchy from Dalmally to Bridge of Orchy there is a forestry road bridge across the River Orchy just below the Eas Urchaidh *(Falls of Orchy)*. Park nearby and cross the bridge to follow the forestry track up the Allt Broighleachan to its end at a hidden meadow. Several tracks beaten out by all-terrain vehicles branch off from there. Take the one which crosses the stream N; there is a footbridge at (232333), not visible from the track, which may be useful in wet weather. Almost at once turn W on another track

which continues for 2km to the edge of the forest on the watershed.

Turn N to the ruined shielings of Airigh Chailleach and climb steeply NW to reach the hill's crest high on the An Sgriodan ridge. The stony summit is a splendid viewpoint, being surrounded by such hills as Ben Cruachan, Starav, Stob Ghabhar and Ben Lui. (6½km; 730m; 2h 50min). To the NE, down a step beyond the cairn, there is a small, deep lochan. A descent due S from there leads back to the ruins of the shieling and the route of ascent. Do not attempt any other way through the dense forest.

In dry weather conditions, and with transport prearranged, an exit down Glen Strae gives a pleasing traverse. Descend NW from the summit lochan to the Airigh Challtuinn shielings and follow the river for 2½km down to the estate track which leads in a further 6km to the B8077 road near Dalmally.

Beinn Udlaidh; 840m; (OS Sheet 50; 280333); *dark (or gloomy) hill*
Beinn Bhreac-liath; 802m; (OS Sheet 50; 303339); *speckled grey hill*

These two hills, bounded by Glen Orchy, Glen Lochy and the A82 road between Tyndrum and Bridge of Orchy, offer a short but varied day's walking. Their flanks are extensively afforested and access has to make use of the few gaps remaining. New plantings in Glen Orchy stretch from Invergaunan to Arichastlich, and Invergaunan is perhaps the best starting point for the traverse of the two hills.

Walk up the Allt Ghamhnain for about 1km then bear S more steeply onto the N ridge of Beinn Udlaidh. A remarkable line of quartz rock is reached; it is a prominent feature of the hill, clearly seen from

the N from as far away as Loch Tulla. It crosses the ridge to form part of the cliffs of Coire Daimh. The ascent up the N ridge to the extensive flat summit is stony, but easy. (4km; 710m; 2h 10min).

Continue SE, then ENE down to a broad col at about 600m and climb, steeply at first, to the fairly flat top of Beinn Bhreac-liath. (6½km; 920m; 3h). The circuit can be completed by walking down the long easy-angled N ridge of the hill to return to the starting point at Invergaunan. If a second car is available, a descent from Beinn Bhreac-liath can be made E to the S edge of the Coille Bhreac-liath forest, which is

Beinn Bhreac-liath and Beinn Udlaidh seen from the north across Loch Tulla   *G.S. Johnstone*

followed down Coire Chalein to the A82 road. This route gives the shortest ascent of Beinn Bhreac-liath, and the traverse described above could equally well be done in reverse.

The shortest ascent of these two hills starts and finishes at Arinabea in Glen Lochy where the streams create breaks in the forest by which it is quite easy to reach the col between them.

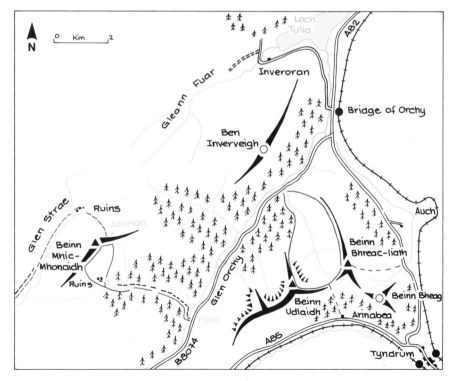

Looking south-west from Creach Bheinn towards the islands of the Firth of Lorn   P. Hodgkiss

Creach Bheinn; 810m; (OS Sheet 50; 024422); *bare (or windswept) hill*

The sprawling mass of this hill, with a great expanse of afforestation covering its west flank, is very obvious from the main road (A828) on the north side of Loch Creran. Seen from higher hills to the north and east, however, its lack of any distinctive shape makes it less readily identified.

Start from the A828 road just N of Druimavuic House near the head of Loch Creran where a metal gate at (007451) leads to a path through the trees. Initially this path skirts the stone wall bounding the policies of the house, but it soon reaches a second gate in open ground and continues E up the N side of the Allt Buidhe, though faint and intermittent in its upper reaches, to the bealach (560m) between Creach Bheinn and Beinn Sgulaird. From the bealach a well-defined ridge leads SW over Creag na Cathaig for 1km, before rising steeply due W to the NE top of Creach Bheinn (803m). From there a short descent and reascent lead SW for 1km to the large cairn on the main summit. (7km; 850m; 3h).

From the top one looks SE to Loch Etive and SW down the Firth of Lorn, and on a clear day a happy hour could be spent with a map picking out the islands and their hills. Closer at hand, Creach Bheinn has a rich crop of spring flowers, with purple saxifrage particularly evident under the hill's granite crags.

An alternative route to Creach Bheinn, shorter and steeper, but one that might be preferred by those planning to continue the traverse to Beinn Sgulaird, is to cross to the S side of the Allt Buidhe about 300 metres beyond the upper limit of the forest on that side of the stream and climb steeply through heather to gain the W ridge of the hill at Meall nan Caorach. Continue along this ridge over Meall Garbh to the NE top and so to the summit. (5km; 850m; 2h 30min).

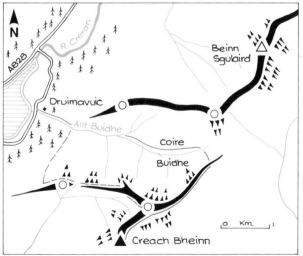

Looking south-west from the Glen Coe peaks down Glen Etive to Beinn Trilleachan   *P. Hodgkiss*

Beinn Trilleachan; 839m; (OS Sheet 50; 086439); *hill of the sandpipers*

As one approaches down Glen Etive, Beinn Trilleachan increasingly dominates the view, which is often further highlighted by morning sunshine glinting from the famous Etive Slabs, the great 200m sweep of granite (named the Trilleachan Slabs on the OS map) on the east face of the hill above Loch Etive. The distinctive shape of Beinn Trilleachan, often likened to an upturned boat, is most apparent when it is seen end-on from the Glencoe mountains to the northeast.

An old cross-country route, not shown on any modern map, connecting the heads of Loch Etive and Loch Creran, provides the first kilometre of the approach to Beinn Trilleachan. It starts at the edge of the forest at (111453) about 300 metres NE of the road end. The path is little used, and being cut through shallow top-soil on the underlying granite, it is often wet. It does, however, provide straightforward access and can be left after about 40 minutes (at a height of about 200m) to climb steeply SW onto the spine of the hill. The first top marked on the OS map, Meall nan Gobhar (590m), is barely noticeable, but from that point the ridge becomes rocky with small tors of granite appearing. Also the sense of exposure on the left becomes increasingly impressive, culminating at the next top (767m) where the cairn is poised directly above the great sweep of the Etive Slabs. There is a short steep descent of about 70m followed by a more gentle slope with less exposure leading SW to the summit. (5½km; 920m; 2h 50min).

Once the angle of ascent eases, at about the 700m level, the views both down and across Loch Etive are truly spectacular, and redolent of mountain ranges on a grander scale. Returning NE along the ridge, the Glencoe and Blackmount peaks are laid out ahead in satisfying complexity.

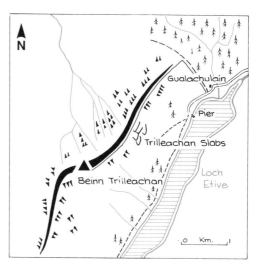

Looking towards the summit of Fraochaidh from the lochan on the NE ridge   P. Hodgkiss

Fraochaidh; 879m; (OS Sheet 41; 029517); *heathery hill*

There is a fine view of this hill from the A828 road at Duror of Appin, but any ascent from the west side involves penetrating a barrier of afforestation, and is not advised. Despite the obviously greater height and mass of its northern neighbour Beinn a'Bheithir, Fraochaidh, when climbed over its long undulating NE ridge, gives the impression of being a much larger hill than its actual height would suggest.

Start from East Laroch, Ballachulish, along the minor road on the W side of the River Laroch. The tarmacadam soon gives way to a Landrover track and, when it dwindles, a good path continues S. After 3½km, at a cairn, drop left from the path to make an easy crossing of the River Laroch. The right of way shown on the OS 1:50000 map as a path leading SSW over to Glen Creran is faint and intermittent, but a stiff climb of 170m through thick grass does end unmistakably on the Mam Uchdaich (390m), unnamed on the OS map. There, where the right of way crosses a stile into the forested slopes above Glen Creran, turn SW and follow a faint path beside the deer fence, then over the humpy crest of the first top (626m).

Descend SSW and cross a knoll to reach a lochan, and keep going in the same direction to the next top (718m). Continue along the ridge, which then narrows and becomes rockier, dropping 80m and turning W over two more knolls. The iron stanchions of an old fence appear before the final ridge climbs WNW for 200m to finally level out and turn WSW to the cairn of Fraochaidh and a splendid view down Loch Linnhe. (10km; 1020m; 4h).

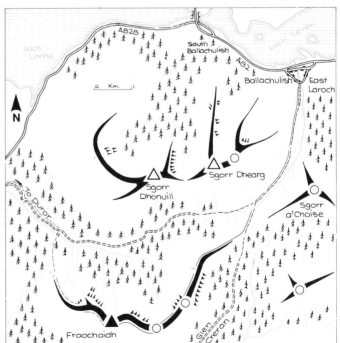

If transport is available at Duror, Fraochaidh can be traversed, provided one is willing to engage a short section of old and trackless forest. Descend the main ridge WNW, then W and finally NW to a lochan at (013529). From there drop steeply due N to the forest edge. There is no firebreak, but 15 minutes of struggle through trees and drainage ditches bring one to a forest track, and a right turn leads down by zig-zags to a footbridge at (014541). From there a forest road leads to Duror.

Meall Lighiche from Aonach Dubh a'Ghlinne   *P. Hodgkiss*

Meall Lighiche; 772m; (OS Sheet 41; 095529); *doctor's hill*

Truly retiring, Meall Lighiche is hemmed in on all sides by other hills, but it can be seen in the view up Gleann Leac na Muidhe from the main road through Glen Coe from a point west of the National Trust for Scotland's Visitor Centre. Its western slopes are rounded, dropping to the forests of Glen Creran, but the eastern flank falls precipitously from the outlying top Creag Bhan (719m) to the head of Gleann Leac na Muidhe. Because of the encircling hills and the afforestation on the western side of Meall Lighiche, the only reasonable approach is from Glen Coe, but this route follows a fine narrow glen through rugged mountain scenery.

One kilometre W of the National Trust for Scotland car park on the A82 road, a Landrover track runs S on the W bank of the Allt na Muidhe. Follow it to a bridge across the burn and through the farm, Gleann-leac-na-muidhe. The track continues further than shown on the OS 1:50000 map, and ends after 2½km at a confluence of streams.

Cross to the W bank of the Allt na Muidhe and follow a faint path W for 300 metres. Turn S and climb the steep, terraced grass slope for 450m to the small cairn on Creag Bhan. From it there is a particularly fine view in the northern arc of Beinn a'Bheithir and Ben Nevis. Level ground continues SSW for 200 metres before the final ridge climbs easily due W along a line of old iron fence posts. The summit cairn of

Meall Lighiche sits on a slab of quartz-embedded schist, and from it there is a magnificent view down Glen Creran and out to Mull. (5km; 730m; 2h 20min).

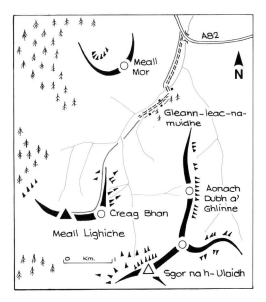

Beinn Maol Chaluim from Glen Etive   *H.M. Brown*

Beinn Maol Chaluim; 907m; (OS Sheets 41 and 50; 135526); *Calum's bare hill*

Beinn Maol Chaluim, like Meall Lighiche, is a retiring hill, hidden behind the greater Glen Coe peaks. A fleeting glimpse of it can be caught from the A82 road through Glen Coe, looking up Fionn Ghleann from a point not far west of the National Trust for Scotland car park. From Glen Etive, only the south-east top (847m) can be properly seen.

Approaches to the hill can be made either from Glen Coe to the north or from Glen Etive to the southeast, but the former involves some heavy going in the wild Fionn Ghleann, while the route from Glen Etive has the advantage of a high ridge walk in splendid surroundings.

Leave the Glen Etive road at (149496) at the S end of the afforestation in the foot of Gleann Fhaolain. The small area of open hillside below Creag na Caillich is the only gap in the trees on the NW side of the Glen Etive road. Climb very steep grassy ground beside the forest fence, turning left once past some rocky bluffs to gain the S ridge of Beinn Maol Chaluim. After 1km of straightforward climbing, crags at about 500m block progress. These are best turned on the right, requiring a traverse of about 300 metres. A scrambling route through the crags is possible, and gives pleasant moderate climbing in dry conditions. After another 1km the southern group of minor tops is reached, and in front of one is the prospect of an aerial ridge with the splendid backcloth of Bidean nam Bian's south face. The ridge stretches NE for 1km and is an easy walk to the summit of Beinn Maol Chaluim. (4km; 820m; 2h 20min).

A grand circuit can be made by descending N to the bealach at the head of Gleann Fhaolain, climbing Bidean nam Bian by its steep SW side and returning to Glen Etive along the ridge over Stob Coire Sgreamhach.

Stob Dubh; 883m; (OS Sheet 50; 166488); *black peak*

From whatever point on the Glen Etive road one views this hill, it is steep, dark and intimidating. Its SW facet is deeply scored by a gorge making the hill instantly recognisable from other heights around the foot of Glen Etive. Stob Dubh is almost completely encircled by the greater peaks of the Blackmount and Glencoe, and lies at the hub of a huge wheel of ridges with the only break provided by Glen Etive. Its outlier, Beinn Ceitlein, is included in this description, and the traverse of the two peaks makes a good round.

Leave the Glen Etive road at (137468) down a private road, not easily seen from above when driving down the glen. After crossing the River Etive on a bridge high above deep pools, take the track NE for just over 1km to another smaller bridge over the Allt Ceitlein. Above looms the uncompromisingly steep SW ridge of Stob Dubh, rising 850m in 2km. Underfoot the going is excellent on short grass, and the minor crags at roughly half height are easily turned, mainly on the right. Once above the last of these bluffs, the angle eases and the cairn is soon reached. (4½km; 900m; 2h 30min).

To continue to Beinn Ceitlein, there is first a steep descent ESE of 120m before a broad ridge curls up NE to the first and higher of two tops, 845m. The descent can be made SE down steep, rough ground for a few hundred metres, then bear S across the eastward-flowing stream in Coire Dubh-mor to reach the headwaters of the Allt Ceitlein. Follow its N bank, along which a path soon appears that leads back to the bridge at the foot of the stream.

Stob Dubh from the head of Loch Etive   H.M. Brown

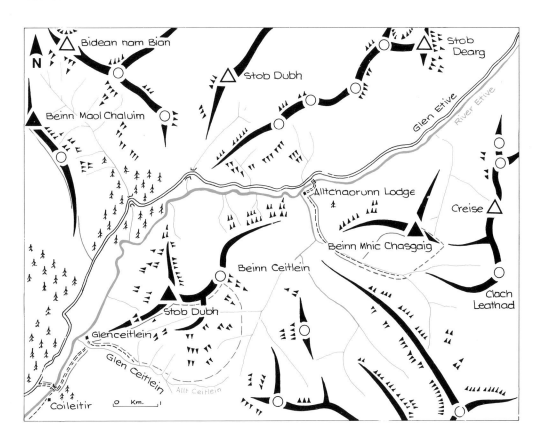

Looking up the west ridge of Beinn Mhic Chasgaig from the Allt a'Chaorainn   *P. Hodgkiss*

Beinn Mhic Chasgaig; 864m; (OS Sheets 41 and 50; 221502); *MacChasgaig's hill*

Beinn Mhic Chasgaig is hemmed in to the north, south and east by the larger mountain ridges of Buachaille Etive Mor and the Blackmount, but it does present a bold front to Glen Etive, above which its north-west wall extends for 3km. From Alltchaorunn one sees a shapely cone, apparently ringed high up by crags, with a strangely isolated little patch of forest on its north flank. A direct route can be made up this west ridge and the crags can be turned, but a more circuitous and easier-angled route passing through a spectacular ravine is described below.

Start at the bridge over the River Etive at (198513).

Looking north from Beinn Mhic Chasgaig to the Buachaille Etive Mor and Beinn a'Chrulaiste   *D. J. Bennet*

This bridge has a corrugated iron gate some 2m high, which is often locked. If access there is not possible, the only alternative approach from Glen Etive is to wade across the river, and this may pose a problem except when it is low, and likely to remain so while you are on the hill.

From the far side of the bridge a track goes to Alltchaorunn, and beyond there a good path follows the E bank of the Allt a'Chaorainn. (There are some wide, deep pools worn from the granite bedrock that are ideal for swimming). In 1km a junction of burns is reached; follow the Allt Coire Ghiubhasan, keeping to its N bank for 100 metres, then hunting carefully downhill for a wire-rope aiding the descent to a single-plank bridge. Roughly 30m above the bridge on the S bank a stalker's path follows the burn

through a glen so narrow and steep-sided as to have the atmosphere, if not the scale, of a Himalayan defile.

Follow the path for 1km until it drops almost to the burn, and an open gorge on the SW flank of Beinn Mhic Chasgaig appears. Cross the burn and climb steeply up the E side of this gorge, veering E once the angle eases, to reach the summit plateau with the cairn at its N end. (4½km; 750m; 2h 20min).

An alternative route follows the path beside the Allt Coire Ghiubhasan for a further 1½km until SW of the col between Beinn Mhic Chasgaig and Clach Leathad. Climb easily to this col, from where Clach Leathad and other Blackmount tops can be included in the traverse.

Map on page 69.

Beinn a'Chrulaiste from the south-east   G.S. Johnstone

Beinn a'Chrulaiste; 857m; (OS Sheet 41; 246567); *rocky hill*

Although Beinn a'Chrulaiste appears as a great lump of a hill compared with its more elegant and majestic neighbours,its ascent is most rewarding for the views from the summit.

The most convenient starting place is at Kingshouse Hotel where there is car parking space and the assurance of refreshment upon return. Go N up the Allt a'Bhalaich for 1½km to a height of about 350m, and then bear WNW up a broad ridge. This is more rugged than the map indicates, with some rocky outcrops, and leads directly to the summit. (3km; 600m; 1h 40min).

The return to Kingshouse can be varied by descending WNW at first, then NE and E to traverse the broad ridge over the twin tops of Meall Bhalach.

The W ridge of Beinn a'Chrulaiste, starting

from Altnafeadh, is a pleasant route, particularly on the descent, for there is a splendid view of the Glen Coe peaks.

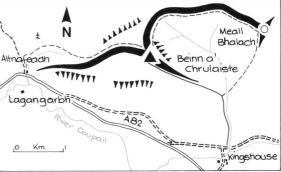

Garbh Bheinn from the north across Loch Leven   *H.M. Brown*

Garbh Bheinn; 867m; (OS Sheet 41; 169601); *rough hill*

Garbh Bheinn is an isolated peak between the Aonach Eagach ridge to its south and the head of Loch Leven to its north. The West Highland Way contours the east end of the hill as it descends towards Kinlochleven. This fine hill has been largely neglected because it is surrounded by higher and better known peaks, and is to some extent hidden by them. The best roadside viewpoint for the hill is from the layby at the highest point on the B863 road along the south side of Loch Leven, from which point one is looking directly up the west ridge.

The west ridge provides a good route of ascent for Garbh Bheinn. Cars can be left at two small laybys near the bridge over the Allt Gleann a'Chaolais 300 metres E of the Caolasnacon caravan site. From the E side of the bridge follow a prominent path up the Allt Gleann a'Chaolais for 60 metres and then a faint path which leads onto the the ridge and continues between rocky outcrops. The crest of the ridge can be followed

throughout over a succession of false tops. During the ascent there are views back across Loch Linnhe to the Ardgour hills and, towards the top, close views of the little seen N face of the Aonach Eagach.

Alternatively, a slightly easier ascent can be made by continuing along the path beside the Allt Gleann a'Chaolais for a further 1km before ascending N to the first col on the W ridge, which is followed to the top. (3km; 850m; 2h 10min).

The top has two cairns. The first of red igneous rock appears to be the higher, though the second of white stones gives the better view over the Glen Coe hills, the Mamores and Ben Nevis, and E along the length of the Blackwater Reservoir. The return can be made back down the W ridge, or by a steeper descent S from the first col on the ridge to the path beside the Allt Gleann a'Chaolais. Another possibility is to complete the traverse down the NE ridge to join the West Highland Way near Kinlochleven.

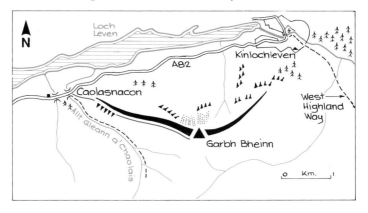

Sgorr na Ciche from Loch Leven   *H.M. Brown*

Sgorr na Ciche (Pap of Glencoe); 742m; (OS Sheet 41; 125594)

The very prominent peak above Glencoe village is Sgorr na Ciche, more commonly known by its anglicised name, the Pap of Glencoe. It forms the true western end of the long ridge which extends for 11km from the Devil's Staircase along the north side of Glen Coe, the central and highest part of this ridge being the Aonach Eagach.

Sgorr na Ciche may readily be climbed as the end of a traverse of the Aonach Eagach, the route to it from Sgorr nam Fiannaidh involving about 2km of quite rough ridge walking. It also gives a very pleasant half day's outing when climbed by itself from the road bet Glencoe village and the Clachaig Hotel.

At the edge of the wood at (111586) there is space to park a few cars. Cross the road and start up the marked farm track, taking the right fork across the burn where the track divides. A clear path goes from the end of this track up the bank and continues along the SE side of the prominent gully which leads to the col between the Pap and Sgorr nam Fiannaidh. From the col easy scrambling leads directly to the summit, or alternatively there is a cairned path which avoids all difficulties up the NE ridge. (2½km; 720m; 1h 50min).

The descent is best made by the same route.

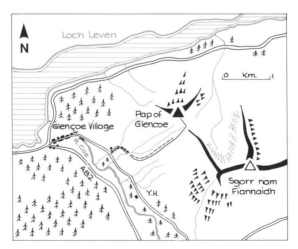

Loch Ossian and Leum Uilleim   *D.J. Bennet*

SECTION 4

Loch Leven to Loch Ericht

Mam na Gualainn and Beinn na Caillich from Kinlochleven   *H.M. Brown*

Mam na Gualainn; 796m; (OS Sheet 41; 115625); *pass of the shoulder*

This hill is situated between Loch Leven and the western end of the Mamore Forest mountains, and although it is dwarfed by its near neighbours, if offers magnificent views, particularly of the Beinn a' Bheithir massif beyond Ballachulish.

The shortest ascent of this hill is from Callert on the B863 road on the north side of Loch Leven. There is a right of way from there to Lairigmor which starts some distance E of Callert House at (097605). The right of way is followed for about 2km, almost to its highest point, and then one climbs the WSW ridge of Mam na Gualainn direct to the summit. (4km; 790m; 2h 20min).

A much more enjoyable walk can be had by traversing the whole ridge between Kinlochleven and Callert, thus including the eastern summit, Beinn na Caillich (764m). This entails the use of two cars. The traverse from east to west will normally give the best views.

Follow the West Highland Way from the western edge of Kinlochleven for about 2km to the point at about 250m where a path branches off to the left to cross the Allt Nathrach. Follow this path across the stream and up the steep nose of the E ridge of Beinn na Caillich, and continue along the ridge to the summit. A delightful 2½km ridge walk follows which ends at Mam na Gualainn. (7km; 950m; 3h 10min). It is equally possible to start the traverse from Mamore Lodge, but the height gained by car may have to be paid for in the form of a parking fee at the lodge.

From the summit of Mam na Gualainn the descent goes down the WSW ridge to reach the right of way leading down to Callert.

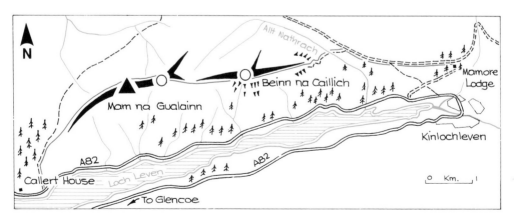

Glas Bheinn; 789m; (OS Sheet 41; 259641); *grey hill*

This rather undistinguished hill is situated in the seldom visited hill country to the east of the Mamores, midway between Kinlochleven and the head of Loch Treig.

The only route to Glas Bheinn which is readily accessible from a public road starts in Kinlochleven. From the Grey Mare Waterfall car park a good path leads steeply up through fine oak and birch woods to skirt the NW flank of Meall an Doire Dharaich. The track from Mamore Lodge to Loch Eilde Mor is reached and followed for ½km before taking another path going E round the end of the loch to the dam at

its outlet. Cross the top of the dam and continue along the path for 2½km to the Meall na Cruaidhe shoulder on the broad SW ridge of Glas Bheinn, and climb this ridge to the top. (8½km; 790m; 3h 20min).

An alternative and more attractive ascent can be made from Staoineag bothy on the S side of the Abhainn Rath, 2km SW of the head of Loch Treig, but the approach to the bothy itself involves a long walk. From the bothy cross the Allt Gleann na Giubhsachan and climb the long NE ridge past the tiny Lochan a' Chuirn Dheirg. (5½km; 500m; 2h 10min).

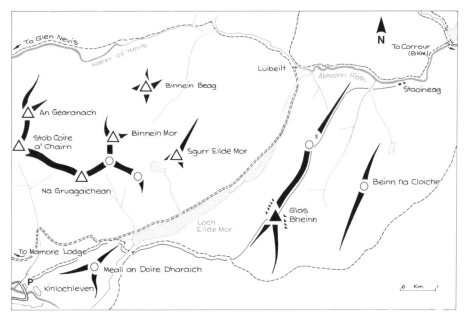

Leum Uilleim; 906m; (OS Sheet 41; 331641); *William's leap*

Lying to the south-west of Corrour Station on the West Highland Line, Leum Uilleim can provide a short yet attractive expedition on the north edge of Rannoch Moor. Its isolated position in the heart of the Central Highlands makes it a splendid viewpoint, and the walking on the hill is good almost everywhere. The big north-east facing Coire a' Bhric Beag is the most prominent feature of the hill, and the traverse of the ridges round this corrie is a good circuit.

Corrour Station and the Loch Ossian Youth Hostel are the only two practicable starting points. From the station go W along a stalker's path to its end in 1½km at the 500m contour. Continue W more steeply for ½km to reach the ridge which leads pleasantly over Tom an Eoin for 2km to Beinn a' Bhric (876m), which is the W top of Leum Uilleim. Descend steeply E, avoiding incipient crags, and climb the uniform slope to the main summit. (6km; 580m; 2h 20min).

The return to Corrour goes along the NE ridge, steeply down the rocky nose of Sron an

Lagain Ghairbh, and then across increasingly boggy ground to the station.

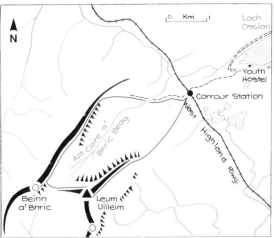

Meall na Meoig and Beinn Pharlagain from Carn Dearg   *I.A. Robertson*

Meall na Meoig of Beinn Pharlagain; 868m;
(OS Sheet 42; 448642); *hill of whey (pharlagain perhaps grassy hollow)*

Beinn Pharlagain lies on the rim of Rannoch Moor and verges on some of the most remote country south of the Great Glen. To its north is the forest of Ben Alder, to the west the hills of Loch Ossian and Loch Treig, and to the south-west Rannoch Moor. Only to the south and south-east, near the head of Loch Rannoch, is there any human habitation within 7 or 8 km of this hill. Access to it is either by road along Loch Rannoch, or by train to Rannoch station.

The historic route to the Highlands, The Road to the Isles, leaves the B846 road 2½km E of Rannoch Station. Follow this track NW then N for 3km to the bridge over the Allt Eigheach, then bear NNE on the E side of the stream to Leacann nan Giomach, the southern end of Beinn Pharlagain. Grass and heather slopes lead N up the undulating ridge, first to an unnamed top of 807m then NE, down and up to Pt 838m. Meall na Meoig is a further ¾km NW and its top is marked by a substantial cairn. (7½km; 660m; 2h 50min). The last part of the ridge is quite broad and featureless, but two lochans on its NE side may be guides to navigation in mist.

One can either return by retracing one's steps along the ridge, or alternatively by descending WSW to reach and follow the path down the W side of the Allt Eigheach to rejoin The Road to the Isles. To extend the walk by a considerable distance, one can continue N for 3½km along the broad ridge to Sgor Gaibhre and return by Carn Dearg and its undulating S ridge, which also leads to The Road to the Isles. This gives a round trip of about 23km along broad grassy ridges which give pleasant easy walking.

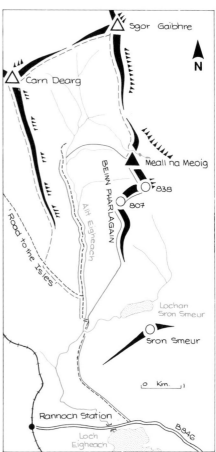

Cruach Innse (left) and Sgurr Innse from the Lairig Leacach bothy   D. Scott

Sgurr Innse; 808m; (OS Sheet 41; 290748); *peak of the meadow*
Cruach Innse; 857m; (OS Sheet 41; 280763); *hill of the meadow*

These two peaks are well named, the massive Cruach rising above the Insh flats on the south side of the River Spean, with the shapely Sgurr appearing over its east flank. They are particularly well seen from the area around Roy Bridge. Both are fairly steep all round their upper slopes, especially on the east and on the south-west above the Lairig Leacach. The only rock of any note is on the Sgurr, but although very sound it is too short and discontinuous to give anything more than scrambling.

The best route is to traverse both these tops. Take the narrow public road on the S side of the River Spean to its end just below Corriechoille where the right of way to Rannoch is indicated by a signpost. A private road goes S for 3km to the site of the old railway built by the British Aluminium Company for the construction of the tunnel from Loch Treig to the factory at Fort William. No objections have been made to date to climbers driving to this point. Continue on foot up the road through the forest and over the Allt Leachdach. A short distance beyond the bridge leave the track and climb steepening grass and heather to the NW ridge of Cruach Innse, and continue up this ridge to the flat stony summit of the hill. (From Corriechoille: 5½km; 750m; 2h 30min).

Descend SE along the broad stony ridge for ½km, then bear S as the ridge steepens and becomes more rocky above the broad col. Cross the col (589m) and climb SE to the foot of the steep upper rocks of Sgurr Innse. A narrow path makes a rising traverse leftwards across scree and boulders, with some optional mild scrambling, to the N shoulder of the hill and an easy walk up to the summit. (8km; 970m; 3h 30min). Descend by the same route to the 589m col and slant down W to rejoin the track in the Lairig Leacach.

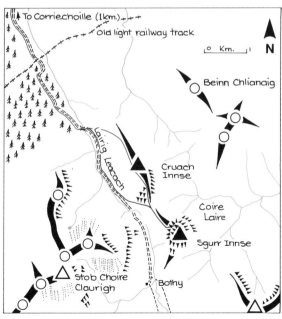

The Fara from Loch Ericht   H.M. Brown

The Fara; 911m; (OS Sheet 42; 598844)

There can be few people driving along the A9 road who have not cast a glance towards The Fara as they passed by the head of Loch Ericht, but fewer will be aware of the fine hillwalk that this long ridge offers. Although the top is at the north-east end of this ridge, and gives a round trip of only 3 hours from Dalwhinnie, to confine one's activity only to this part of The Fara is to miss a longer and more rewarding expedition.

The most direct approach is from Dalwhinnie, and as the slopes above Loch Ericht are now extensively forested, route-finding is a matter of avoiding the forests. From Dalwhinnie station go S across the level crossing (where there is limited parking) and follow the private road along the NW side of Loch Ericht for about 2½km to a point (615836) where there is a gap between newer and older sections of the forest. From there climb NW up the slope through this gap. At the top of the forest follow a broken fence and a dry-stane dyke directly to the massive summit cairn. (4½km; 550m; 2h).

The walk can be extended by traversing the ridge of The Fara to Meall Cruaidh, descending SW then S to the track near Ben Alder Lodge and returning to Dalwhinnie along the private road by Loch Ericht.

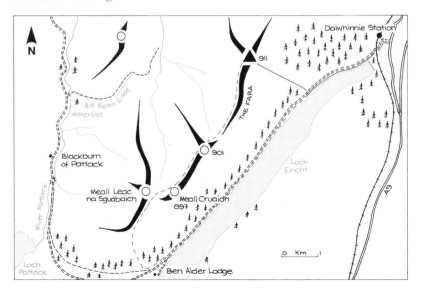

Looking across Loch Ericht to Stob an Aonaich Mhoir   P. Hodgkiss

SECTION 5

The Southern Grampians: Loch Rannoch to Glen Garry

Stob an Aonaich Mhoir; 855m; (OS Sheet 42; 537694); *peak of the big crest*
Beinn Mholach; 841m; (OS Sheet 42; 587655); *shaggy mountain*

These two rather elusive hills are described together largely because they share a desolate and neglected corner of the Central Highlands. Access routes to them are long and tedious, and climbing them together might be regarded as a possible option, but only one which should be adopted by strong walkers on long summer days.

Stob an Aonaich Mhoir is the highest point of the long ridge that encloses the east side of Loch Ericht. The ascent may be easy, but the approach from the south is long and uninteresting, a 12km tramp along a tarred road that has to be retraced on the return journey. If a bicycle could be used for this approach it would be a great advantage. This road starts at Bridge of Ericht on the N shore of Loch Rannoch; the gate at its start is usually locked, but the keeper whose cottage is nearby will open it on request. The road leads to Coire Bhachdaidh Lodge and a hydro-electric power station on the side of Loch Ericht. From its highest point bear NW directly up slopes of grass and heather to the summit of Stob an Aonaich Mhoir, which is a splendid perch with views up and down Loch Ericht. (13½km; 650m; 4h 10min).

Beinn Mholach's big cairn crowns a craggy hill which must be one of the least visited summits in Scotland. The vast expanse of moor between it and Loch Rannoch has a great atmosphere of space. From Annat on the N side of Loch Rannoch a right of way goes N to Duinish and Loch Garry, and this is the easy route from the S, particularly if a bicycle is used for the first 4 or 5km of the way. The alternative track starting at Craiganour is not a right of way, but it joins the Annat route after 2km. Beyond this meeting of the two tracks bear NW across the moor on the N side of the Caochan an Leathaid Bhain, passing NE of Sgurran Dearg to reach and climb the steeper SE slopes of Beinn Mholach. (9km; 650m; 3h 10min).

Dalnaspidal Lodge and the right of way along the W side of Loch Garry also provide a possible approach to Beinn Mholach, and a bicycle might be used for 5km to the S end of the loch. Cross the footbridge at (614675) and climb the NE ridge of Beinn Mholach over Creag nan Gabhar. (From Dalnaspidal: 10km; 440m; 3h).

The Loch Garry approach is the best one for the traverse of both hills. From Beinn Mholach wend over or round the intervening hills WNW towards Stob an Aonaich Mhoir. The return journey by the Allt Feith Gharuiareagan and the Allt Shallain is long and demanding, crossing trackless country that gives heavy going.

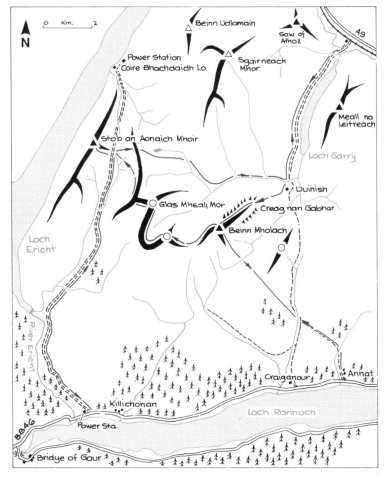

Beinn a'Chuallaich across Loch Rannoch   H.M. Brown

Beinn a' Chuallaich; 892m; (OS Sheet 42; 684618); *hill of the herding*

This is a rather self-effacing hill, but it gives a pleasant short ascent, and a superb summit view. In winter there is often good skiing on the east-facing side of the hill, which holds snow well. The traverse of the hill is particularly worthwhile, provided of course that one has suitable transport arrangements at one's disposal.

The shortest ascent is from the east, and although there are recent forestry plantings on that side of the hill not shown on the OS map, they can be avoided. One possible starting point is at a bend on the B847 road at (707616) where a stalker's path leads W to a small bothy. Climb WNW to reach the col between Meall a' Chuallaich and its N top, Meall nan Eun, and finish with a short climb up the NW ridge to the summit where there is a large cairn and a trig point. (3km; 590m; 1h 40min).

A pleasant traverse can be continued, with splendid views to the west, by descending W from the summit, avoiding some small crags, to reach a stalker's path in ½km. This leads down S to the road beside Dunalastair Water. A longer continuation of the traverse goes SW down the open hillside to the Allt Mor which is followed S, crossing to its W bank by a bridge just above the trees and finally descending a steep path beside the dramatic waterslide of the burn to reach Kinloch Rannoch.

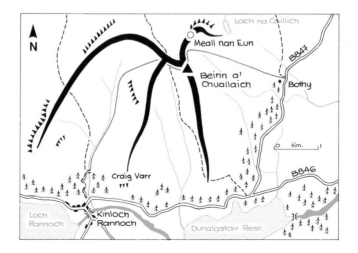

The Sow of Atholl from Dalnaspidal   *H.M. Brown*

Meall na Leitreach; 775m; (OS Sheet 42; 639703); *hill of slopes*
The Sow of Atholl; 803m; (OS Sheet 42; 625742)

The Pass of Drumochter, with the A9 road and railway using its deep trench to break through the Grampians, is a famous travellers' route. The first proper road through the pass was constructed by General Wade in the early 18th century. If the many route improvements since then, the line of electricity pylons and the noise, bustle and fumes of traffic now give the pass the impression of being a major line of communication, a climb up the hills at its sides shrinks man's work into perspective. Seen from the hillsides high above it, the moraine-filled pass appears as if the scouring work of the glaciers had been only yesterday.

The Sow of Atholl is the fanciful name given to balance its near neighbour to the north, An Torc, better known as the Boar of Badenoch. Originally The Sow was Meall an Dobhrachan *(watercress hill)*. Both The Sow and Meall na Leitreach can be easily climbed from Dalnaspidal, in a single day if one wants, for the ascent to each one is less than 400m. Their slopes are easy grass and heather, which in winter may well give delightful skiing. The flat ground surrounding Dalnaspidal Lodge is apt to flood, particularly in winter and spring, so follow the track towards Loch Garry, and use the bridges shown on the map.

As one climbs S up to Meall na Leitreach's undulating summit plateau there is quite a dramatic view northwards through the Pass of Drumochter, with the Sow rising steeply on its W side. The summit of Meall na Leitreach is reached almost 1km across the plateau. (3km; 370m; 1h 20min).

The Sow of Atholl is best climbed by its broad SE ridge, which gives a less spectacular view eastwards towards the lower country of Atholl. It can conveniently be climbed as the first stage in a longer traverse of the hills W of Drumochter Pass. (3km; 400m; 1h 20min).

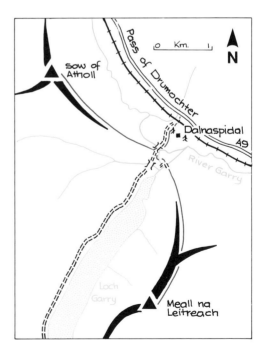

Looking north through the Gaick Pass from the slopes of An Dun   D.A. Baird

SECTION 6

The Southern Grampians: Glen Garry to Glen Shee

An Dun from the track to Sronphadruig Lodge   J. Renny

Maol Creag an Loch; 876m; (OS Sheet 42; 735807); *hill of the crag of the loch*
An Dun; 827m; (OS Sheet 42; 716802); *the fort*

An Dun is in Section 5 of this guidebook, but is included with Maol Creag an Loch in Section 6 because the two hills are conveniently climbed together.

These two naked hills, flat plateaux on top, are walled about by some of the steepest and most unrelenting hill slopes in Scotland. Wedged between them is bleak Loch an Duin and the path of the historic Gaick Pass which links Atholl to Badenoch. The approaches to the pass and the hills above it are all long and lonely, but time can be saved by using a bicycle on these private roads, which are rights of way. At the head of Glen Tromie it is possible to cycle to the north end of Loch an Duin on a bulldozed road which ends there. The deep gash between the two Corbetts at Loch an Duin is only traversed by a footpath.

The road northwards from Dalnacardoch Lodge on the A9 road is the shortest and most popular approach, and leads in 9km to the neglected lodge of Sronphadruig at the southern entrance to the narrows of the Gaick Pass. From the lodge climb E up a short steep slope to a col and then turn N along the ridge which is edged by the screes and crags of Creag an Loch. This ridge eventually merges with the large plateau on which the summit of Maol Creag an Loch stands at its northern end. (12km; 550m; 3h 40min).

The eroded tableland so characteristic of the Grampians is strikingly seen from this top.

Rather than attempt the very steep descent W or NW down to the pass, it is better to return to Sronphadruig Lodge by the uphill route and start the ascent of An Dun from there. The S ridge or the slopes further W connecting it to Vinegar Hill are the easiest ways up and down this Corbett, which rises like some gigantic motte, very much reflecting its Gaelic name. (16km; 900m; 5h 10min)

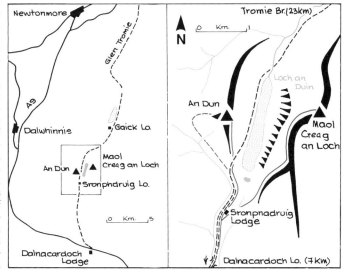

Looking south from Achlean to the distant plateau of Leathad an Taobhain   H.M. Brown

Leathad an Taobhain; 912m; (OS Sheet 43; 822858); *slope of the rafters*
Carn Dearg Mor; 857m; (OS Sheet 43; 824912); *big red cairn*

These two rounded hills are situated far up Glen Feshie, Carn Dearg Mor overlooking Glenfeshie Lodge, and Leathad an Taobhain 5½km to its south in the vast tract of featureless hills and undulating plateaux between the headwaters of the River Feshie and the Minigaig Pass. The name on the OS map appears to be given to the W top which is 10m lower than the summit. The Minigaig Pass is an ancient right of way much used in the past by drovers taking their beasts from Speyside to Atholl.

Starting from Achlean in Glen Feshie, follow the E bank of thr river S for just over 1km and cross a wooden bridge to the private road on the W bank. Continue along this road to a point just before Glenfeshie Lodge where a rough track continues S for 2km to two solitary trees on the flat floor of the glen. (It is possible to cycle to this point, but the last part of the track is not a right of way, so it is advisable to ask permission).

Continue SW along the track which climbs steadily up the steep-sided glen to Lochan an t-Sluic. Beyond the loch the track forks, and the left branch is followed

S on a gradually rising line round a series of heathery corries. This track ends at 847m on the summit of Meall an Uillt Chreagaich. A faint path continues SSW downhill to cross a col just W of the source of the River Feshie. There are the ruins of a small stone-built bothy on the south-facing slope just W of the col. The ascent of the final 150m S to the summit of Leathad an Taobhain is straightforward, still following a faint path. (14km; 680m; 4h 20min). The W top is 1km away across an expanse of tussocky grass.

Retrace the outward route as far as the junction of the tracks ½km SW of Lochan an t-Sluic, and take the other track which climbs steeply NNW towards the SW ridge of Carn Dearg Mor. A zig-zag path reaches this ridge which is followed for ½km NE to the summit. (20km; 1070m; 6h 20min). Return to Achlean along the route of ascent by Lochan an t-Sluic and Glen Feshie. It is also possible to descend NNE from Carn Dearg Mor along a broad ridge over Carn Dearg Beag to reach a track which goes down to Glen Feshie at Carnachuin.

Meallach Mhor; 769m; (OS Sheet 35; 777909); *big hump*

This hill, lying between the upper Feshie and Tromie glens, is very much off the beaten track, and is seldom climbed. From any direction it involves a long walk-in, but with the private road (which is a right of way) up Glen Tromie tarred for much of its length the easy option is to use a bicycle. It is possible to cycle 10km from Tromie Bridge right to the foot of the hill.

Glen Tromie is attractively wooded in its lower reaches as far as the lodge at Lynaberack, which resembles more a modern council house. Then the landscape is bleaker as far as Bhran Cottage and the confluence of the Allt Bhran and the River Tromie, which is also the junction of the historic drovers' roads over the Gaick and Minigaig passes.

Leave the road ½km beyond Bhran Cottage and

climb E up the shallow corrie of the Allt an Tulaich, or more directly up the W ridge of Meallach Mhor directly to the summit. (From Tromie Bridge: 12km; 520m; 3h 40min).

It is quite possible to traverse E from Meallach Mhor for 5km to reach Carn Dearg Mor, the lowest point of the broad intervening ridge being about 540m. However, the best way to combine the ascent of these two hills is to walk (or cycle) up Glen Feshie to Carnachuin and continue up the hill track on the W side of the glen which eventually leads SW up the Feith Mhor towards the col between them.

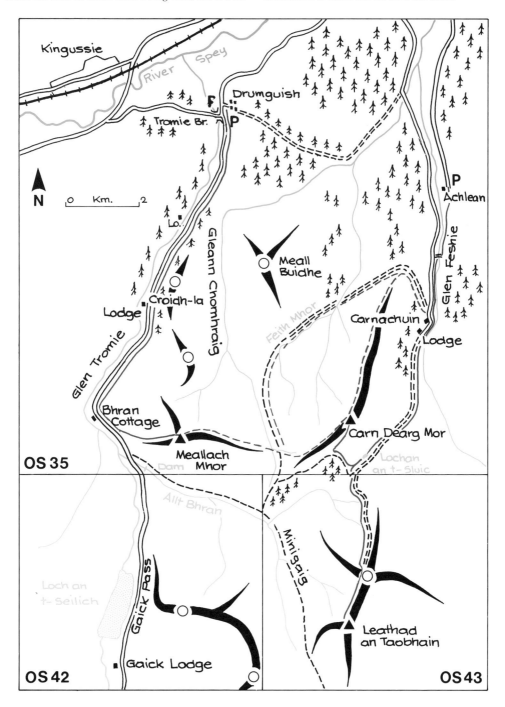

The approach to Beinn Bhreac up Glen Bruar   *G.S. Johnstone*

Beinn Bhreac; 912m; (OS Sheet 43; 868821); *speckled hill*

This is another very inaccessible hill right in the heart of the expanse of featureless country at the headwaters of the Tarf Water and the River Feshie. Most hillwalkers will find this a rather taxing expedition because of the distance to the hill from the nearest point on any public road. It is possible to walk in from Achlean in Glen Feshie, but this is even longer than from Bruar, so the latter is recommended as the starting point.

Leaving the Falls of Bruar car park, follow the path which is signposted to the upper bridge. Cross the bridge and climb up through open forest to join an overgrown forest road which is followed N until it ends at a deer fence. Continue up this fence to join the Glen Banvie forest road which is followed until it turns E at its highest point. A bulldozed estate road (marked as a single dotted line on the OS map) leads NW to cross the River Bruar below Cuilltemhuc to join the right of way to Bruar Lodge at the southern end of the Minigaig Pass.

Continue a further 5km to Bruar Lodge. It is quite possible to reach the lodge by following the right of way along the estate road from Calvine on the A9 road. The distance is nearly the same, and there is the possibility of using a mountain bicycle along this rough and in places steep road.

Beyond the lodge continue along the track for a further 1km beside the Bruar Water and then follow a good stalker's path NE up the steep slope on the N side of the Allt Beinn Losgarnaich. There is no path over the very rough and boggy watershed, but once on its N side there is a faint path for over 1km on the hillside E of the stream.

This path disappears before reaching the next very flat and featureless watershed between the Allt a'Chuil and the Tarf Water. There are some small cairns on the N side of the watershed, but they appear to have no particular significance. The ascent of the final 220m up the regularly shaped cone of Beinn Bhreac is then straightforward. (18km; 870m; 5h 30min).

The only feasible return is by the route of ascent, unless one wishes to descend N to the headwaters of the River Feshie and continue for a further 20km down Glen Feshie to Achlean, thus completing a long and arduous crossing of one of the wildest tracts of hill country in the Scottish Highlands.

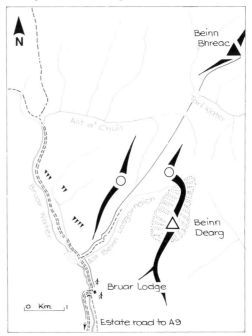

Looking south-east from Beinn Dearg over the summit of Beinn Mheadhonach   *G.S. Johnstone*

Beinn Mheadhonach; 901m; (OS Sheet 43; 880758); *middle hill*

This hill, which forms a narrow ridge on the north-west side of Glen Tilt, is best seen from the new A9 road to the south-east of Blair Atholl. From there, looking north, it is the prominent conical hill sharply outlined by two deep glens on either side.

Starting from Old Bridge of Tilt, the route follows the private road up Glen Tilt, first on the W side of the river, then on the E side to reach Gilberts Bridge. Alternatively, one can follow the old right of way along a very pleasant footpath high on the E side of the glen; this path drops down to the river near Gilberts Bridge.

Cross the bridge to the W bank and take the forestry road N. Leave the road after about 300 metres and follow the original path which takes a lower line through the conifer plantation and along the W bank of the River Tilt to a stone bridge across the Allt Mhairc which rushes through a narrow linn under the bridge. From this bridge follow the path NNW, gradually ascending grassy slopes above the Allt Mhairc to another stone bridge 200 metres above its confluence with the Allt Diridh.

Climb NW to reach the S ridge of Beinn Mheadhonach. Deep heather on the lower slopes makes for heavy going as there is no path, but higher up the heather becomes shorter and finally gives way to moss on the narrow plateau. Pass a large cairn on the E side of the ridge about half way up, and reach the summit at the N end of the narrow plateau. The cairn is quite small, and should not be confused with three smaller cairns passed on the ridge before reaching the top. (10km; 750m; 4h 30min).

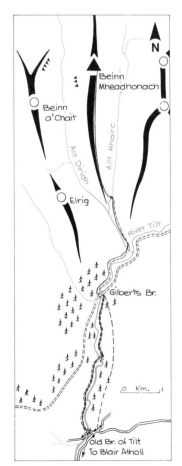

Looking north-east from Ben Vrackie to the flat dome of Ben Vuirich   G.S. Johnstone

Ben Vuirich; 903m; (OS Sheet 43; 997700); *hill of roaring*

This hill may be ascended either from Glen Brerachan on the road between Pitlochry and Kirkmichael, or from Loch Moraig above Blair Atholl. As the former route requires traversing much trackless peat bog, the latter one is recommended.

From Blair Atholl it is possible to drive to Loch Moraig. From there walk ENE along an estate road across the S slopes of Carn Liath before descending SE to a bridge across the Allt Coire Lagain. The abandoned steading at Shinagag is 300 metres further on, but turn left before reaching it and head NNE following a rough estate road which passes a line of shooting butts before turning ENE across the S slopes of Meall Breac. The road ends at more butts. The following 2km heading E to the S ridge of Ben Vuirich is trackless peat bog and heavy going; how-ever, once the ridge is reached, the last 1½km N to the rather flat summit is pleasant walking. (11km; 720m; 3h 40min).

It is possible to return by a different route without adding distance. Descend W from the summit and cross the low ridge N of Stac nam Bodach to join an estate road coming up from Glen Loch. Follow this road SW over the watershed, but leave it where it descends steeply towards some old shielings. Con-tinue traversing SW until the hillside on the left becomes less steep. At this point an estate road is visible to the SW on the other side of the Allt Coire Lagain. If the river is not high it can be crossed to reach this road, which is followed back to Loch Moraig. If the crossing is not possible, then a detour to the bridge at Shinagag is necessary.

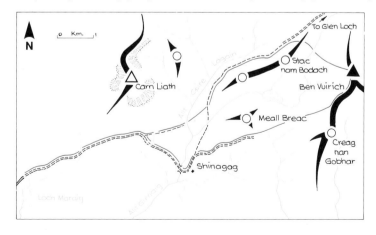

The approach to Ben Vrackie by the path from Moulin   *G.S. Johnstone*

Ben Vrackie; 841m; (OS Sheets 43 and 52; 951632); *speckled hill*

On a good day this hill must be one of the best viewpoints in the Southern Highlands, commanding views south down Strath Tay, west beyond Loch Tummel to Schiehallion and north to Beinn a' Ghlo and many other hills. Being close to Pitlochry, it is also a very popular hill with a well-trodden path all the way to the summit.

The starting point of the path is at a small car park which is reached by taking the road from the centre of Pitlochry to Moulin and turning into a short lane behind the Moulin Inn. From the car park follow the path ascending through pleasant mixed woodland to a gate which gives access to the open hillside. The obvious path goes NNE to a shallow col to the NW of Creag Bhreac, where it divides. On the OS map the path is shown as traversing below the dam of Loch a' Choire, but as the terrain there is normally rather wet and boggy, it is better to take the left-hand path to cross the dam itself and join the lower path just beyond. The final 320m to the summit are up the steep slopes to the E of the craggy SW face of Ben Vrackie. The view is rewarding, with the added bonus of an indicator for those who are not familiar with the surrounding hills. (4km; 640m; 2h 10min).

A less-frequented alternative route of ascent is to start from the north end of the Pass of Killiecrankie. (It is best to park on the old A9 road at the National Trust for Scotland Visitor Centre and walk up the private road to Druid which goes under the new A9). Once on the NE side of the road, climb SE towards Meall Uaine and from there continue NE along an un-

dulating ridge to Meall na h-Aodainn Moire. Descend to the NW end of Loch a' Choire and climb the last 320m keeping to the left of the steepest slopes on which there are considerable rocky outcrops. (5km; 700m; 2h 20min).

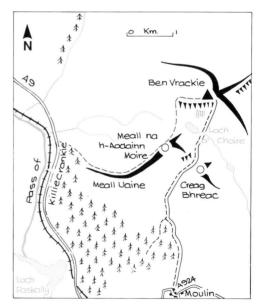

Ben Gulabin from Spittal of Glenshee   *H.M. Brown*

Ben Gulabin; 806m; (OS Sheet 43; 101722); *hill of the curlew (whimbrel)* or *hill of the beak*

Ben Gulabin lies between Gleann Beag and the glen which comes down from Dalmunzie Hotel to the Spittal of Glenshee. North of the Spittal on the A93 road there are two signs at (114714) warning southbound traffic of bends in the road ahead. At the more northerly of those signs there is a parking space with a gate giving access to Ben Gulabin. From the gate a very good track leads up to the col between it and Creagan Beithe. On the slopes of the latter hill will be seen an old ski pylon and below it a ruined hut. Opposite those remains of an early ski development, a strip of grass provides a route to the top of Ben Gulabin free from the heather which covers this side of the hill. (2½km; 450m; 1h 20min). Return by the same way.

Ben Gulabin can also be the end point of a long traverse of the hills on the west side of Gleann Beag, starting at the Ski Centre at the Cairnwell Pass, but suitable transport arrangements would have to be made. There is a twice-weekly bus service in July.

Leaving the Ski Centre, head WNW up Butchart's Corrie towards the col at its head and then go S along the ridge in the direction of The Cairnwell for 300 metres. Turn SW along the broad ridge which rises and falls over Carn an Sac to Carn a' Gheoidh. There go S and follow the ridge to Carn Mor. Continue S to Creagan Bheithe and descend the SW side of this ridge to join the track from Gleann Beag. Follow this to the col at (107728) and climb SW to Ben Gulabin. (9½km; 600m; 3h 10min). Descend by returning to the col and down the track to Gleann Beag.

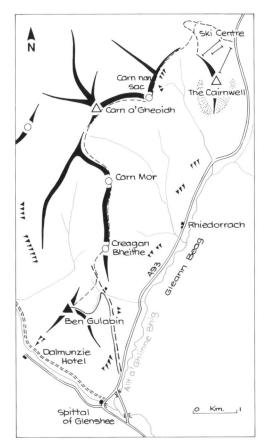

Morrone above Braemar   *G.S. Johnstone*

Morrone; 859m; (OS Sheet 43; 132886); *the big nose*

Morrone lies on the west side of the Clunie Water a few kilometres south-west of Braemar. It is a featureless hill, taking away much of the sun from the village during the winter, but it is well worth walking up for the very fine view from the summit, cluttered though it is with three huts and a pylon.

Walk or drive up Chapel Brae to the car park by the pond. Then follow the private road to an indicator. Originally it was intended to site this 17m higher, and not all the points shown on it are visible from its present position. Head towards the track going to the left, crossing it immediately to follow a path slanting upwards round the knoll where the indicator should have stood. At first the path is rather faint, but after 30 metres it becomes clearly defined and is so all the way to the top of Morrone. (2½km; 430m; 1h 20min).

Return by the same way, or alternatively walk on SW past the summit to the top of a Landrover track heading S. This is an old hill track now used by work parties for access to the summit huts. Follow it down to Glen Clunie opposite Auchallater farm, 3½km S of Braemar, and return to the village by the minor road on the W side of the river. (7km from the summit of Morrone).

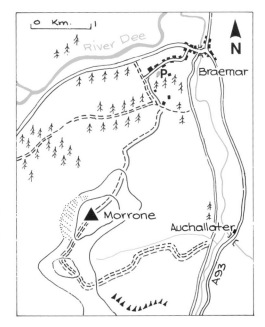

Monamenach from Glen Shee H.M. Brown

SECTION 7

The Southeast Grampians: Glen Shee to Cairn o'Mount

Monamenach; 807m; (OS Sheet 43; 176707);
middle hill

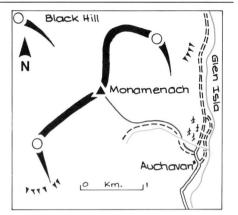

This hill stands on the watershed between Spittal of Glenshee and the head of Glen Isla. Although a rounded heathery hill, it is quite steep and craggy in places on its east side above Glen Isla.

Monamenach is most easily accessible from Glen Isla. Start at Auchavan, at the end of the public road in the glen, and follow a path NW up a burn to a col at about 610m. From there the summit rises steeply to the NW. (2km; 450m; 1h 20min).

There are good views from Monamenach into the glens on either side, and up to the higher hills to the north. It can easily be included in a longer traverse to Creag Leacach and Glas Maol, returning to Glen Isla by the old Monega drove road.

Mount Blair from Glen Shee   H.M. Brown

Mount Blair; 744m; (OS Sheet 43; 167629); *hill of the plain*

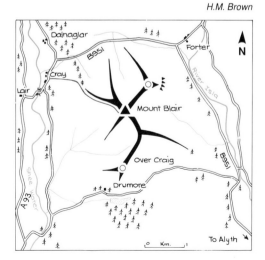

The sweeping, symmetrical cone of Mount Blair is well seen from Glen Shee and Glen Isla. Standing boldly between those two glens, it is a heathery sprawl typical of the lower Grampians, but it is re-deemed by excellent walking and by being a notable viewpoint. The lower slopes are rough, with some crags and scree, but these are easily avoided; higher up the going improves markedly with some good paths. The hill has a long history, with prehistoric sites, some famous wells, and even a suicide's grave under the summit cairn.

Start from Cray (146636) on the B951 road at the first gate on the right to the N of the church. Make a direct ascent E to the conifer plantation then follow the district boundary fence, shown on the OS map, at first SE, then ESE to the top. (2½km; 440m; 1h 20min).

Creag nan Gabhar from Glen Clunie   *I. Brown*

Creag nan Gabhar; 834m; (OS Sheet 43; 154841); *hill of the goats*

Creag nan Gabhar lies between Glen Callater and Glen Clunie. The narrower, northern end of its ridge rises steeply from Auchallater farm (4km south of Braemar) to Sron Dubh and continues south over Sron nan Gabhar for 3km, rising gradually to the summit. At Auchallater the ridge is closely hemmed in by Clunie Water and the Callater Burn, but it is 3km wide at its southern end. The walk between Sron Dubh and Creag nan Gabhar gives good views in all directions. There is a car park at the foot of Glen Callater up which the easiest route starts. Walk up the Callater road for about 1¾km to the point where the Landrover track to Sron Dubh leaves it on the right. Follow this track as it winds its way up to the Sron and then along the broad crest to Sron nan Gabhar, where it fades out. Beyond this point the going is good over dry ground with short heather. Turn SW for the final 400 metres to the summit of Creag nan Gabhar. (6km; 490m; 2h 10min). Reverse the route for the descent.

The more adventurous walker can traverse the hill from S to N, but unless two cars are used, this will involve walking back along 5km of road at the end of the day. There is a twice-weekly bus service in summer which might be useful. Cars can be parked at the AA box (140834) beside the A93 road in Glen Clunie. Cross the grassy stretch of land on the E side of the road and follow a path, intermittent at first, up an unnamed glen. The path goes on the S side of the glen until after 1½km it drops to the burn. Find a suitable crossing place and continue E up the path, which becomes very indistinct, for a further 1½km until a line of stones (marking the path to Lochcallater Lodge) becomes prominent. Follow the path until it is

crossed by a Landrover track, and take this track up-hill, finishing just below the shoulder of Creag nan Gabhar about 1¼km ESE of the summit. Beyond this there is a short flat stretch which is boggy, but the going is good thereafter for the final 1km to the summit. (4km; 440m; 1h 40min). Complete the traverse by reversing the route of ascent described in the preceding paragraph.

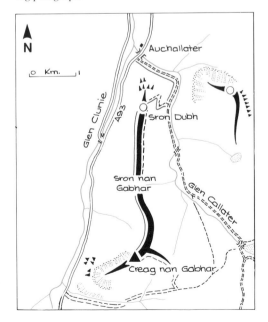

Conachcraig from Glen Muick   A. Watson

Conachcraig; 865m; (OS Sheet 44; 280865); *combination of rocks*

Conachcraig is a big, rough, bouldery hill of three summits and some small cliffs, rising a few kilometres east of Lochnagar on the west side of Glen Muick. It stands prominently in a number of well-known views of Lochnagar from Deeside, and looks especially fine when seen from above the Linn of Muick. It should be noted that the name Conachcraig on the OS map is marked at pt 850m, 1km NE of the true summit.

Start at the car park at the end of the public road in Glen Muick, a few hundred metres NE of Spittal of Glenmuick. Take the track for 1½km to Allt-na-giubhsaich, and then follow the Lochnagar footpath through the pine wood until it joins another track ½km beyond the trees. This track rises above the rocky gorge of Clais Rathadan and then reaches the col at 700m where the Lochnagar path branches off to the left, and a grand view opens out down Glen Gelder. A short climb NE from there leads to the highest point of Conachcraig. (5km; 470m; 2h).

The shortest return is by the route of ascent. However, a good traverse of the tops of Conachcraig can be made by going NE for 1km along a broad ridge to Pt 850m, and then NW for ½km to the bouldery summit of Caisteal na Caillich (862m). Return to Pt 850m and descend its E ridge to the little col at Carn an

Daimh, and from there go SE down heathery slopes to the pine wood of Glen Muick where a track leads back to Allt-na-giubhsaich and Spittal of Glenmuick.

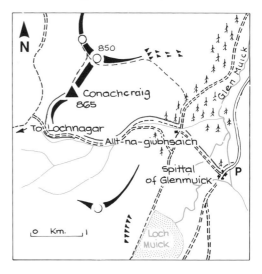

The Craigs of Loch Wharral   *D. Green*

Ben Tirran, 896m; (OS Sheet 44; 374746)

The highest top on the great undulating plateau between Glen Esk and Glen Clova, Ben Tirran has its
own little windswept plateau. The best approach rises
above the magnificent corrie enclosing Loch Wharral.

Start at Wheen on the B955 road up the E side of
Glen Clova. From there a track leads N up the moor,
eventually becoming a footpath climbing up the side
of the corrie above Loch Wharral. The point where the
path crosses the burn at the top of the corrie offers a
very fine view down past the loch and into Glen
Clova. The path peters out shortly above there, the
gradient eases and an easy walk E leads to the summit
of Ben Tirran. (5km; 650m; 2h 20min). A short detour
to a cairn ½km SW of the summit gives a grand view
along Glen Clova.

A good return route is round the top of the Craigs
of Loch Wharral and then down a path W of Loch
Wharral. An even better, but longer, alternative is to
go along the top of the Craigs of Loch Wharral to
Green Hill (870m), and then descend by a path down
the E side of Loch Brandy to the public road beside
the hotel at Clova, 3½km from the starting point.

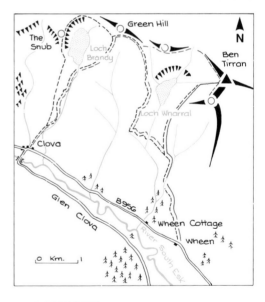

Mount Battock; 778m; (OS Sheets 44 and 45; 549845)

Mount Battock is the most easterly of the higher
hills of the Mounth, and the most easterly Corbett. Its
extensive upland plateau displays a considerable area
of short arctic-alpine vegetation. As it stands between
Deeside and the Mearns, it gives spacious views over
the lowlands of north-east Scotland as well as the
Cairngorms and the higher Mounth hills to its west.

The shortest route to it is from the south, from
Millden Lodge in Glen Esk (541791). However, a better route approaches from the east and on the return
may include Clachnaben, one of the most outstanding
of Scotland's lower hills.

For this approach start immediately S of Spital Cottage on the B974 road in Glen Dye. Follow the gravel
road across the bridge over the Water of Dye, and
along the river to Charr and beyond. At the point
where the Burn of Badymicks joins the Water of Dye,
take the right fork up a bulldozed track and later

Clachnaben   *A. Watson*

branch off it leftwards by a path to a hut at 550m. From there another bulldozed track climbs W. Follow it until it starts to traverse to the right, and leave it to head straight uphill to the summit of Mount Battock. (11km; 560m; 3h 30min).

Return to the hut and then continue E along the bulldozed track over the plateau to the Hill of Edendocher. From there the striking granite tor and top of Clachnaben (599m) rise about 1km to the NE. Clachnaben gives a very fine view of the lowlands of north-east Scotland, featuring in the old rhyme:

> *"Clochnaben and Bennachie*
> *Are twa landmarks fae the sea."*

An electrified deer fence runs for miles on Clachnaben and the ridge to its W, but stiles offer shock-free crossings at the main points where paths intersect it. From Clachnaben a path goes E downhill to a mature wood where a rough vehicle track goes down the S side of the burn past Miller's Bog and then to the B974 road S of Spital Cottage.

(From Mount Battock: 13km; 3h. From Clachnaben: 5½km; 1h 20min).

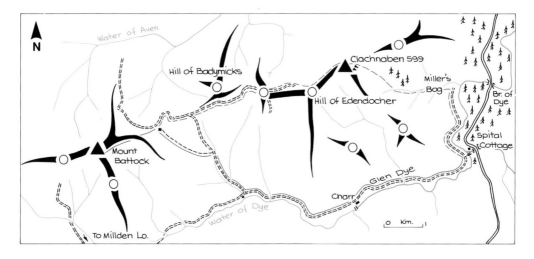

Looking from Loch an Eilein across Rothiemurchus Forest to Meall a'Bhuachaille   *D.J. Bennet*

SECTION 8

The Cairngorms and Buchan

Sgor Mor from Glen Luibeg   H.M. Brown

Sgor Mor; 813m; (OS Sheet 43; 006914); *big peak*

Sgor Mor is the highest top of the hill which extends westwards from the Linn of Dee between Glen Lui and Glen Dee. Its traverse gives a much more interesting walk than might be expected from its appearance on the map.

From the Linn of Dee car park at (063897) follow the estate road W along the N side of the Dee for almost 5km. This road goes below fragmentary schistose rock outcrops scattered among Caledonian pines and passes ruined farm settlements on the river flats before reaching White Bridge. A path continues along the N bank past Chest of Dee where the river cascades splendidly over a series of rock ledges.

Leave the footpath at the next side stream and slant up the steepening hillside to ascend the southern spur of Sgor Mor. The underlying rock changes from Moine schist to Cairngorm granite, and you clamber up broken granite blocks and then walk easily over swelling ice-polished slabs to the summit cairn. (8km; 470m; 2h 40min). Nearby is a summit slab with a fine circular pothole scoured out by wind blast.

A broad ridge of ice-worn granite, interspersed with patches of gravel, leads ENE for about 3km to Sgor Dubh (741m). This offers pleasant high-level walking against the stupendous backcloth of the main Cairngorm massif. From Sgor Dubh drop SE down the widening shoulder of the hill for 2km, eventually trending S down steeper slopes amid broken rock, long heather and Caledonian pines to rejoin the gravel road leading back to the Linn of Dee. (16km; 4h 50min).

This hill could easily be traversed en route by anyone walking south from the Lairig Ghru to the Linn of Dee.

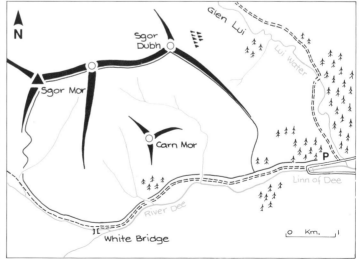

Carn na Drochaide across the River Dee   H.M. Brown

Carn na Drochaide; 818m; (OS Sheets 43 and 46; 127938); *hill of the bridge*

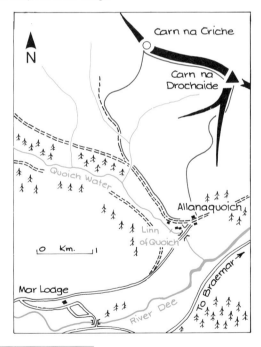

This hill rises from the floor of the Dee valley opposite Braemar, and forms the watershed between it and Gleann an t-Slugain. Start from the end of the public road near Linn of Quoich, where cars may be parked at (117912). It is easy to go direct from there to the summit of Carn na Drochaide over the Carn Dearg spur, but it is more interesting to take the slightly longer route described below.

Pass to the left of the house to reach the derelict cottage at the Linn of Quoich. Cross to the right to leave the wood and gain the track leading NW. Follow this for 3km, gaining height gradually. As the track fades out, strike NE up the hillside to the SW ridge of Carn na Criche (737m). A faint vehicular track can be followed ESE all the way from there along a broad heathery ridge to Carn na Drochaide. (6½km; 490m; 2h 20min).

The summit is decorated with several cairns and has fine views towards Beinn a'Bhuird and Ben Avon. The best feature of Carn na Drochaide, however, is the outstanding view of Braemar spread out below in the Dee valley. It continues to attract you on the way down the broad SSW ridge over Carn Dearg. This descent offers easy going; stony at first, but later on heather. There is a faint path lower down which reaches the road through a gap in the trees to the right of the main plantation and just SW of Allanaquoich farm. (9½km; 3h).

Carn Liath; 862m; (OS Sheets 36 and 43; 165977); *grey cairn*
Culardoch; 900m; (OS Sheets 36 and 43; 194988); *big back high place*

These two hills form the divide between upper Glen Gairn and the Dee valley. They are separated by the 650m Bealach Dearg through which passes an old route connecting Braemar and Tomintoul by way of Loch BuILG. They are smooth-sided hills, without crags or significant corries, but they enjoy a setting of great charm and offer magnificent views across the Gairn to Ben Avon. A bicycle is useful for access to them. Grouse shooting and deer stalking are actively carried out on these hills in season.

Culardoch from the south   W.D. Brooker

From Invercauld take the estate road leading NW from the Keiloch sawmill, leaving the car at (186916). In about 1½km take the first road on the right, winding uphill through mature firs to an iron gate. Further on are scattered birches and then another coniferous plantation. Emerging onto the open hillside, the road passes round a shoulder to enter the Glen Feardar basin, enclosed by Carn Liath to the NW and Culardoch on the N, and after dipping to a hollow clad with heather and birch trees it crosses the Allt Cul by a wooden bridge.

After a further 400 metres, leave the road and go NW following the headstream of the Allt Cul to its source in a shallow corrie. Ascend the slope W and cross a ruined but conspicuous stone wall to reach the summit ridge of Carn Liath, where there is a prominent cairn at 860m. The named summit is about 250 metres N of the abrupt termination of the wall and has no significant cairn. (8km; 570m; 2h 50min). Carn Liath has some half dozen tops of similar height on a bumpy summit ridge shaped like a wide **H**. The two highest are both shown as 862m and lie 1km apart. An hour is sufficient time to visit the other tops and descend E to reach the shelter of the stable hut at the Bealach Dearg.

To continue to Culardoch, follow the road NE for 1km to reach a level shoulder at 730m, and leave it at a sharp bend to ascend E up the heathery slope to the summit cairn at 900m. (13½km; 890m; 4h 30min). Return via the Bealach Dearg, or else descend S more steeply to intersect a track which leads back to the Allt Cul bridge.

If only Culardoch is being climbed, an alternative approach is from Knockan (220936) near Inver, via the deserted farmhouses of Ratlich and Achtavan, and then by the head of Glen Feardar. (9km; 590m; 3h).

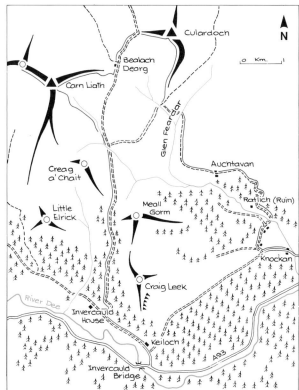

Brown Cow Hill   *A. Watson*

Brown Cow Hill; 829m; (OS Sheets 36 and 37; 221044)

This smoothly contoured hill lies on the watershed between Glen Gairn and the upper reaches of the River Don. It is as exciting as its name suggests, and is separated from the higher and more interesting Ben Avon massif by the deep narrow trough of Glen Builg and its loch.

The public car park for Corgarff Castle is a convenient starting place for this hill. Leave the A939 road at (259087) by a grassy track which after about 200 metres gives access to the gravel road going from Cockbridge farm SW along the Cock Burn. In about 300 metres the track crosses to the W side of the burn, gains height and passes through a scattered plantation of mixed conifers. Veering to the W, it ascends more steeply beside a small stream to end at about 600m just below the wide boggy saddle which separates Brown Cow Hill from Carn Oighreag.

A line of grouse butts leads S up the slope to the gently rising brow of the hill. Pass through a zone of peat hags and then swing to the SW up another gentle slope to the summit area. This forms a broad ridge some 3km long at a height of just over 800m. Like much of the hill, it is clad in a rich tundra of short heather, blaeberry, crowberry and cloudberry, interspersed with sphnagnum and occasional mossy puddles. It provides easy walking in dry conditions, but its wide convex slope makes for testing navigation in thick mist. The named top of Brown Cow Hill is the first small cairn, but the true summit is the centre top of 829m, a further kilometre to the W. (7km; 430m; 2h).

The ridge continues over Meikle Geal Charn (named for the white quartz stonefield at its summit) and Little Geal Charn, and then curves back NE past

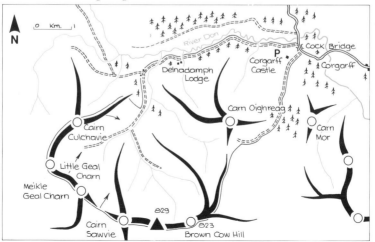

the Well of Don to Cairn Culchavie. It offers a pleasant walk with attractive views over Glen Builg to Ben Avon. It is easy to descend from this horseshoe at any point to join the hill road which leads down the Don valley to Inchmore and thence back by a good road past Delnadamph to Corgarff. (Complete horseshoe circuit: 19km; 560m; 5h 10min).

Brown Cow Hill is also easily climbed by its S side from Corndavon Lodge in Glen Gairn. Access to the lodge from the A939 road is helped by the use of a bicycle.

Morven from the east   *H.M. Brown*

Morven; 872m; (OS Sheet 37; 377040); *big hill*

Morven is the prominent haystack-shaped hill which rises abruptly from the farmlands of Cromar. As an outlier of the higher hills, it often carries patches of snow and is well seen from Deeside. It has several obvious routes of ascent, and the two described below are representative of them.

The shortest and most direct route is by the E side to a level shoulder from which a ridge leads to the top. One kilometre S of Logie Coldstone on the A97 road a minor road is signposted to Groddie. In 3km a fork at (410044) provides parking place and a gate gives access to a track leading W across undulating pastureland towards the lower slopes of Morven. Pass the deserted farmhouse of Balhennie by a gate on its S side and in another 100 metres reach the open hillside beyond the end of a drystone dyke.

Ascend steeply for over 300m by a heathery slope with small cairns marking an exiguous path in its upper part. At the 600m contour the angle falls back to a wide platform from which rises the E ridge. There is a cairn and an old fence line leads uphill to gain the ridge at a spur. Follow the fenceposts by a straggle of animal tracks leading W along the wide ridge past a rock outcrop and cairn to the summit. (4km; 660m; 2h).

Another longer route is from the south. About 2km NE of Ballater leave the A93 road 150 metres E of Bridge of Tullich. Pass farm buildings and go through a gate to join a track passing through birches and young pines to enter the glen on the E side of Crannach Hill. Continue up this glen along a track, and at its head reach the wide upland basin of the Rashy Burn. Beyond the burn the steepening southern slopes of Morven lead to the summit. (7½km; 670m; 2h 50min).

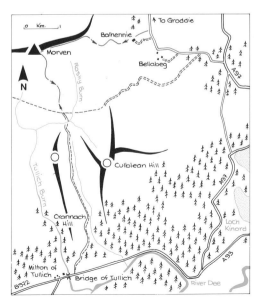

Carn Ealasaid from the Gairn   H.M. Brown

Carn Ealasaid; 792m; (OS Sheets 36 and 37; 228118); *Elizabeth's hill*
Carn Mor; 804m; (OS Sheet 37; 265183); *big cairn*

Carn Mor is the highest point on the Aberdeenshire-Banffshire boundary east of Ben Avon, and also the highest top of the Ladder Hills which form a dividing line between Donside and Glen Livet. Carn Ealasaid and its westerly neighbours Tolm Buirich and Craig Veann are an extension of the Ladder Hills southwestwards along the district boundary, but separated from them by the defile of the Lecht.

The two hills can be done easily in a day from the summit of the Lecht road, but this is not the most attractive way to climb them. The following descriptions give slightly longer, but more attractive trips.

For Carn Ealasaid park at the Allargue Hotel (257092) and take the old road behind the hotel to the uninhabited farmhouse of Loinherry. From there climb NW towards Carn Vaich and continue pleasantly up the ridge over short heather to Carn Ealasaid (3½km; 390m; 1h 30min). The outing can be extended by going N to Beinn a' Chruinnich (776m) and then SE to Carn Mhic an Toisich, passing ski pylons on the way to Carn Meadhonach. Descend a short distance W and join a wide track which goes down to Loinherry. (2h from Carn Ealasaid).

For Carn Mor the best approach from the east is by the Water of Nochty, which is about 3km from Bellabeg in Strathdon. Leave the Glen Buchat road just before Torrancroy (cars can be parked at the nearby bridge over the Nochty) and take what is known as the Ladder route past the site of the former house of Auchernach to the farm of Aldachuie. From there a forestry road leads to the ruin of Duffdefiance. The name is curious and is said to date back to a time when a crofter, Lucky Thain, came over

the hills from Glen Livet and squatted there. He was able to build a house and have the lum 'reekin' before he was challenged by the local laird, a Duff, and so he sat there in defiance of him.

At this point a steep ascent of 190m leads to a wide ridge with a final pull up another 150m to the highest point of the path on the ridge just NE of Dun Muir. Carn Mor lies about 1½km SW across grassy, sometimes boggy ground. (7km; 480m; 2h 30min).

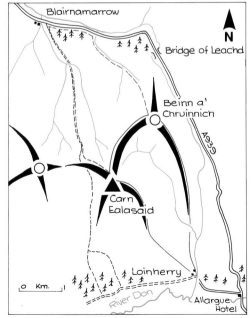

Looking north from Carn Mor to Ben Rinnes and Corryhabbie Hill   *H.M. Brown*

If approaching from Glen Livet, park near the church at Chapletown and head for East Auchavaich, then past the ruin at Corry and on to Corrunich. The route then follows the path up the Ladder Burn into a lovely grassy corrie and up to the ridge near Dun Muir to join the route from Donside.

To climb both hills in a single day from the A939 road, park at (223152) and walk down the road towards Blairnamarrow. Then follow a track S up a grassy glen and heather slopes to its highest point on the NW shoulder of Carn Ealasaid, and up to the summit. (5km; 400m; 1h 50min). The descent can be made along the line of the district boundary to Beinn a' Chruinnich and then N down to the shooting road which leads to the small car park on the A939 road. (2h 30min for the circuit).

From there walk N up the path towards the large building at the site of an 18th century ironstone and manganese mine. Just before reaching this take a track right up to shooting butts, and then straight up to Carn Liath (792m). Follow the district boundary over Monadh an t-Sluichd Leith (799m) and on to Carn Mor. (4½km; 450m; 1h 50min from the road). A pleasant alternative route back to the road is to traverse the ridge to Carn Dulack (663m) and descend E from there to join the path which leads down to the car park on the A939 road. (3h 30min for the circuit).

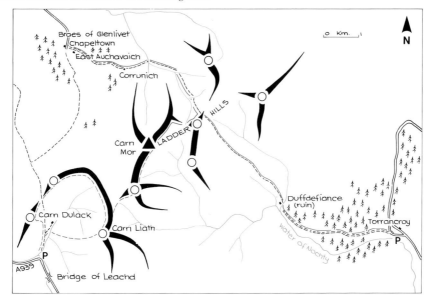

Looking north-west from Corryhabbie Hill to Ben Rinnes   R. Wood

Ben Rinnes; 840m; (OS Sheet 28; 255355); *headland hill*

This fine hill is the second-highest summit entirely in Banffshire, Creag Mhor (895m) being the highest, and it commands a glorious view over the Laich of Moray and across the Moray Firth to the hills of Ross, Sutherland and Caithness. It has a bold and well-defined outline which makes it a prominent landmark, easily identified from all quarters.

Ben Rinnes can be climbed from any side, but the easiest route is undoubtedly from the NE. From the B9009 road, about 5km SW of Dufftown, turn NW up the road to Milltown of Edinvillie and after ½km park at a track which is used to ascend Round Hill, thereafter rising to Roy's Hill. A fairly flat area is crossed before climbing more steeply up a well-worn path to the summit. (3km; 600m; 1h 40min.

An enjoyable traverse, if one's transport arrangements make it possible, is to go W from Ben Rinnes down the broad W ridge to a track near the Burn of Lyneriach, and continue down to Bridge of Avon.

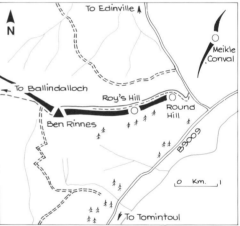

Corryhabbie Hill; 781m; (OS Sheet 37; 281289)

The rounded mass of Corryhabbie Hill is the highest ground in the area enclosed by Glen Livet, Glen Rinnes and Glen Fiddich. The best approach to it is from the B9009 road between Dufftown and Tomintoul. At (267329) turn off and head for Ellivreid farm where cars can be left. Opposite the farm take the track to Sheandow, but instead of going to this ruined building climb straight up the Hill of Achmore (510m). Nice easy walking on grass and short heather takes one gently up to Muckle Lapprach (729m) and then on to the top of Corryhabbie Hill. (5km; 450m; 2h.)

An alternative descent can be made by walking for about 200 metres NE from the summit and joining Morton's Way - a shooting road built by the one-time laird at Glenfiddich Lodge named Morton. Follow the Way NE for about 1km and then start to descend NW, making for a ruin at (275309) in the upper part of the Corryhabbie Burn where three streams join. Cross the bridge at the ruin and walk up past Sheandow to rejoin the track to Ellivreid.

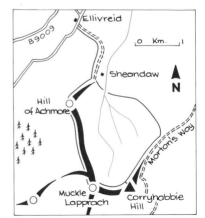

Creag Mhor; 895m; (OS Sheet 36; 057048); *big crag*

Creag Mhor is geographically an inaccessible Corbett, although otherwise it is an easy hill to climb. It lies hidden away in an unfrequented corner of the Cairngorms above the cross-roads of the River Avon and the Lairig an Laoigh, 12km from both Glenmore Lodge and Derry Lodge.

Many hillwalkers have skirted past Creag Mhor, bent on other ploys, but if any hill exemplifies the wisdom of climbing Corbetts along with Munros, rather than after them, it is this one. It can be very readily fitted in to all manner of expeditions, such as walking through the Lairig an Laoigh, visiting Loch Avon, climbing Bynack More or heading for Faindouran Lodge. The easiest approach is from Glenmore Lodge, as Derry Lodge is itself an additional 4½km from the public road at Linn of Dee.

From the end of the public road 150 metres past Glenmore Lodge, walk through the Pass of Ryvoan and, on leaving the pass, take the right fork in the track round to Bynack Stable. The Lairig an Laoigh path rises steadily up the ridge to the SE, dips into Coire Odhar, then crosses another ridge to drop to the Glasath before pulling up again to the top of the pass

at Lochan a'Bhainne between the Bynacks and Creag Mhor. From the pass turn E and climb 160m to the summit of Creag Mhor, which is a granite barn (tor), so it cannot be missed. (12km; 760m; 4h).

A possible alternative to this long approach is to get a lift to the car park in Coire Cas and use the chairlifts to gain quick and easy access to the plateau. From the top chairlift station go ½km SE to the col between Cairn Gorm and Cnap Coire na Spreidhe, and then descend the steep slope SE to The Saddle (807m), the col at the head of Strath Nethy. From there descend to the path along the shore of Loch Avon and go down the river to the Fords of Avon, leaving only 200m of ascent up the broad SW ridge of Creag Mhor. (From the top of the chairlift: 6km; 250m; 2h).

Creag Mhor may be only a minor summit in the context of the Cairngorms, but these mountains, with their long distances and empty spaces, should never be treated casually. The Lairig an Laoigh path is broad and clear, but careless navigation in poor visibility has seen walkers go astray, down the Water of Caiplich for example, so allow plenty of time for this remote Corbett at the cross-roads of the Cairngorms.

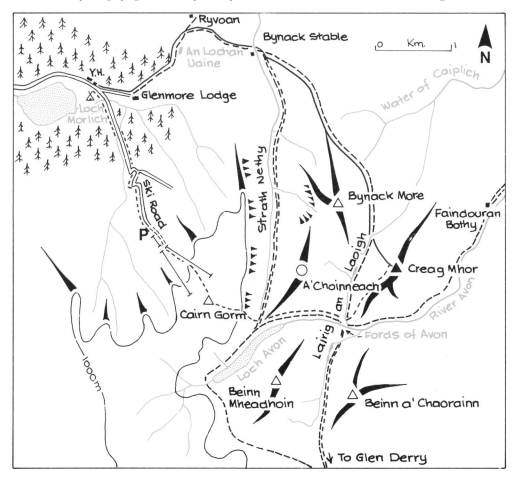

Meall a'Bhuachaille from Loch Morlich   *G.S. Johnstone*

Meall a'Bhuachaille; 810m; (OS Sheet 36; 991115); *shepherd's hill*

Meall a'Bhuachaille is the highest of the three hills which overlook the north side of Loch Morlich in the Glen More Forest Park. They form as grandstand ridge for the view of the northern corries of the Cairngorms, and are themselves a fine profile when seen from the Spey valley. The Queen's Forest rises high on their southern slopes, and Abernethy Forest is to their north, so access to these hills is rather restricted. Meall a'Bhuachaille can be easily climbed up its treeless eastern flank above Ryvoan Pass, and this can be combined with a walk through the pass from Glen More to Nethy Bridge.

The usual start is from Glen More, passing Reindeer House and walking along the road past Glenmore Lodge to Ryvoan Pass. (Cars can be taken to a parking place 150 metres beyond the Lodge). The deep V-gap of Ryvoan Pass is an old outflow channel for the glacier that once occupied Glen More; it is steep and craggy on the east and covered with Scots pine and heather on the west side. Set in the depths of the pass is An Lochan Uaine, a little jewel of a loch which lives up to its name, the little green loch. Soon after leaving the pass, the road forks; keep left to Ryvoan Bothy. From there a waymarked path leads up Meall a'Bhuachaille, giving an easy ascent to the summit. (5½km; 480m; 2h 10min). The big cairn commands a wide view of the Cairngorms, Speyside and the dark, undulating land to the north.

Descend W by the path and just before reaching the col below Creagan Gorm take another path S into the forest and down by a burn back to Glen More.

The traverse can be extended, however, to Creagan Gorm and Craiggowrie, an enjoyable 3km high level walk along the tops of these hills. Unfortunately the effects of erosion along the paths is very obvious, especially at the peaty cols. From Craiggowrie a marked path (posts) leads down to the forest and through it to Badaguish.

The return to Glen More can be made by one of two forest roads: either direct to the W end of Loch Morlich and back along the main road, or along a rising traverse in the forest to drop down to the main road opposite the Glen More shop. Despite the effects of erosion, this is an excellent circular walk.

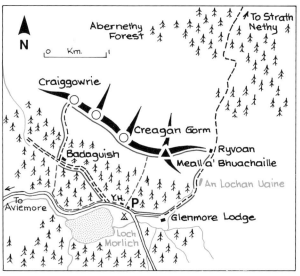

Looking north-east across the Abernethy Forest from Meall a'Bhuachaille   *G.S. Johnstone*

Geal Charn; 821m; (OS Sheet 36; 090127); *white hill*

This unobtrusive, unpretentious hill stands in an area which has excellent cross-country walking, and it could well be included in (for example) a long walk from Nethy Bridge to Tomintoul. Starting from Dorback Lodge, however, the ascent of the hill by itself is barely half a day's walk.

The minor road to Dorback Lodge turns off the link road between Nethy Bridge and the A939 and goes south-east for 4½km towards the Braes of Abernethy: dark,rolling, heathery hills which are typical of the lower Cairngorms. The road ends at a turning place, but one can park in a nearby quarry. Descend and cross the Dorback Burn (which downstream cuts through fluvial deposits) to reach Upper Dell. Take the bulldozed track up past a series of kettle lochs, ignoring a right fork, until the track ends on the skirts of Geal Charn. Continue up the broad ridge, with green-rimmed Coire an Uillt Mhoir on the left, and the summit is soon reached. (4½km; 450m; 1h 50min). The views northwards are pleasing: the Hills of Cromdale, Ben Rinnes and distant Morven in Caithness.

The Dorback Burn may well involve a paddle to start the day. In wet weather it and even the streams crossed by the bulldozed track may prove impracticable to cross. In this case go round the back of Dorback Lodge and follow the estate track up the Allt Mor as far as the watershed, then climb SW to reach Geal Charn.

The approach to Geal Charn from the NE can be lengthened and improved by starting at Bridge of Brown and using the paths to the E or W of Tom an t-Suidhe Mhoir to reach Dorback. Another long approach to the hill starts at Forest Lodge in the Abernethy Forest (accessible by car from Nethy Bridge or Boat of Garten), and follows a forest road

round the S side of Carn a'Chnuic to a point high on the W side of Geal Charn, 2km from the summit.

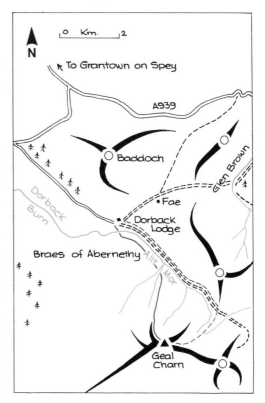

On Bennachie, looking towards Mither Tap from Oxen Craig   *W.D. Brooker*

Bennachie; 528m; (OS Sheet 38; 682223); *hill of the pap*

Bennachie is the best known and probably the most popular hill in Aberdeenshire. Its shapely outline can be seen from most parts of the Northeast, and as the rural population there hold it in great affection, it is inevitable that legend and verse should have grown around the hill.

It is not a single peak, but a ridge 5km long with several tops, the highest of which is Oxen Craig. This summit is, however, far exceeded in prominence by the Mither Tap (518m) with its large granite tor. The Tap affords excellent views, not only of the rich agricultural flatlands of the Northeast, but also of the Upper Donside hills, with the eye being drawn to the not-too-distant Cairngorms.

There are four car parks around the hill, from which paths lead to the various tops. The most northerly is the Back o' Bennachie car park at Puttingstone. About 3km east is Pittodrie farm car park, and 2km south is another near Tullos. On the south side of the hill there is Esson's car park near Lower Woodend. An hour from any of these points is sufficient to reach the Mither Tap.

The Tap itself is a granite tor with its N and W faces reaching a height of about 25m, affording a few climbs in the grooves and on the pancake-like formation of the slabs. The summit can be easily reached by the broken rocks on the E side, below which can be seen a circular wall, the remains of a prehistoric fort.

Various combinations of ascents and traverses can be done using two cars, or even by leaving bikes at the foot of the planned descent route. The best traverse is from the Back o' Bennachie car park over all the tops, including Millstone Hill, and down to Esson's car park. (8km; 550m; 2h 40min).

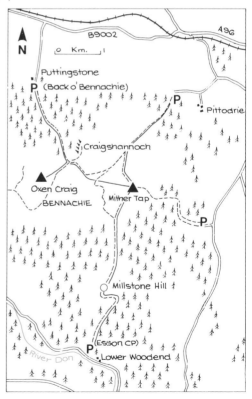

The Buck of Cabrach   *A. Watson*

The Buck of Cabrach; 721m; (OS Sheet 37; 413234); *Gaelic 'bucaidh'- knob or pimple*

The Buck of Cabrach, with its markedly pointed shape, is a very conspicuous landmark in the north-east of Scotland. Local people usually call it "the Buck i' the Cabrach". On the west side of the summit there are small granite outcrops of a similar formation to those on Bennachie. From the top good views can be had across the Moray Firth, and on a clear day the Caithness hills are easily seen.

The easiest access to the hill is from the B9002 road just over 1km SE of its junction with the A941, where there is space for parking at (426250). From there the final cone of the hill rises to the SW beyond a stretch of level moorland, and the top can be reached without difficulty in about an hour.

If a longer day is desired, a traverse using two cars can be made by continuing S from the Buck to Bridge of Buchat. From the summit of the Buck follow the line of the district boundary in a generally southerly direction over Mount Meddin, Dun Mount, Creag an Eunan, Meikle Firbriggs Hill and Millhuie Hill, from which a descent S leads to Bridge of Buchat. This traverse gives a 4 hour walk from the B9002 road.

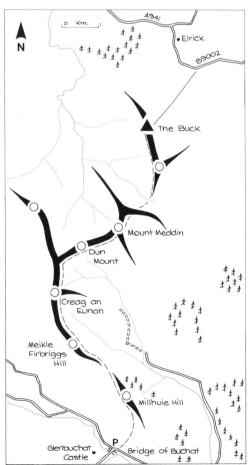

The Parallel Roads of Glen Roy and Beinn Iaruinn   *G.S. Johnstone*

Section 9

Glen Roy to the Monadh Liath

Beinn Iaruinn; c800m; (OS Sheet 34; 296900); *iron hill*
Carn Dearg (East of Glen Roy); 834m; (OS Sheet 34; 345887); *red cairn*

Glen Roy, a delightful and typical Highland glen, has a unique feature, the Parallel Roads, which have given it an international geological fame. These parallel lines scored horizontally along the steep hillsides are the old shore-lines of natural lochs created by dams of ice as big glaciers periodically blocked the foot of the glen during the Ice Ages.

After 5km of twisting road up the glen, the farmland and woods are left behind and there is a car park and view-point from which the character of the upper glen can be seen, with the Paral-lel Roads prominent across the flank of Beinn Iaruinn. The narrow public road continues for a further 8km to end at Brae Roy Lodge. There are three Carn Deargs in Glen Roy, the southernmost one rising opposite Beinn Iaruinn. These two hills are described together, but they have to be climbed separately. However, as each one by itself is only half a day's climb, it is quite possible to do both in a single day.

Beinn Iaruinn is most easily climbed by the ridge bounding Coire nan Eun, starting from the road bridge (308891) over the burn draining from it. Follow the ridge in a clockwise direction up and round this craggy little corrie. It is quite rough going , with al-most 1km of bleak plateau before gaining the summit. (2km; 600m; 1h 30min). The hills to the west of Loch Lochy spring into view as the plateau is reached. The descent can be made by the same route, or by contin-uing the circuit round the corrie to drop down steep slopes on its N side.

The Carn Dearg on the opposite side of the glen is the most attractive of the three hills of this name in Glen Roy. A pleasant circuit can be made by the cor-

Carn Dearg from Brunachan, Glen Roy   H.M. Brown

ries on either side of Carn Brunachain, as the NW spur of the hill is called. Start at the footbridge 1km down from Brae Roy Lodge (330909)and walk downstream to Brunachan (where quern stones were once quar-ried), then follow the burn steeply up into Coire Dubh. The crags and gullies can be avoided and the angle eases for gentle walking to the summit, the new view this time being to the Creag Meagaidh hills. (5km; 630m; 2h 10min). Return N to descend Coire na Reinich, keeping to the right bank of the burn once down into the corrie.

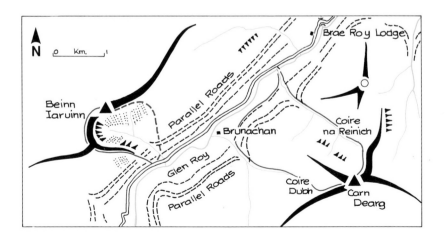

Carn Dearg (South of Gleann Eachach); 768m; (OS Sheet 34; 357948); *red cairn*
Carn Dearg (North of Gleann Eachach); 815m; (OS Sheet 34; 349967); *red cairn*

The unique character of Glen Roy has been described on the preceding page. The two Carn Deargs near the head of the glen, on either side of its subsidiary Gleann Eachach, dominate the rather desolate country to the north of the junction of Glen Turret with Glen Roy.

It is possible to drive to Brae Roy Lodge and park cars just below the lodge. A private road continues up Glen Roy, but at Turret Bridge take the left fork to its end at a sheep fank in Glen Turret. Sheep tracks and footpaths continue up the glen. Cross the Allt Eachach and traverse the slopes on its NW side up the glen to the watershed at 570m. The two Corbetts lie roughly N and S of this col, each one only about 1km distant from it, both appearing as rather featureless lumps in a neglected corner of the country. The ascent of both is easy from the col. (9km; 800m; 3h 20min).

Instead of returning by Gleann Eachach, the descent can be made down the SW ridge of either hill, depending on which one has been climbed first. A longer, but more interesting return is to go E from the col between the hills down the N bank of the Allt Dubh. A path is reached on the E side of the Allt Creag a'Chail (which may be difficult to cross in spate), and ½km further on there is a footbridge

Carn Dearg (South) from Brae Roy Lodge   R. Wood

across the Allt Chonnal. Cross this and descend to the road in Glen Roy 6km above Brae Roy Lodge.

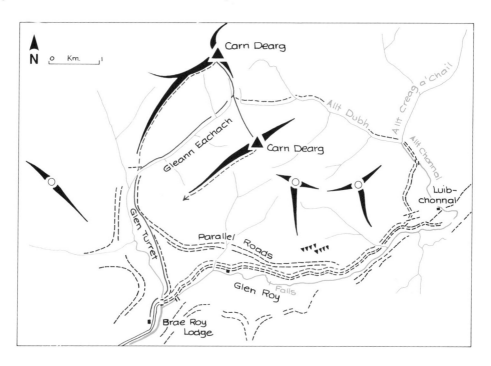

Gairbeinn from Melgarve   *H.M. Brown*

Corrieyairack Hill; 896m; (OS Sheet 34; 429998); *hill of the rising glen*
Gairbeinn; 896m; (OS Sheet 34; 460985); *rough hill*

The Corrieyairack is a very ancient pass, used by drovers and travellers before being finally made into a military road by General Wade's soldiers in 1731. The Jacobite army crossed it in 1745. The two hills described here, which are of equal height and both nearly Munros, lie to the north and east of the pass above the Allt Yairack. This stream joins the River Spey near Melgarve, which is the furthest point up the Spey to which one can drive, 15km from Laggan Bridge.

From Melgarve follow Wade's road NW for 5km to the top of the Corrieyairack Pass, at first along a straight section of road, then up a series of zig-zags as the road climbs the headwall of Corrie Yairack. Elec-

tricity transmission pylons marching alongside the road detract from any feeling of wilderness in this remote corrie. From the pass a straightforward ridge of 1½km leads NE then N to Corrieyairack Hill. (7km; 540m; 2h 30min). The view from the summit is better than might be expected, particularly W to Ben Tee and the Glen Garry hills.

The traverse to Gairbeinn is undulating, with an intermediate hill, Geal Charn (876m) to be crossed. The march line is a fence along the district boundary, a useful navigational aid in misty conditions. (11km; 800m; 3h 50min). Descend SSW down a broad slope towards a little knoll (586m), then bear SE directly towards Melgarve.

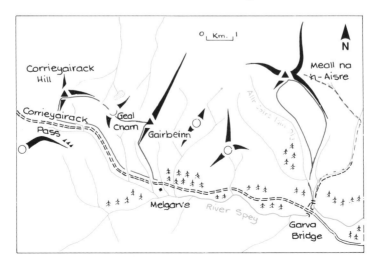

Meall na h-Aisre from the Allt Coire Iain Oig   D. Green

Meall na h-Aisre; 862m; (OS Sheet 35; 515000); *hill of the defile*

This featureless hill stands in remote country between the Monadh Liath hills and the Corrieyairack Pass. However, it offers an easy ascent from the south, starting from the upper reaches of the River Spey.

From Laggan take the public road W to Garva Bridge, a fine old bridge built by General Wade. From there go N and cross the footbridge over the Allt Coire Iain Oig at (522958), and climb N up the open hillside to the broad crest called Leathad Gaothach. Continue NW over a rocky top (844m) and reach the summit of Meall na h-Aisre across the shallow hollow of Coire Gorm. (6km; 630m; 2h 30min).

It is also possible to follow the Allt Coire Iain Oig to its source in Coire Iain Oig and climb the S slopes of the hill. An alternative descent can be made SE to reach the stalker's path on the E side of the Allt Talagain.

Map on page 117.

Carn a'Chuilinn; 816m; (OS Sheet 34;416034); *cairn of holly*

This is an isolated summit in the Glendoe Forest south-east of Fort Augustus. The obvious line of approach is by the private estate road which leaves the A862 at (403090), but this may cause antagonism locally. It is better to park about 1km further east near the bridge over the Allt Doe, and start from there.

Climb up beside the waterfall on a path which higher up joins the private road, and continue S along it into Glen Doe. When this road makes a tortuous change of direction SE, continue up a stalker's path S to the steeper upper slopes of Carn a'Chuilinn. Climb directly up to the craggy summit, which overlooks a maze of lochans on its E side. (6km; 620m; 2h 30min).

If the area is to be savoured for its exceptional roughness and isolation, it may be more interesting to make the ascent from Loch Tarff along the stalker's path from there to the Dubh Lochan, followed by 4km of very rough walking to Carn a'Chuilinn. The route described above can then be used for the descent.

The simplest route in many ways is to walk up the Corrieyairack road S from its start near Fort Augustus until opposite Creagan na Cailliche, then drop down and cross the River Tarff and climb the hill from the SW. In spate conditions this route is not practicable for there is no bridge across the river.

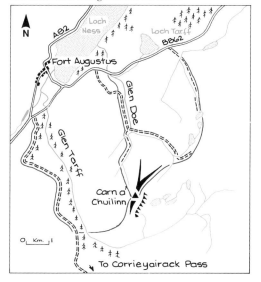

Carn a' Chuilinn from Loch Tarff   *R. Wood*

Carn na Saobhaidhe; 811m; (OS Sheet 35; 600145); *cairn of the den (fox lair)*

The northern section of the Monadh Liath mountains, lying between the Great Glen and the upper River Findhorn, is perhaps the least-known part of the range. Essentially a plateau, the hills lack the more dramatic mountain characteristics of ridge, peak or corrie. In misty conditions navigation on them is quite challenging. Their redeeming features and attraction to the hillwalker are the very fine glens which dissect this extensive plateau and give access to it. One of the finest of these glens is Strath Dearn, which contains the headwaters of the River Findhorn. Carn na Saobhaidhe is on the watershed between the Findhorn and the river draining north-west into Loch Mhor which has the distinction of having the shortest name, the River E.

Leave the A9 road just after the Slochd summit if going north, or before Tomatin if going south and follow the old A9 road to Findhorn Bridge. From there a public road goes up Strath Dearn as far as Coignafearn Old Lodge, where there is a locked barrier and limited parking space on the south side of the road. A private estate road continues for a further 7km past Coignafearn Lodge to the cottage of Dalbeg. Strike W up the bulldozed track that follows the Allt Creagach. Leave the track after 2½km and follow the Allt Odhar W past waterfalls. The going on the plateau is extremely toilsome because of extensive peat hags, but the worst may be avoided by following the burn which has worn through the layers of peat and provides reasonable walking on its banks. Continue up the Allt Odhar to the second of two tributaries which join it from the NW, which is followed towards the summit of Carn na Saobhaidhe. (14km; 420m; 3h 50min). There is a very small cairn which may or may not be on the summit, which is very flat. Return by the same route. A bicycle can be used with advantage as far as Dalbeg.

An alternative route is from Strath Nairn to the north. Leave the B851 road at (605246) where there is limited parking by the telephone kiosk. Follow the private road to Drumnaglass Lodge for 2½km and then take the track through fields and over the River Farigaig at (596222). Follow the track up the Allt Uisg an t-Sidhein, then take the right-hand fork at (604187) which crosses the Aberchalder Burn. This is followed to its source, from where the summit lies about ½km W. (13km; 570m; 3h 50min).

These two routes can be combined in a very long and interesting traverse.

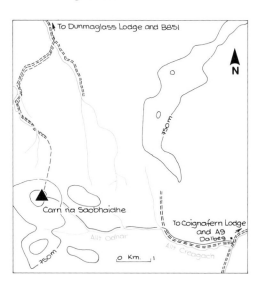

Carn an Fhreiceadain from Kingussie   H.M. Brown

Carn an Fhreiceadain; 878m; (OS Sheet 35; 726071); *watcher's (lookout) cairn*

This extensive flat hill is situated on the edge of the Monadh Liath mountains behind Kingussie, and its position makes it an excellent viewpoint across the River Spey to the glens of Tromie and Truim.

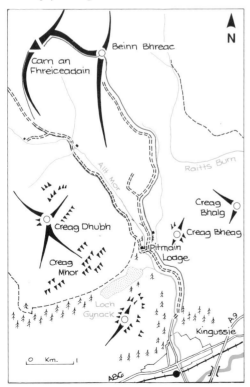

Take the road to the golf course on the north side of Kingussie, and park near the caravan site and club house. Walk behind the club house and cross the Allt Mor by a footbridge to reach the road on the east side of this stream. Follow the road to a bridge just before Pitmain Lodge. Do not cross the bridge, but take the track going right and pass an old building. Follow the track N then NW to the summit of Beinn Bhreac. The map indicates that the track finishes at about 750m on the S shoulder of this hill, but it continues over it to Carn an Fhreiceadain. (8km; 630m; 2h 50min).

On the descent, go SW from the summit past a large cairn and then S down a broad ridge to reach a track which is followed down the Allt Mor to Pitmain Lodge. The grounds of the lodge may be avoided by re-crossing the Allt Mor just before reaching the trees.

Creag Dhubh; c757m; (OS Sheet 35; 677973); *black crag*

Creag Dhubh, rising abruptly from flat Strathspey, is a hill of dominant character, well seen from many directions and giving a summit view which is unrivalled in the region. Along its south-east side steep crags and scree slopes rise above the A86 road. To its north Glen Banchor separates the hill from the main Monadh Liath range; southwards the River Truim flows in to join the Spey in an area of rich greens, birches and lochans. "Creag Dhubh!" is the war cry of the Clan MacPherson, and this is their territory. Cluny's Cave, a hide-out for clansmen and their chiefs in the terror after Culloden, is situated in the cliffs to the south-west of the hill.

Creag Dhubh is a popular hill for rock climbers, the crags above Lochain Uvie rising in tiers of intimidat-

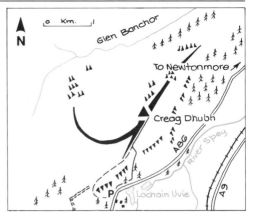

ing steepness. Beside the A86 road below the cliffs there is a small car parking place which makes a convenient starting place to climb the hill. Make a rising traverse NE below the cliffs and the worst of their screes, then follow the edge of a plantation to gain the heathery and craggy slopes above the tree-line. Bear left to gain the crest of the SW ridge of the hill and follow this over several false tops to reach the summit cairn. (2km; 500m; 1h 20min). The hill is quite rugged and calls for careful route-finding, so it should not be underestimated.

On the descent the steep lower slopes can be avoided by continuing down the SW ridge to reach a track which leads to the A86 road 1½km SW of the day's starting point.

The Cairngorms from Geal-charn Mor   G.S.Johnstone

Geal-charn Mor; 824m; (OS Sheet 35; 837124); *big white hill*

This hill is the highest point of the Kinveachy Forest, which lies between the River Spey and the River Dulnain. It is a superb viewpoint for the Cairngorm Mountains on the opposite side of the Spey valley.

There is ample space for car parking off the main A9 road at Lynwilg (882107) beside the bridge over the Allt na Criche. Follow the estate road NW up the finely wooded glen called An Gleannan, climbing gradually in 2km above the trees onto the open hillside. Continue along the road until it reaches the watershed near a memorial. From there climb SW up a broad ridge which gives pleasant walking to the summit of Geal-charn Mor. (6km; 600m; 2h 20min).

The descent may be made by the same route, but a good circuit can be completed by descending E to reach a path which continues SE to Ballinluig farm, from where there is a 1½km walk along tracks and paths back to Lynwilg.

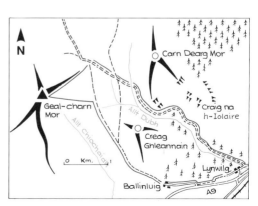

The wilds of Ardgour and Moidart from the north, Beinn Resipol in the centre beyond Loch Shiel   *D.J. Bennet*

SECTION 10a

Morvern, Sunart, Ardgour and Moidart

Beinn Resipol; 845m; (OS Sheet 40; 766655); *from old Norse, homestead*

Situated 4½km north of Loch Sunart and about midway between Strontian and Salen, Beinn Resipol is a very prominent and isolated mountain. It gives a fairly short and easy climb which is rewarded on a good day by one of the finest views along the west Highland coastline, extending to the Cuillin of Skye, Ben Nevis and Ben More in Mull.

Two routes to Beinn Resipol are described, which if one's transport can be arranged make an excellent traverse. From Strontian one can start 2km N of the village near Ariundle and follow the old miners' track NW towards the old mines in Coire an t-Suidhe (Corrantee). From the highest point of the path go W over Meall an t-Slugain and up the E ridge of Beinn Resipol. (7km; 750m; 3h).

The other route starts at Resipole farm and caravan site, 4km WSW of Beinn Resipol. Follow a track, which in less than 1km becomes a good footpath, up the SE side of the Allt Mhic Chiarain. For 1½km this path goes through very pleasant woodland high on the steep side of the burn, then it emerges onto the open hillside. The path tends to disappear, but continue due E along the burn to finally climb the hill's W ridge to the summit. (5km; 850m; 2h 40min).

Beinn Resipol from Loch Sunart   *R.D. Walton*

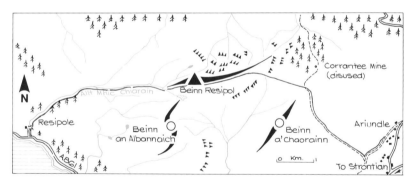

Ben Hiant; 528m; (OS Sheet 47; 537632); *holy hill*

This hill lies within the great volcanic ring complex which forms the western part of Ardnamurchan, a world renowned place of study for geologists. For hillwalkers the attraction of Ben Hiant is almost as great, for it is a superb viewpoint. The best ascent of the hill is from the NE, leaving the narrow B8007 road near its high point 1½km S of Loch Mudle at (551641). Climb steeply towards the lower part of the NE ridge and follow it along a path round to the steeper slopes below the summit. Just below the final steep rise to the top the path branches. The right-hand path traverses upwards across a rocky and somewhat exposed slope which can be slippery when wet, and leads to a short grassy ascent to the top. The left-hand path is less obvious, but leads round to avoid steep ground and approach the top from the S. (2km; 370m; 1h 10min).

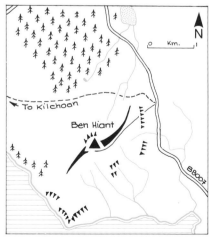

The hills of Morvern seen from Lismore   *D.J. Bennet*

Fuar Bheinn; 766m; (OS Sheet 49; 853564); *cold hill*
Creach Bheinn; 853m; (OS Sheets 40 and 49; 871577); *hill of spoil*

These two hills are the highest in the district of Morvern. With their lower outliers they form a well-defined horseshoe ridge round Glen Galmadale above Loch Linnhe. The complete traverse of this ridge is a good hillwalk and the best way to climb both hills, although the drops between successive tops give a lot of up and downhill work. A much shorter approach to Creach Bheinn is from Glen Tarbert to its north, climbing the NW ridge above the cliffs of Coire Dhuibh, but this is not a particularly good way if one wants to include Fuar Bheinn.

The west side of the horseshoe has a succession of small corries overlooking Glen Galmadale, but they are not very impressive when seen at close quarters. More impressive is the east side of Druim Maodalaich, the eastern arm of the horseshoe. It falls steeply in a long line of broken cliffs of red granite, cut by many dykes which form tree-filled gullies above the narrow B8043 road. This steep and rocky hillside is home for a herd of wild mountain goats which can often be seen from the roadside below.

The best starting point for the traverse is near the bridge over the Galmadale River. Walk SW along the B8043 road for a few hundred metres and climb steeply beside a plantation to gain the SE ridge of Beinn na Cille (652m). The ridge is grassy, with many outcrops of granite, for this hill is within the area of Strontian granite which extends further S to the huge Glen Sanda quarry.

From Beinn na Cille continue NNW down to the col at 460m and climb the broad ridge to Fuar Bheinn. Only if one keeps well to the E side of the ridge does one get any impression of the corries above Glen Galmadale. From Fuar Bheinn descend NW then N to the broad featureless col, the Cul

Mham. From there climb just over 300m up a broad stony ridge to Creach Bheinn. Just N of the summit

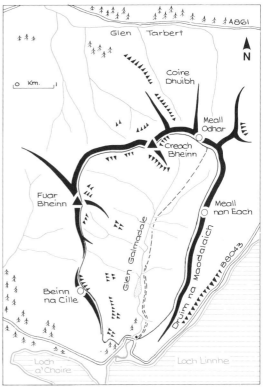

Looking south from Creach Bheinn to Fuar Bheinn and Beinn Mheadhoin   *R.D. Walton*

there is a dry stone walled enclosure that may have been built as a look-out at the time of the Napoleonic wars. It is marked on the Second Series 1:50,000 map as 'camp'. It must have been a very cold one. (8km; 1260m; 4h).

Descend NE down a narrower rocky ridge and then bear E and SE across the col at the head of Coire

Dhuibh and up the rounded Maol Odhar (794m). From there it is possible to descend directly SSW down a grassy spur to the head of Glen Galmadale, but the traverse continues SE then S over Meall nan Each (591m) and along the knolly ridge of Druim na Maodalaich, with fine views across Loch Linnhe, to return to the foot of Glen Galmadale.

Beinn Mheadhoin; 739m; (OS Sheet 49; 799514); *middle hill*

On the opposite side of the inlet of Loch a'Choire from the Creach Bheinn group just described, stands Beinn Mheadhoin. Its north-east face is a series of fine corries above Kingairloch House, but the south-western slopes of the hill are inaccessible and uninteresting, dropping to Glen Sanda and the featureless moorland typical of the interior of Morvern.

The most direct approach to the hill is through the policies of Kingairloch House, and should only be taken with discretion or permission. The road to the house along the north shore of Loch a'Choire is private, and there is a shorter approach down a footpath through the forest just north-west of the house. From North Corry go SW along a path to the Old Mill and climb the ENE ridge of Beinn Mheadhoin, which is quite narrow high up and leads directly to the summit. (From the B8043 road: 6km; 740m; 2h 40min).

On a fine day it is worthwhile to continue the traverse SE along the Beul Choire nan Each ridge and descend one of the bounding spurs of Coire Reidh to return to the head of Loch a'Choire.

An alternative route that may be preferred as it avoids the need to walk through the policies of Kingairloch House starts a few kilometres up the B8043 about 1km down from the outflow of Loch Uisge. Climb up Coire Shalachain onto the twin flat

tops of Meall na Greine, descend to the tiny lochans at the Bealach a'Choire Bhain and continue up the broad NW ridge of Beinn Mheadhoin, passing a false top and another tiny lochan before reaching the true summit. (5km; 740m; 2h 30min).

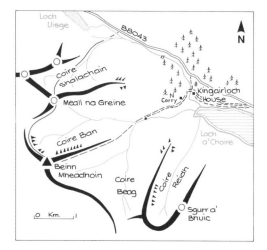

Garbh Bheinn; 885m; (OS Sheet 40; 904622); *rough mountain*

The summit of Garbh Bheinn seen across the head of   G.S. Johnstone
Coire an Iubhair from Sron a' Gharbh Choire Bhig

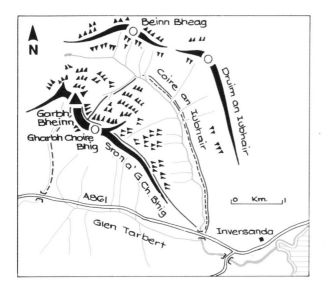

Garbh Bheinn of Ardgour is one of the finest mountains in the western Highlands, and it is certainly the finest and most precipitous mountain in Ardgour. The best view of it is from the east, looking across Loch Linnhe from Glen Coe or Ballachulish from where the jagged outline of the mountain is very obvious. From closer at hand, the full extent of the crags on its north-east face above Coire an Iubhair is best seen from the ridges on either side of that corrie. Despite its steep and rocky character, Garbh Bheinn is relatively easy of access by hillwalkers, although it should be treated with respect in adverse weather conditions.

Of three or four possible routes of ascent, probably the best starts at the foot of Coire an Iubhair, where cars can be parked off the A861 road at the old bridge over the Abhainn Coire an Iubhair. Cross to the W side of the stream and climb the long, but easy-angled ridge of Sron a'Gharbh Choire Bhig. There is a good deal of bare rock, but there are traces of paths up the ridge through and between the many rock outcrops, and the going is easy to the cairn at the top of the Sron (823m).

From that point there is a superb view of the south face of Garbh Bheinn across the head of Coire an Iubhair, as well as eastwards to the Glen Coe mountains. Descend the broad rocky ridge NW to a col (748m) and climb N up steep and rocky, but perfectly easy slopes to reach the W ridge of Garbh Bheinn a short distance W of the summit, which is perched right on the edge of the precipitous south face. (5km; 880m; 2h 40min).

The return may be varied by descending the route of ascent to the 748m col, and going steeply down from there NE into the head of Coire an Iubhair. There is a path of sorts which leads down between crags and boulders to the more level floor of the corrie where the path on the E side of the stream leads back to the day's starting point.

The shortest route of ascent is up Coire a'Chrothruim from a point on the A861 road through Glen Tarbert 2km due S of the summit of Garbh Bheinn. The climb is a toilsome mixture of steep heather, scree and gravelly waterslides and, while not particularly difficult, is not recommended.

A very fine, but rather long traverse can be made round Coire an Iubhair, starting on the E side of the corrie up the ridge of Druim an Iubhair to Sgorr Mhic Eacharna. Continue over Beinn Bheag (736m) and steeply down to the pass on the N side of Garbh Bheinn, the Bealach

Feith 'n Amean. The ascent from this pass up the N ridge of Garbh Bheinn is quite steep and the upper section of the ridge is rocky, but perfectly easy, lead-ing over the tops of the buttresses on the mountain's NE face. The descent of the Sron a'Gharbh Choire Bhig completes a fine traverse.

Looking across Loch Linnhe to Sgurr na h-Eanchainne and Beinn na Cille   *H.M. Brown*

Sgurr na h-Eanchainne; 730m; (OS Sheets 40 and 41; 896658); *peak of the brains*

Sgurr na h-Eanchainne is a very shapely peak which is well seen from the A82 road between Fort William and Ballachulish. Its summit rises very stee-ply above Loch Linnhe at Corran Ferry, so it is conspicuous in views up and down the Great Glen. For the same reason it commands a superb prospect up and down Loch Linnhe and across it to Glen Coe. Its ascent in good weather is, therefore, highly recom-mended, despite the fact that it is not quite the highest hill in its massif, being just overtopped by the flat mass of Meall Dearg Choire nam Muc (734m), 2km to the west.

On the north-west side of Ardgour village there is an extensive fluvio-glacial sand and gravel terrace, pock-marked here and there by 'kettle-hole' lochans. (These are the melt-out holes where large masses of glacier ice were embedded in the gravels at the time of the last Ice-Age). Go N along the A861 road for about 2km from the ferry to a cattle grid at (014658) just beyond the Clan Maclean burial ground. Access to the open hillside can be gained on the N side of the stream below Beinn na Cille (a name often wrongly attributed to Sgurr na h-Eanchainne).

Cross to the S bank of the stream and climb steeply uphill beside it, but before the col between the two hills is reached, turn W then S and climb up to the sharp summit of Sgurr na h-Eanchainne. (2km; 730m;

1h 50min).

The descent can be varied if desired by going to the highest point of the massif, Meall Dearg Choire nam Muc, round the rim of the well-formed Coire Dubh. The top is of no great interest, and the view from it is inferior in every way. Descend steeply down a rough hillside to Loch nan Gabhar and Sallachan, keeping E of the cliffs shown on the OS 1:50,000 map.

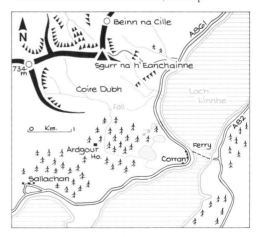

Sgurr Dhomhnuill from Sgurr na h-Ighinn   R. Wood

Sgurr Dhomhnuill; 888m; (OS Sheet 40; 889679); *Donald's peak*

Sgurr Dhomhnuill is the highest peak in Ardgour, and because of its height and pointed appearance it is a conspicuous landmark when seen from many distant viewpoints. It stands at the head of the Strontian Glen, and is one of several peaks surrounding the headwaters of the River Scaddle.

Although it is possible to climb Sgurr Dhomhnuill from Glen Scaddle, the walk up that glen is very long. The best approach to the mountain is from Strontian to its south-west, and two routes are possible.

The most scenically attractive route is up the Strontian Glen from the car park at the entrance to the Ariundle Nature Reserve. Walk up the glen through a fine natural forest of oak and take the upper path leading to the disused Feith Dhomhnuill mines. Cross the stream to the E and climb onto the Druim

Leac a'Sgiathain, a narrow ridge leading to Sgurr na h-Ighinn (766m). Descend N to a col at 682m and climb the S ridge of Sgurr Dhomhnuill in two steps to the summit. (8½km; 970m; 3h 30min).

The alternative route starts at the highest point of the road from Strontian to Loch Doilet at 342m. Go ENE along a broad, featureless ridge studded with little lochans to Druim Garbh, and from its highest point (803m) descend SE and climb the NW ridge of Sgurr Dhomhnuill which gives a good scramble almost all the way to the top. (6km; 750m; 2h 40min). Although this route is shorter than the one described above, the terrain on the Druim Garbh ridge (particularly its lower part) is likely to be very confusing in bad visibility. The two routes described can be combined to give a fine traverse.

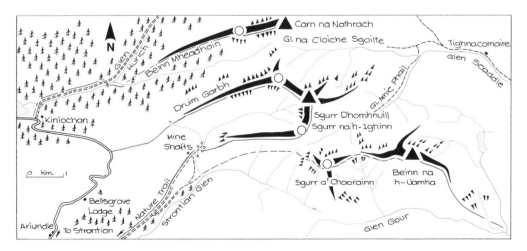

Looking south-east from Sgurr Dhomhnuill over Beinn na h-Uamha to Glen Coe   *G.S. Johnstone*

Beinn na h-Uamha; 762m; (OS Sheet 40; 917664); *hill of the caves*

Beinn na h-Uamha is a remarkably rocky hill on the north side of Glen Gour several kilometres west of Sallachan. With its twin peak, Sgurr a'Chaorainn (761m) which is 2½km to its west, it form a high ridge to the south-east of Sgurr Dhomhnuill on the north side of the watershed between Glen Gour and the Strontian Glen. The traverse of this ridge from Sallachan to Strontian is a very good day's walking, and use can be made of the bus service between Ardgour village and Strontian.

Starting at Sallachan, a good track is followed on the S side of Glen Gour to Loch nan Gabhar and the ruined cottage of Tigh Ghlinnegabhar. About 4km up the glen a crossing of the River Gour must be made and the SE ridge of Beinn na h-Uamha is climbed. There is a conspicuous knoll about half way up the ridge, which is rocky for much of its length, and leads directly to the summit. (7½km; 770m; 3h).

Continue W down a broad ridge to the col at 556m and climb more steeply to Sgurr a'Chaorainn. From there descend steeply W to the Strontian Glen and go down this glen to reach the path and track which leads very pleasantly through the oakwoods of the Ariundle Nature Reserve to the road 2km N of Strontian.

Carn na Nathrach; 786m; (OS Sheet 40; 887699); *cairn of the adders*

This hill is situated right in the heart of the wilds of Ardgour, and is the highest point of a long ridge (to which the name Beinn Mheadhoin is given) which extends from the lower reaches of Glen Hurich near Loch Doilet to Glen Scaddle. Glen Hurich, including the entire western perimeter of the Beinn Mheadhoin ridge, is extensively forested, and some of this forest is now being felled, so access to the hills may be impeded by felling and re-afforestation.

The closest approach to Carn na Nathrach is from Glen Hurich as it is possible to drive along the narrow and very steep public road from Strontian to Loch Doilet and the little forestry village of Polloch. From Kinlochan near the E end of Loch Doilet walk (or cycle) up the forestry road in Glen Hurich for 2km and cross the River Hurich. Continue E on the road on the N side of the Allt an Dubh Choirein to the point where it crosses the ridge of Beinn Mheadhoin. Strike uphill through the remains of the forest and gain the open ridge of Beinn Mheadhoin which is followed for 4km over a few knolls and a final narrow section to Carn na Nathrach. (8km; 800m; 3h 20min).

A number of possibilities exist for different descents. It is possible to continue the traverse E along the Beinn Mheadhoin ridge, descend to Glen Scaddle and walk for many kilometres down this glen to the road beside Loch Linnhe. If returning to Kinlochan, one can return along the ridge to the 602m knoll and descend N from there down a steep ridge on the W side of the prominent gully W of Creag Bheag. This leads to a forest road on the S side of Glen Hurich 6½km from Kinlochan. (On the ascent it is possible to cycle up this road, thus minimising the walking distance to the hill).

Looking north up Glen Hurich to Druim Tarsuinn and Beinn Mheadhoin   *G.S Johnstone*

Stob a'Bhealach an Sgriodain (Druim Tarsuinn); 770m; (OS Sheet 40; 854727); *peak of the pass of screes (transverse ridge)*
Sgurr Ghiubhsachain; 849m; (OS Sheet 40; 875752); *peak of the fir-wood*
Sgorr Craobh a'Chaorainn; 775m; (OS Sheet 40; 896757); *rowantree peak*

These three mountains lie in the north-west corner of Ardgour, almost isolated from the neighbouring parts of the western Highlands by the long lochs Shiel and Eil. The heads of these two lochs are separated by about 5km over a col which is only 15m above sea-level. Especially near Loch Shiel the hills are steep-sided and rocky, with Sgurr Ghiubhsachain being one of the finest peaks, not only in this area, but in the whole of the west. It is not to be treated too lightly, especially in winter. The most convenient access to these hills is from the A830 road from Fort William to Glenfinnan at a point about 2km before reaching Glenfinnan.

In the list of Corbetts the name Druim Tarsuinn has been applied to the 770m top which is the highest point on the long line of peaks between the heads of Glen Scaddle and the Cona Glen. This is probably incorrect, as the name is not apposite and moreover has been shown by the Ordnance Survey as applying to the ridge to the north-west of the Bealach an Sgriodain over which the old path from Glenfinnan to Glen Hurich passes. Local enquiry has failed to come up with an explanation. The 770m summit is well-defined and quite separate from its neighbouring peak Meall Mor. The name Stob a'Bhealach an Sgriodain is therefore suggested for it.

No matter what its name, it is an enticingly remote hill; 14km up the Cona Glen from Loch Linnhe, 11km up Glen Hurich from Loch Doilet, which is itself not altogether easy of access from Strontian with the additional complexity of felling and re-afforestation in Glen Hurich near Resourie bothy. The best route to the hill is from Callop cottage, 2km east of Glenfinnan just off the A830 road. Even this route involves some descent and reascent to cross the head of the Cona Glen.

Leave the A830 road at (925794) and park near the locked gate at the bridge over the Callop River. From the bridge follow the path S past Callop cottage and up the W side of the Allt na Cruaiche. In spate conditions the Allt Coire na Leacaich is surprisingly difficult to cross, but is easy in dry weather. The path continues to a pass overlooking the head of the Cona Glen, where it divides. Go straight downhill to cross the Cona River at a prominent meander loop. (If this river is in spate, crossing will be very difficult, and an easier point will have to be found upstream). Climb SW up the W side of the stream which comes down from the col W of Meall Mor on pleasantly low-angled rock and grass to reach the col itself. From there the ridge W to Druim Tarsuinn is rocky and knolly. (9km; 890m; 3h 30min).

The easiest descent is WNW to the Bealach an Sgriodain, then down to the Cona Glen and up the path to the col at the head of the Allt na Cruaiche. The path between the Cona River and the col is none too distinct, but beyond the col the going is easy back to the day's starting point.

Sgurr Ghiubhsachain from Glenfinnan   *D.J. Bennet*

The traverse of Sgurr Ghiubhsachain and Sgorr na Craobh Chaorainn also starts at the bridge over the Callop River. Follow the forest road NW then SW along the shore of Loch Shiel for 5km to Guesachan cottage. Climb Sgurr Ghiubhsachain by its very fine N ridge, best reached by going up the Allt Coire Ghiubhsachain for some way and then traversing onto the ridge above its steep and rocky lowest part. After reaching the ridge climb steeply through rocky bluffs where care is needed in misty weather. Some scrambling can be found. Cross the shoulder of Meall a'Choire Chruinn and climb the final steep slopes to the apparent summit, from where a horizontal ridge leads to the large cairn on the true top. (7½km; 850m; 3h 10min).

Descend steeply ESE down slabs and grass, then easily along the ridge round the head of Coire Ghiubhsachain to Sgorr Craobh a'Chaorainn. This peak has a steep W face and a rocky summit where any slight difficulty can be circumvented on the E side of the ridge. (10km; 1040m; 4h). Continue downhill NE over Meall na Cuartaige to join the path in the Allt na Cruaiche glen, which leads back to the bridge over the Callop River.

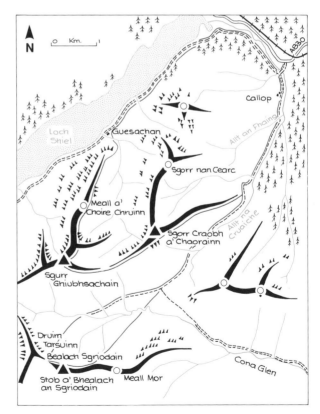

Stob Coire a' Chearcaill from the Cona Glen   *R. Wood*

Stob Coire a'Chearcaill; 770m; (OS Sheet 41; 107727); *peak of the circular corrie*

Stob Coire a'Chearcaill is the highest hill in the north-east corner of Ardgour. It presents a uniformly dreary appearance towards Loch Eil, but from a point 2km south of Fort William the view of the summit across Loch Linnhe is a much more impressive sight, with crags rising above Coire a'Chearcaill at the head of Gleann Sron a'Chreagain.

The shortest route to the top, by 1km, is by the north flank, starting from a point (024770) just over 1km E of Duisky on the A861 road beside Loch Eil. At that point (near a cattle grid on the E side of a large plantation) a gate gives access to open hillside. Go through open woodland for a short distance and then head straight uphill. A ruined fence appears intermittently and leads onto the Braigh Bhlaich ridge a short dis-

tance E of the summit. Follow the crest W round the corrie and up to the top where a huge cairn lies a few metres back from, and apparently higher than, the triangulation pillar. (4½km; 770m; 2h 20min).

A slightly longer, but more attractive approach, is by Gleann Sron a'Chreagain. Unfortunately parking near the foot of this glen is very restricted as access to steadings and fields must not be blocked. From the road a track leads W through fenced, stock-grazing land for about 2km to a point about 150 metres before the last fence. A gate, slightly above the path, leads to open country from which the Braigh Bhlaich ridge can be reached and the first route joined. This route can be used by carless parties from Fort William, using the Camusnagaul ferry.

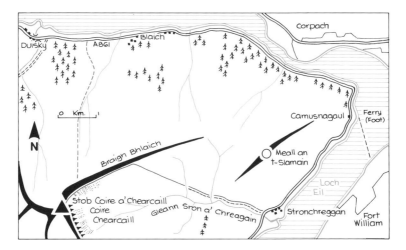

Beinn Odhar Bheag (right) from Beinn an Tuim   *D.J. Broadhead*

Beinn Odhar Bheag; 882m; (OS Sheet 40; 846778); *little dun-coloured hill*
Beinn Mhic Cedidh; 783m; (OS Sheet 40; 828787); *MacCedidh's hill*

Moidart is rough, sparsely populated country that is bounded on the east by Loch Shiel, on the west by Loch Ailort and on the north by the A830 road from Fort William to Mallaig. The highest hills in the district lie near its northern and north-western edge, and are readily accessible from the nearest roads; their southern flanks are much more remote and inaccessible.

Beinn Odhar Bheag, with its slightly lower twin Beinn Odhar Mhor, and Beinn Mhic Cedidh are in the north-east corner of Moidart, accessible from Glenfinnan and one or two points on the A830 to its west. If it is wished to start and finish the traverse of these hills at the same point, then the most convenient point is at the east end of Loch Eilt.

The burn which flows into Loch Eilt at its E end, the Allt Lon a'Mhuidhe, is surprisingly deep and difficult to cross, but there are stepping stones close to a roadside parking place about 200 metres E of the E end of the loch. (In spate conditions, or if the level of Loch Eilt is high, these stepping stones may be of little help). Once across the burn bear W parallel to the railway through scattered birches and reach the Allt a'Choin Bhuidhe. On its W side climb up to the col at the foot of the N ridge of Beinn Mhic Cedidh, and continue up this well-defined ridge, which becomes quite narrow and rocky near the summit. (4½km; 750m; 2h 30min).

Descend E to the Bealach a'Choire Bhuidhe and climb the NW ridge of Beinn Odhar Bheag directly to its summit. (6½km; 1150m; 3h 30min). It is a fine vantage point high above Loch Shiel.

Traverse the ridge N along the edge of some fine corries above Loch Shiel to reach Beinn Odhar Mhor (870m). From there descend the NW ridge, which is quite well-defined at first, but lower down tends to merge with the steep NW side of the hill. At the foot of this slope the Allt a'Choin Bhuidhe is reached and followed down to rejoin the uphill route.

If the burns are in spate, access to these hills may best be made from the A830 road near its high point about 2km E of Loch Eilt. From there one can climb S up the rough Coire Odhar to Beinn Odhar Mhor.

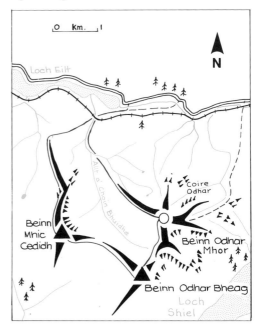

The Rois-Bheinn group from Loch nan Uamh   *G.S. Johnstone*

Rois-Bheinn; 882m; (OS Sheet 40; 756778); *hill of showers*
Sgurr na Ba Glaise; 874m; (OS Sheet 40; 771777); *peak of the grey cow*
An Stac; 814m; (OS Sheet 40; 763794); *the stack*

These mountains in the north-western corner of Moidart give very fine ridge walking, largely because of their splendid position close to the western seaboard above Loch Ailort. The views out across the Sea of the Hebrides to the islands of Eigg, Rhum and others are unmatched elsewhere along the west coast. Two possible starting points for the traverse of these peaks and their slightly lower neighbours are at Lochailort and Alisary. The traverse from one of these points to the other is a fine expedition, with a pleasant walk back to the starting point along the A861 road beside Loch Ailort.

Starting at the north end of the group at Lochailort, cars can be parked just off the main road near Inverailort, or near the Glenshian Lodge Hotel. From there a path leads through a little col immediately S of the knoll of Tom Odhar and into the lower part of Coire a'Bhuiridh. Continue up the corrie and cross to the E side of the Allt a'Bhuiridh in order to climb SE up the grassy slopes of Beinn Coire nan Gall. Aim for the lochan at the col between this hill and Druim Fiaclach (869m), and climb the latter by its steep and craggy N ridge.

Druim Fiaclach, although not a Corbett, is possibly the finest peak of this group. Its main feature of interest is the SE ridge, which is narrow and has on its crest a number of small tooth-like pinnacles which give the hill its name, *toothed ridge.*

Descend SW from Druim Fiaclach along another fine ridge to a small col and re-ascend S to a tiny lochan perched on the crest of An t-Slat-bheinn, turning WSW at the lochan along a narrow ridge to reach the summit of this peak (c820m). This undulating ridge culminates 1km further W at Sgurr na Ba Glaise, which has impressive crags on its north face. (7½km; 1000m; 3h 20min).

Descend steeply NW to the Bealach an Fhiona (701m) where the remains of an old wall are found leading W for 1km to the eastern and higher summit of Rois-Bheinn. (9½km; 1180m; 4h 10min). The wall continues for 700 metres to the western summit (878m), which although it is not the highest point of the mountain, certainly is the best viewpoint.

To reach the last peak of this group, return to the Bealach an Fhiona and descend steeply NNW, still following the broken wall, to the col below An Stac, from where a steep rocky ridge leads directly to its isolated summit. (11½km; 1450m; 5h).

The final descent of the day depends on one's objective. If returning to Lochailort, descend N then NNE over rocky ground to Seann Cruach (521m), and continue NE to rejoin the path near the Tom Odhar col, a short distance from Lochailort.

If making a traverse of the group to Alisary, descend W from An Stac down steep ground with many rocky outcrops to Coire na Cnamha.   Go down the

Rois-Bheinn from Sgurr na Ba Glaise   R. Wood

corrie to the E corner of the forest on the S side of the Alisary Burn and descend a narrow path on the S side of this burn (keeping close to the forest high above the burn) to reach the A861 road beside Loch Ailort 4km from the day's starting point.

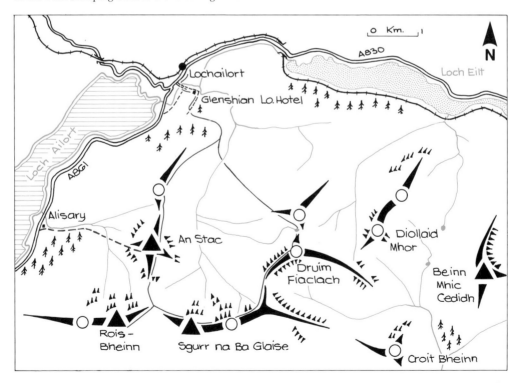

SECTION 10b

Loch Eil to Glen Shiel

Sgurr an Utha; 796m; (OS Sheet 40; 885839); *peak of the udder*

Although rather a retiring mountain, without any dominant features, Sgurr an Utha well justifies its Corbett status. It is the highest point, albeit by only a few metres, of the well-defined group of extremely rocky hills immediately to the north-west of Glenfinnan. This massif is bounded on the north by the deep gash of the Chaol-ghlinne, on the east by Glen Finnan, on the west by the Allt Feith a'Chatha and on the south by the A830 road from Glenfinnan to Mallaig.

The shortest route to this hill starts where the A830 road crosses the Allt Feith a'Chatha (875817); there is space for parking W of the bridge. Follow the forest track which starts from the roadside just E of the bridge through forest plantings not shown on the 2nd Series Ordnance Survey 1:50,000 map. In a few hundred metres the track emerges onto the open hillside and turns NE towards the ridge of Druim na Brein-choille above the Allt an Utha, and this is a convenient route to gain height easily. Leave the track before it turns away from the burn and cross the latter to gain the SW ridge of Sgurr an Utha. (In spate conditions one can reach the foot of this ridge, without the problem of crossing the burn, by crossing a bridge at the confluence of the Allt an Utha and the Allt Feith a'Chatha). Climb the SW ridge up extremely rocky ground over knolls and slabs to reach the well-defined summit, with a small cairn perched on the edge of the steep slopes above the Chaol-ghlinne. (2½km; 690m; 1h 50min). The summit is a very fine viewpoint.

Sgurr an Utha from Loch Beoraid   H.M. Brown

On the return one can go E to the col between Sgurr an Utha and Fraoch-bheinn (790m) and climb the latter hill if wished before descending SW to reach the end of the forest track quite high up on the Druim na Brein-choille.

The hill can also be climbed by the WSW ridge, reached by crossing the bridge at the foot of the Allt an Utha and climbing N to Sidhean Mor. This is a steep and laborious route, wending a way through crags,and it becomes mildly adventurous in winter.

If one arrives at Glenfinnan by train, the best route to the hill is directly N from the station up the Tom na h-Aire ridge, which is quite steep and rocky, and curves round NW to reach Fraoch-bheinn. The descent to Glenfinnan can most easily be made by dropping S from the col between Sgurr an Utha and Fraoch-bheinn and going down the Allt a'Choire Dhuibh.

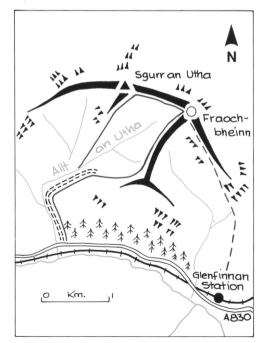

Streap and Sgurr Thuilm from the north   *G.S. Johnstone*

Streap; 909m; (OS Sheet 40; 946863); *climbing hill*

Streap is the highest summit on the long undulating ridge which separates Glen Finnan from Gleann Dubh Lighe, and it can be climbed equally well from either glen. The route from the latter is scenically more attractive and offer the possibility of a traverse over Streap Comhlaidh.

For the Gleann Dubh Lighe approach leave the A830 road at (799931) and follow the forest road up the W side of the burn to a point opposite the Dubh Lighe bothy, and reach the open hillside above the forest plantings. Climb NW below Beinn an Tuim to reach the col between that hill and Stob Coire nan Cearc (887m). Traverse the rocky, undulating ridge over the intermediate knoll (844m) and descend to the col SW of Streap. The final ridge above this col narrows considerably and becomes a steep-sided knife-edge (possibly rather intimidating to the inexperienced) leading directly to the summit of Streap, a magnificent perch.(8km; 1050m; 3h 40min).

Descend SE and climb a short distance to Streap Comhlaidh (898m). The return to the Dubh Lighe goes down the S ridge of this peak to a possibly difficult crossing of the burn if it is in spate. On the E side a path leads S to join a recently made extension of the forest road, which is followed down the glen past the Dubh Lighe bothy and over the Dubh Lighe to join the uphill route.

For the Glen Finnan approach, follow the private road up the glen to Corryhully bothy. Cross the River Finnan by a footbridge near the bothy and make a steep ascent to the col between Beinn an Tuim and Stob Coire nan Cearc, where the route described above is joined and followed to Streap. (7½km; 1050m; 3h 30min).

To return to Glen Finnan, descend the SW ridge of Streap and go down a curious diag-onal shelf (indicated on the Ordnance Survey map) on the NW flank of the hill to return to Corryhully.

Braigh nan Uamhachan; 765m; (OS Sheet 40; 975867); *slope of the caves*

This is the northern and culminating point of the long ridge between Gleann Dubh Lighe and Gleann Fionnlighe. The main part of this ridge is a gently undulating crest which stretches north from Na h-Uamhachan (691m) and gives a very pleasant high-level walk.

The Gleann Dubh Lighe approach to Braigh nan Uamhachan goes to the Dubh Lighe bothy by the route for Streap described above. From the bothy continue N along the road for about 1km to the fence at the edge of the planting and there head NE uphill to Na h-Uamhachan. The first part of the climb is hard going through tussocky grass, but higher up it is eas-

ier. Once on the ridge there is easy walking over Sron Liath and along 1½km of well-built wall to the top of Braigh nan Uamhachan. (8km; 850m; 3h 20min).

The approach up Gleann Fionnlighe starts from the A830 road just W of the end of Loch Eil and follows the private road to Wauchan and on up the glen for 2km. A bicycle can be used to that point. There is tree planting along the SE flank of Na h-Uamhachan not shown on the Ordnance Survey map. Once past this planting, make a rising traverse N across the E face of Sron Liath to reach the ridge at the col ½km S of Braigh nan Uamhachan. (8km; 760m; 3h 10min).

The summit of Braigh nan Uamhachan from Sron Liath   G.S Johnstone

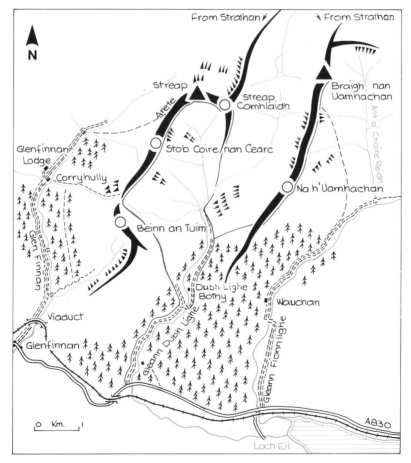

Meall a'Phubuill; 774m; (OS Sheet 41; 029854); *hill of the tent*
Beinn Bhan; 796m;(OS Sheets 34 and 41;141857); *white hill*

The curving through-valley formed by Glen Loy and Gleann Suileag is bounded on the north and west by a 25km-long ridge of hills of which Beinn Bhan is the eastern termination, with Meall a'Phubuill about two-thirds of the way along to the west. The traverse of this ridge is long and tedious, but as neither of the two Corbetts makes a full day's walking on its own, the ascent of both in a day from Glen Loy might be considered.

For the Glen Loy approach to Meall a'Phubuill, park near Achnanellan and follow the right of way W to the rather struggling wood of Brian Choille. Beyond the trees bear up easily NW to reach the crest of Druim Gleann Laoigh at about (051852) some way W of the lowest point. A dry stone dyke can be followed W along the ridge to Pt.747m, passing a cairn which serves no discernable purpose. Follow the wall down to the deep col E of Meall a'Phubuill where it peters out and a fence turns S towards Gleann Suileag. Breast the slopes ahead to reach the broad summit of Meall a'Phubuill. (7km; 760m; 2h 50min).

Return by descending to the col and following the fence down towards Gleann Suileag, passing in the burn a long water-slide of fragmental dark rock. This is the agglomerate of a volcanic vent - a rare phenomenon for the western Highlands. About half way down the burn, cross it and bear ESE to regain the path in the glen and return along it to Achnanellan.

Meall a' Phubuill from Gleann Suileag   *D.J. Bennet*

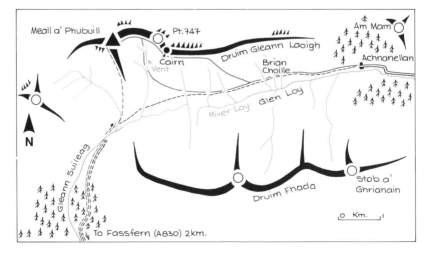

Beinn Bhan from the foot of Glen Loy   *G.S. Johnstone*

Meall a'Phubuill can equally well be climbed from Fassfern on the A830 road. It is possible to cycle up the track on the E side of Gleann Suileag to the N edge of the forest. From there continue along a good path to Glensulaig cottage and climb Meall a'Phubuill by its S flank

Beinn Bhan is a bulky hill with a 2km-long summit ridge which is almost level, forming a crescent round Coire Mhuilinn. This gives a convenient circuit which is best made by starting up the W side of the corrie, as the route thereafter is easier to follow in mist.

Park near the presently derelict house at Inverskillavulin. On either side of the burn issuing from the corrie above the slopes are fenced off, but there is ample room between fence and burn on each bank for a way to be made easily but steeply to the lip of the corrie and the open hillside above. Starting up the W side of the burn, aim to reach the lip of the corrie well to the SE of the cairn indicated on the Ordnance Survey map. The route round Coire Mhuilinn is straightforward and in mist a line of fence posts is a useful, if intermittent guide. The summit trig point of Beinn Bhan is not too easy to locate in thick mist. (4½km; 750m; 2h 20min). To descend, go about 150 metres WSW from the top, then S, curving gradually SW to regain the lip of the corrie. Then go down the E bank of the stream.

Beinn Bhan can also be climbed from the B8004 road 1½km NE of the foot of Glen Loy. Go up beside the forest and over Monadh Uisge Mhuilinn, an easy but dull route relieved by the excellent views up the Great Glen and towards Ben Nevis.

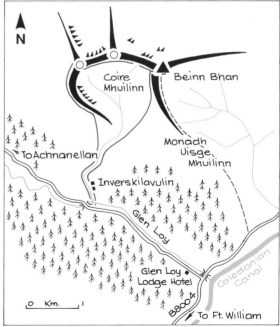

Looking up Gleann Cia-aig to Meall na h-Eilde   D.J. Bennet

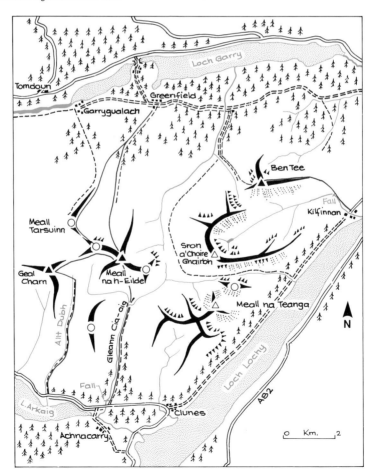

Ben Tee; 901m; (OS Sheet 34; 241972); *fairy hill*

Ben Tee is the very obvious conical hill rising above the forests in the angle where Glen Garry joins the Great Glen. From points to the west in Glen Garry, and the north-east up the Great Glen it is the most prominent of the group of hills of which it is part.

The shortest route to it is from Kilfinnan, which is reached along the narrow public road from Laggan Swing Bridge between Loch Oich and Loch Lochy. There is a path up the NE side of the Kilfinnan Burn, but this goes to the Kilfinnan Fall. The better way to Ben Tee is to climb directly NW up the grassy hillside a few hundred metres NE of the burn to reach a stile over a fence near (271968). From there continue WNW across featureless rising moorland which gradually steepens and becomes rockier as the summit of Ben Tee is approached. (4km; 860m; 2h 20min).

An alternative route from the northwest starts at the bridge over Loch Garry at (195022). From the bridge follow the private road to Greenfield and through the forest E to the foot of the Allt Ladaidh. Another forest road goes S up this burn for 2km to the foot of the Allt Bealach Easain. It is possible to cycle to that point. Continue up the path on the NE side of the Allt Coire Easain and climb steeply to the summit of Ben Tee. (9km; 810m; 3h 30min).

Ben Tee from Glen Garry   *R. Wood*

Meall na h-Eilde; 838m; (OS Sheet 34; 185946); *hill of the hinds*
Geal Charn; 804m; (OS Sheet 34; 156943); *white cairn*

These hills, only slightly lower than the neighbouring Loch Lochy hills to their east, have much the same character as them. Meall na h-Eilde and its adjacent hills Meall an Tagraidh, Meall Coire nan Saobhaidh and Meall Tarsuinn form a fine undulating ridge which is well seen from Glen Garry to their north. Geal Charn is a more isolated, rounded hill rising above the east end of Loch Arkaig. Good paths lead in from both Loch Arkaig to the south and Loch Garry to the north, but the former approach is shorter and probably more often used.

The best starting point for the southern approach is at the Eas Chia-aig, a fine waterfall at the west end of the Dark Mile on the road to Loch Arkaig. From the car park climb steeply uphill along a fine path through the forest to reach a road which is followed N up Gleann Cia-aig, continuing along a path beyond the end of the forest to a footbridge at (187928). On the N side of the Allt Cam Bhealaich climb N towards the Bealach an Easain and then NW to the rounded summit of Meall na h-Eilde. (6km; 790m; 2h 40min).

Descend NW to the Bealach Choire a'Ghuirein and climb W along the easy-angled ridge to Meall Coire nan Saobhaidh. From there descend SW down the broad ridge to the little lochan at the Bealach Carn na h-Urchaire and finally climb more steeply to Geal Charn, from where there is a very fine view westwards. (10km; 1040m; 4h).

Descend SE to reach the end of the track (previously a good stalker's path) which goes down the Allt Dubh to Achnasaul, leaving a 2½km walk along the Loch Arkaig road back to the Eas Chia-aig.

On the north side of these hills there is a network of paths and forest roads starting from Greenfield. The path S from Greenfield is the most direct, but care is required not to lose it in deep heather and recently planted trees. The road which goes E, then back WSW is a longer, but surer route to the S edge of the forest, and a bicycle can be used to reach the start of the path up the N ridge of Meall Tarsuinn to start a traverse to Meall na h-Eilde. On the return the path down the Allt Coire nan Saobhaidh can be used.

Fraoch Bheinn and Sgurr Mhurlagain from the south-west   *G.S. Johnstone*

Sgurr Mhurlagain; 880m; (OS Sheet 33; 012944); *peak of the bay-shaped inlet*
Fraoch Bheinn; 858m; (OS Sheets 33 and 40; 986940); *heathery hill*
Sgurr Cos na Breachd-laoigh; 835m; (OS Sheets 33 and 40; 948947); *peak of the cave of the bonny calf*

Going west from the hills described in the preceding page, the first of the big hills at the west end of Loch Arkaig is Sgurr Mhurlagain. Although it has no particular character or interest for the climber, its rocks are unusual, being largely made up of a beautiful pale granite gneiss which marks the junction between the smooth granulite hills to the east and the rugged schist mountains to the west.

The public road along Loch Arkaig ends close to the west end of the loch, but there seems to be no objection at the present time to cars being driven a further 1km along a rough road and parked near Strathan. It is not possible to drive further, either up Glen Dessarry or Glen Pean. Sgurr Mhurlagain presents a broad grassy flank towards Loch Arkaig above Murlaggan cottage, and it can be climbed from almost any point along the road near there in less than 2 hours. Another possible route that allows Sgurr Mhurlagain to be combined with Fraoch Bheinn is the long, easy-angled SW ridge which can be easily reached by taking the path from Strathan up the Dearg Altt to the col between the two hills. From this col the upper part of the SW ridge leads in less than 2km to the summit. (5km; 830m; 2h 30min).

To the west of Sgurr Mhurlagain, Fraoch Bheinn (despite being slightly lower) is a more interesting hill, particularly on its north side where narrow ridges and steep rocky corries overlook Glen Kingie. Fraoch Bheinn is the most easterly of the craggy schist mountains which stretch westwards into the Rough Bounds of Knoydart. It is separated from its neighbours by two passes, each with a stalker's path, which go from Glen Dessarry to Glen Kingie; the Dearg Allt (c460m) to the east and

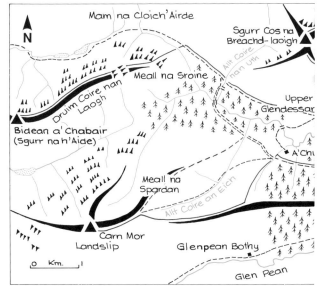

Sgurr Cos na Breachd-laoigh from Sgurr Beag   *G. Blyth*

the Feith a'Chicheanais (c360m) to the west.

The ascent of Fraoch Bheinn from Strathan is very straightforward, either directly up the well-defined SSW ridge or up the path on the E side of the Dearg Allt to the point where a ruined fence crosses the path. Cross to the W side of the stream by a footbridge and climb steeply NW through small rocky bluffs to reach the SSW ridge, which is followed to the top.

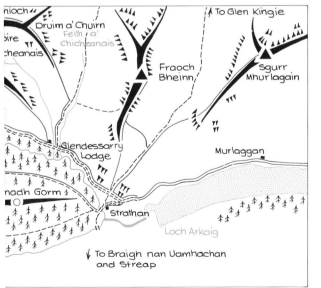

If time permits, it is worthwhile to continue N for a short distance along the almost level summit ridge leading to the north top (854m) to look down at a huge rock-slip on the E side of the hill at the head of Coire na Cloiche Moire. This slip is delimited by fissures which seem to cut right through the turf. As Fraoch Bheinn is steep-sided, it is best to return to Strathan by the SSW ridge, unless one wants to continue W to include Sgurr Cos na Breachd-laoigh in the traverse. In that case go down the SSW ridge for about ½km and descend smooth slopes W towards Glendessarry Lodge to reach the Allt Feith a'Chicheanais at about the 300m contour at the foot of the SE ridge of Druim a'Chuirn.

Sgurr Cos na Breachd-laoigh is the highest point of a horseshoe-shaped ridge to the north-west of Glendessarry Lodge; Druim a'Chuirn (815m) being the other high point of this ridge near its east end. There is a prominent little pinnacle, called A'Chioch, half way along the narrow crest of the ridge.

The best circuit of this ridge is to take the path N from Glendessarry Lodge for about 1km and then climb the SE ridge of Druim a'Chuirn. Continue very pleasantly along the ridge past A'Chioch to Sgurr Cos na Breachd-laoigh. (From Strathan: 6km; 850m; 2h 50min). Return directly to the lodge down the easy-angled SE ridge.

Bidean a' Chabair from Druim Coire nan Laogh   *D.J. Bennet*

Carn Mor; 829m; (OS Sheets 33 and 40; 903910); *big cairn*

The summit of Carn Mor is the highest point of an 11km-long ridge between Glen Pean and Glen Dessarry. The eastern half of this ridge rising above Strathan and over Monadh Gorm is dull and its lower slopes are forested, but the western half beyond the bealach at the head of Coire nan Eich takes on all the rugged and steep-sided character of the hills of the Rough Bounds. The termination of the ridge above the head of Loch Morar is as rough and rocky as any of Carn Mor's more famous neighbours.

The approach to this hill is along the road on the north side of Loch Arkaig as far as Strathan, where one must park one's car and start walking, or cycling. Proceed along the well constructed forest road up Glen Dessarry on the south side of the River Dessarry to a point just beyond A'Chuil bothy. There is a good deal of afforestation on the south side of the glen. Beyond the bothy there is a gap in the forest and it is possible to climb SW onto the main ridge of the hill.

One route is up Coire nan Eich to the bealach at its head from where the way gets steeper and much rockier as one goes W, and it takes a surprisingly long time to reach the summit of Carn Mor, only 1¾km distant from the bealach. The alternative route is up the ridge of Meall nan Spardan; this route bypasses the bealach and leads directly to the summit of Carn Mor. (8½km; 800m; 3h 20min, or less if one cycles from Strathan). A small cairn on one of the several knolls of the summit area marks the top; it is not easy to find in thick mist.

There are stupendous views from the ridge between the bealach and the summit downwards into Glen Pean over the fissured slopes of the huge landslip which has fallen from the summit towards Lochan Leum an t-Sagairt. It is one of the largest landslips of its kind in the Highlands, and a descent down the fissured part of the S face of the hill should be avoided, especially in snow conditions.

Bidean a'Chabair (Sgurr na h-Aide); 867m; (OS Sheets 33 and 40; 889931); *peak of the hawk (peak of the hat)*

About 5km west of Glendessarry Lodge, Glen Dessarry divides into two passes. On the north the Mam na Cloich'Airde leads to Loch Nevis, on the south Gleann an Lochan Eanaiche leads to Loch Morar.

Although recent afforestation in upper Glen Dessarry has somewhat spoiled the approaches to these two passes, they remain amongst the wildest and most spectacular through routes in Scotland. Between them rises the steep-sided, rocky ridge of Sgurr na h-Aide, whose western end separates the upper reaches of Loch Nevis and Loch Morar. The highest

point of this rugged ridge is called Bidean a'Chabair; seen end on from Loch Arkaig it forms a sharp cone, often mistaken for Sgurr na Ciche. Its ascent is a long and fairly rough climb.

There are two ways up Glen Dessarry from Strathan. The right of way to Loch Nevis and Inverie goes along the private road to Glendessarry Lodge and Upper Glendessarry and continues as a footpath up the glen on its north side to the pass at its head. If one has a bicycle, the better way is along the forest road on the south side of the glen; this road goes as far as the junction of the Allt Coire nan Uth and the

River Dessarry at (930934), and it is easy to cycle that far. There is a one-plank bridge across the River Dessarry at that point, and a path on the north side leads up to join the right of way.

Going to Sgurr na h-Aide, continue along the right of way for about 1km past the Allt Coire nan Uth until beyond the forest, and cross the headwaters of the River Dessarry to reach the foot of Meall na Sroine, the eastern end of the Sgurr na h-Aide ridge. Climb steeply up this rocky nose and continue along the undulating ridge of Druim Coire nan Laogh over knolls and past little lochans to the final steep rise to Bidean a'Chabair, which needs some easy scrambling if climbed direct. (11½km; 880m; 4h 10min, much less if cycling).

The western summit (859m) is ½km away along a fine ridge without too much of an intervening drop. It gives a splendid view west along the extremely rugged ridge that separates Loch Nevis from Loch Morar.

It is possible, but not advisible, to climb the north flank of Sgurr na h-Aide from the Mam na Cloich'Airde. The hillside is steep and slabby. The south side of the hill above Gleann an Lochain Eanaiche is even steeper and rockier, and is definitely not a hillwalkers' route. Return to Glen Dessarry by the route of ascent.

Sgurr an Fhuarain from Sgurr Mor, with Glen Kingie and Sgurr Mhurlagain to the right   G. Blyth

Sgurr an Fhuarain; 901m; (OS Sheets 33 and 40; 987980)

Sgurr an Fhuarain is very much a lone Corbett among Munros, standing as it does on the long mountain range between Gairich and Sgurr na Ciche. It is more likely to be climbed as part of the traverse of this ridge than by itself. Access to Sgurr an Fhuarain is not entirely easy as to its north is the expanse of Loch Quoich, and to the south one has to cross a pass from Loch Arkaig to Glen Kingie before the foot of the hill is reached.

From Strathan go up to Glendessarry Lodge and N from there over the pass of the Feith a'Chicheanais. Leave the path just N of the pass and descend to cross the River Kingie as directly below the Sgurr Mor - Sgurr an Fhuarain col as possible. In spate conditions the Kingie is difficult to cross and it may be necessary to go upstream.

Once on the N side of the river climb easily, if steeply, to the col and then E along a ridge-path to the summit of Sgurr an Fhuarain. (8km; 1000m; 3h 30min).

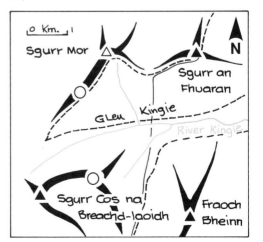

Sgurr a'Choire-bheithe from the west   J. Renny

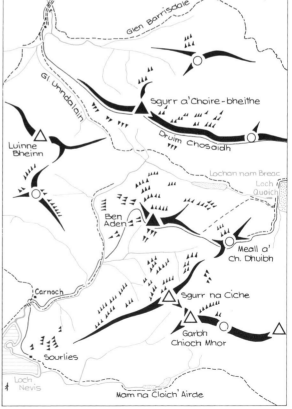

Ben Aden and Sgurr a'Choire-bheithe lie near the west end of Loch Quoich on the eastern boundary of Knoydart. This is one of the most rugged and remote parts of the Highlands, and also one with the highest rainfall; any expedition into this area must therefore be undertaken with due consideration for the weather. The distance to these two mountains from the nearest public road is quite considerable, access involves river crossings that may be difficult and even dangerous, and there is not much by way of shelter or accommodation in the area for climbers and walkers.

The bothy at Sourlies, which is reached by a 13km walk from Strathan through Glen Dessarry to the head of Loch Nevis, is very small. There is a bothy adjacent to the keeper's house at Barrisdale on Loch Hourn, reached by a 10km path along the loch-side from Kinloch Hourn, but it too has limited accommodation. The approach to these two mountains from the nearest point on a public road is along the north shore of Loch Quoich, starting at (986036) on the road to Kinloch Hourn. The way goes along the loch-side, which is pathless for the first 5km, but the going is fairly easy. Then the Abhainn Chosaidh has to be crossed. There is no bridge and this is a notoriously difficult crossing, definitely impossible when the river is high. Beyond it a good track leads in a further 4km to the west end of Loch Quoich. The 'easy' way to reach the head of Loch Quoich is by canoe or small dingy, and it is possible to launch such a craft at (994034) where there is access to the water's edge from the Kinloch Hourn road, but beware of submerged rocks when the water is low.

Ben Aden from the west end of Loch Quoich   *D.J. Bennet*

Ben Aden; 887m; (OS Sheets 33 and 40; 899986); *hill of the face*

Ben Aden is a superb mountain and a worthy companion to its higher neighbour Sgurr na Ciche, with which it may be climbed. It is steep and rocky on all sides. In particular, the great 600m high N face overlooking Lochan nam Breac is a feature of the mountain which dominates the pass from Loch Quoich to Loch Nevis. The ascent of Ben Aden is a good test of hillwalking skills, for it needs good routefinding, especially in bad weather when the best way through the many crags and slabs is not easily found.

From Sourlies bothy the approach goes up the River Carnach to its junction with the Allt Achadh a'Ghlinne. From there climb the SW face of the mountain, keeping to the left (N) high up to avoid steep rocks below the summit and gain the NW ridge.

Climb this ridge, passing a couple of knobs or false tops before the true summit is reached. (7km; 890m; 3h 10min).

From the W end of Loch Quoich one can take the path shown on the Ordnance Survey map leading up the side of Meall a'Choire Dhuibh (740m). Traverse this peak and continue along the extremely rocky E ridge of Ben Aden, past three lochans and over an intervening knoll. Alternatively, go'W from the head of Loch Quoich along the path to Lochan nam Breac for 1km and climb up the Coire na Cruaiche to reach the E ridge of Ben Aden by steep slopes at the head of this corrie. (From the head of Loch Quoich: 4km; 690m; 2h 10min).

Sgurr a'Choire-bheithe; 913m; (OS Sheet 33; 895015); *peak of the birch-tree corrie*

The summit of Sgurr a'Choire-bheithe is the highest point of a splendid 9km ridge called the Druim Chosaidh which extends from the west end of Loch Quoich to Barrisdale Bay on Loch Hourn. The north and south flanks of the ridge drop steeply from the narrow crest , which has many knolls and little tops along its length. The summit is near the west end of the ridge, dirctly above the Mam Unndalain, the pass between Loch Quoich and Barrisdale.

For those starting from Barrisdale, the ascent is very straightforward. Go S along the path to Gleann Unndalain and climb the long easy-angled WNW ridge which rises for 2km at a very uniform angle to a prominent knoll, beyond which the summit lies 1km due E. (4½km; 940m; 2h 40min).

Staring from the road to Kinloch Hourn, go along the N shore of Loch Quoich as far as the Abhainn Chosaidh. After crossing this river climb up the E end of the Druim Chosaidh, first over Meall an Spardain, then Sgurr Airigh na Beinne (776m) and then along 3km of undulating narrow ridge, which gives a little mild scrambling on its rocky crest, to reach the summit. (11½km; 900m; 4h 20min). If the return along the ridge is too daunting, descend SW from the summit to the Mam Unndalain and return to Loch Quoich along the path past Lochan nam Breac.

This route should not be attempted during or soon after bad weather as the Abhainn Chosaidh is likely to be imposssible to cross, and very dangerous. Only set out on this route in settled, dry weather

Looking west from Sgurr nan Eugallt to Ladhar Bheinn and Loch Hourn   *R. Wood*

Sgurr nan Eugallt; 894m; (OS Sheet 33; 931045); *peak of the death streams (precipices?)*

Sgurr nan Eugallt is a fine rocky mountain overlooking the head of Loch Hourn at the end of the public road to Kinloch Hourn. It is the highest point of an 8km ridge which is parallel to and north of the Druim Chosaidh, and is separated from it by Gleann Cosaidh. The last few kilometres of the road to Kinloch Hourn pass below the succession of wild corries on the north side of the mountain and its eastern extension, Sgurr a'Chlaidheimh. Its summit is a superb viewpoint towards Ladhar Bheinn, Loch Hourn and the Hebrides.

The climb from the road on the northeast side of Sgurr nan Eugallt is simplified by there being a stalker's path up to almost 600m, which takes much of the slog out of the ascent. This path starts at the ruined cottage of Coireshubh, where there is only limited space to park cars. Roadside parking is a problem, and there is none on the very steep and narrow section of the road between Coireshubh and Kinloch Hourn.

From Coireshubh the stalker's path leads well up almost onto the NE ridge of Sgurr nan Eugallt, and this ridge is followed easily to the summit. (3½km; 770m; 2h). The slightly lower peak of Sgurr Sgiath Airigh (881m) lies 1km NW, and is possibly a better viewpoint.

In good weather a very pleasant return can be made by traversing along the main ridge of Sgurr nan Eugallt SE to Sgurr a'Chlaidheimh (c830m). The descent to the road is then down through numerous rocky bluffs and slabby slopes which, as is

the case with so many other hillsides in or near the Rough Bounds, can be quite confusing, even intimidating, in misty conditions, but present no great difficulties when one can see clearly enough to choose a route through their intricacies. It was down this steep hillside that Prince Charles and his small band of men slipped past the Hanoverian troops on a dark night in 1746 to escape northwards to Glen Shiel.

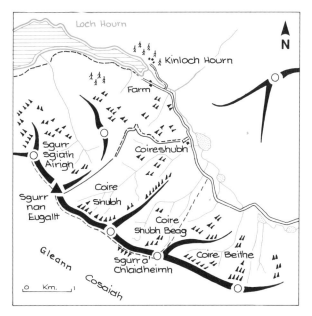

For the magnificence of its setting, nearly surrounded by the sea and sea-lochs, and the rugged grandeur of its mountains, Knoydart is justifiably regarded as the epitome of west Highland landscape and character. Not for nothing is the area known as The Rough Bounds. No road leads into the district, and one must either reach it on foot by long walks through the mountains, or by boat from Mallaig, which is the closest link that the population of Knoydart has with the outside world.

For many years Knoydart was regarded as being difficult of access, with no accommodation available and camping discouraged. However in recent years, possibly with change of ownership, the situation has changed, and it is now possible to get accommodation at Inverie, the only village in the district. As has already been noted, there is a small bothy at Barrisdale adjacent to the keeper's house. Accommodation in it is limited and a small charge is made.

The Mail Service sails from Mallaig to Inverie three days each week (at present on Mondays, Wednesdays and Fridays) and is operated by Bruce Watt Cruises, Mallaig (Telephone 0687 2233). It may be possible by private arrangement to hire a boat for a crossing of Loch Hourn from Arnisdale to Barrisdale.

The walkers' routes to Knoydart are from Strathan to the head of Loch Nevis (as noted already) and from there over the Mam Meadail to Inverie, and from Kinloch Hourn to Barrisdale and on over the Mam Barrisdale and down Gleann an Dubh-Lochain to Inverie. These routes follow rights of way along well-defined paths.

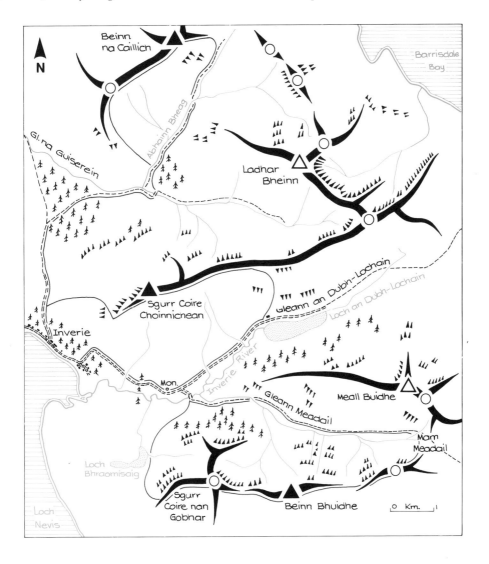

Beinn Bhuidhe from the head of Loch Nevis   R.Wood

Beinn Bhuidhe; 855m; (OS Sheet 33; 822967); *yellow hill*

The southernmost part of Knoydart, between the head of Loch Nevis and Gleann Meadail, is occupied by a single massive mountain - Beinn Bhuidhe. It is a long undulating ridge, about 8km from east to west, with the highest point near its centre. To the south long grassy slopes drop in a single sweep into Loch Nevis; on the north there is a fine series of corries overlooking the right of way in Gleann Meadail.

The complete traverse of the Beinn Bhuidhe ridge is a long expedition, but it gives unexcelled views of Loch Nevis from its narrow head to the more open waters of Inverie Bay. Starting from Inverie, the approach is made by Gleann Meadail to the Mam Meadail. From there climb SW to the first peak on the ridge, Meall Bhasiter. The delights of this undulating high-level walk are then enjoyed westwards to Beinn Bhuidhe. (13km; 1020m; 4h 40min).

Continue to Sgurr Coire nan Gobhar and descend to Loch Bhraomisaig, and thence NE towards the Inverie River and the bridge near the monument. Some care has to be taken when descending in limited visibility. Map on page 151.

Sgurr Coire Choinnichean; 796m; (OS Sheet 33; 791011); *peak of the mossy corrie*

Sgurr Coire Choinnichean is the shapely peak which dominates the landscape of Inverie Bay. It is a very prominent landmark as one approaches Inverie from Mallaig, visible from the moment the boat rounds the headland north of the harbour. It is also a very fine viewpoint, looking westwards over the sea to the Hebrides and eastwards to the mountains of Knoydart's hinterland. For anyone staying in Inverie the ascent of Sgurr Coire Choinnichean is a very pleasant short climb. In fact it is the only short climb from Inverie, although it can be extended by traversing its ridge eastwards.

An easy approach from Inverie may be made along the track to the Mam Uidhe. Once past the forest bear E up open slopes to about 450m where one comes to the extensive level floor of Coire Choinnichean. Beyond this flat corrie the upper half of the peak rises much more steeply. Bear SE past the top of the gorge of the Alt Slocha a'Mhogha to gain the lower part of the narrow SW ridge of Sgurr Chionnichean, and climb this very pleasant ridge to the summit. (3½km; 800m; 2h 10min).

The traverse may be continued by descending the equally narrow ENE ridge, crossing the peak of Stob an Uillt-fhearna and descending the ridge to the Mam Suidheig. From there drop down S to reach the track in Gleann an Dubh-Lochain and follow this for 6km back to Inverie. Map on page 151.

Sgurr Coire Choinnichean above Inverie House   *H.M. Brown*

Beinn na Caillich; 785m; (OS Sheet 33; 796067); *hill of the old woman*

Beinn na Caillich is a craggy hill which rises 4km north-west of Ladhar Bheinn and 7km north of Inverie. It is the most northerly of the Knoydart hills, and dominates the wild and totally uninhabited north-west corner of the peninsula.

The approach from Inverie is by way of the Mam Uidhe track and its north-east branch in Gleann na Guiserein. Ford the river, or if necessary go a short distance E to a bridge near the ruin of Folach, and then bear NW to climb the long slope to Meall Coire an t-Searraich (686m). Continue NE for 2km to the summit of Beinn na Caillich. (9km; 900m; 3h 30min). There are excellent sea-views to the W, SE towards Ladhar Bheinn and E to Loch Hourn.

Return by the same route, or continue E down Carn Dubh to the Mam Li and follow the path down the Allt Mam Li and the Abhainn Bheag to return to Gleann na Guiserein.

Map on page 151.

Looking across Loch Hourn from Corran to Beinn na Caillich
                    J. Cleare/Mountain Camera

Beinn na h-Eaglaise; 804m; (OS Sheet 33; 854120); *hill of the church*
Beinn nan Caorach; 773m; (OS Sheet 33; 871122); *hill of the rowan berries*

These two shapely hills are the eastern outliers of Beinn Sgritheall and add distinction to the finely sculpted skyline of the Glenelg peninsula. They are easily accessible from Arnisdale on the northern shore of Loch Hourn, and taken together make a fine short round, which may be extended to include Beinn Sgritheall to give a longer day.

The traverse of the two Corbetts is best done anti-clockwise, starting with Beinn nan Caorach, thus giving a fairly easy approach along paths and enabling a proper appreciation of the panorama over Loch Hourn and the Knoydart hills on the final steep descent from Beinn na h-Eaglaise. Cars are best parked at Arnisdale. At 400 metres beyond the village a track turns off up Glen Arnisdale, and this is followed for 1½km to a bridge. Go N past the cottage of Achadh a'Ghlinne and climb an excellent stalker's path which zig-zags up the E bank of the Allt Utha. At a height of 300m the fine cascade of Eas na Cuingid is passed. Leave the path a short distance further on, cross the burn and climb the rough but straightforward SSW ridge of Beinn nan Caorach which leads direct to the summit. (5km; 770m; 2h 30min).

Follow a line of old fenceposts NW across a broad col of short-cropped grass and onto the Druim nan Bo. This ridge dips SW to a lower col at 550m from where the NE shoulder of Beinn na h-Eaglaise rises impressively as a narrow ridge leading to the summit. This ridge might give good sport in winter, but sadly its crest is disfigured by a line of tall fenceposts. (7½km; 1040m; 3h 30min).

The linking ridge to Beinn Sgritheall drops very steeply WNW for 200m through outcrops to the Bealach Arnasdail. In wet, misty or snowy conditions it is potentially dangerous. From the bealach steep but straightforward slopes of scree and boulders lead up to Beinn Sgritheall's eastern summit.

The best descent from Beinn na h-Eaglaise to Arnisdale goes SSE over the shoulder of Beinn Bhuidhe which cradles a fine little lochan on its E side. Then descend steeply but without any major obstacles SSW to meet the track in Glen Arnisdale near its end at the public road.

Looking across Loch Hourn to Beinn Sgritheall (left) and Beinn na h-Eaglaise   J. Cleare/Mountain Camera

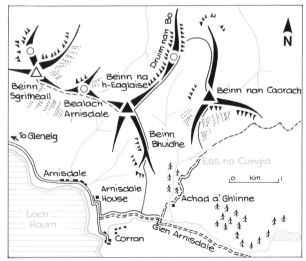

Sgurr Mhic Bharraich from Strath Croe at the head of Loch Duich　　　　　　　*D.J. Bennet*

Sgurr Mhic Bharraich; 781m; (OS Sheet 33; 917174); *peak of the son of Maurice*

Viewed from the northern shore of Loch Duich, the range of hills which culminates in The Saddle makes an intriguing prospect. A complex web of spurs and subsidiary tops rings the depths of Gleann Undalain and all but obscures sight of the crowning summit. Sgurr Mhic Bharraich looms large in this beckoning scene, guarding the entrance to the glen on its west side and forming the outpost of The Saddle's long northern ridge. It is, however, sufficiently detatched and buttressed by corries and crags to form a worthy objective in its own right, and offers a satisfying short day from Shiel Bridge.

The best approach is afforded by the excellent path which begins at Shiel Bridge campsite, where there is ample parking. The path climbs over a rock bar into the glen, then crosses a bridge over the Allt Undalain onto its W bank and continues round the SE flank of Sgurr Mhic Bharraich. After 3km it turns W and climbs out of the glen to Loch Coire nan Crogachan and the pass over to Glen More which provides a walking route between Glen Shiel and Glenelg. On the climb a left fork in the path should be ignored, and the steeper right-hand branch followed uphill between parallel streams to emerge at the lochan at a height of 450m.

Leave the path and cross the outlet of the lochan to climb the rough upper slopes of Sgurr Mhic Bharraich at their easiest point. Heather-clad slopes lead upwards to reach the mountain's E ridge close to the top. There are several knolls on the broad summit area, but the highest

one is unmistakably marked by a fine cairn. (5km; 770m; 2h 30min).

The long E shoulder of the hill gives a fast and easy return to Gleann Undalain, passing over a craggy eminence and then dropping directly down uniform slopes. The path in the glen is regained a short distance above the bridge.

Two other routes to Sgurr Mhic Bharraich are possible. From Moyle in Glen More on the W side of the hill a path leads to the Loch Coire nan Crogachan col, where the route just described is joined. An approach along the hummocky NW ridge from the highest point of the Bealach Ratagain road is also possible, but the roughness of this route and its many undulations outweigh the advantage of the 340m starting height.

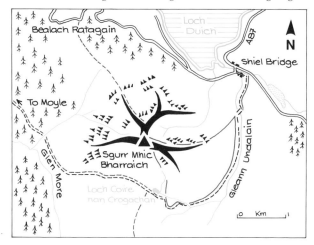

Looking east from Sgurr a'Bhac Chaolais along the South Glen Shiel ridge   H.M. Brown

Sgurr a'Bhac Chaolais; 885m; (OS Sheet 33; 958110); *peak of the hollow of the narrows*

Rough and knobbled in the fashion of the Knoydart hills, yet lacking prominence in any distant views, Sgurr a'Bhac Chaolais is hardly recognised other than an awkward and strenuous obstacle which must be

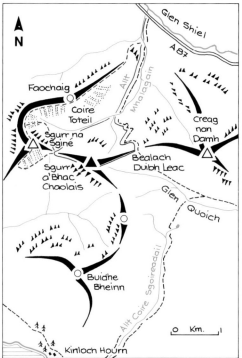

traversed by those wishing to link the Munros of the South Glen Shiel ridge to its east with The Saddle group on its west. Whilst its ascent is most frequently made as the connection in this magnificent ridge walk, the hill merits a more individual appreciation if only for its excellent views of the surrounding higher peaks.

The right of way from Glen Shiel to Glen Quoich over the Bealach Duibh Leac, which starts from the bridge over the Allt Mhalagain in Glen Shiel, provides quick access to the summit. The path initially follows the Allt Mhalagain, crossing to its W bank after a few hundred metres, then climbs steadily into Coire Toteil. Crossing the burn again, the path zig-zags up steep and rough slopes to the pass at 721m, rather indistinctly in places. From the pass a wall and then fenceposts are followed WSW along the ridge and over bluffs and dips to the summit of Sgurr a'Bhac Chaolais. (4½km; 860m; 2h 30min).

To complete the traverse of the hill a descent W is made to the connecting bealach with Sgurr na Sgine, outflanking a craggy steepening on the left. Then easy slopes are followed NE down Coire Toteil to rejoin the path of approach.

A very good circuit of Coire Toteil can be made by continuing the traverse over Sgurr na Sgine and its prominent outlier, Faochag. The direct ascent of Sgurr na Sgine is not advised, and one should either bear WSW below its steep face to reach the SW slopes which can be easily climbed, or head up into the highest part of Coire Toteil from where an easy gully leads to the NW peak of Sgurr na Sgine. The descent of the steep and narrow NE ridge of Faochag leads down to Glen Shiel at the day's starting point.

Beinn Loinne (W Peak), Druim nan Cnamh; 790m; (OS Sheets 33 and 34; 131077); *bony ridge*

While many may have admired the long rocky sprawl of Beinn Loinne on the south side of Loch Cluanie, only a few hillwalkers make the ascent, for it is a long way from any direction. One unconventional approach might be to canoe across Loch Cluanie and make the direct and steep ascent up Coire Beithe. Otherwise the most practicable approach is from the west, starting from Cluanie Inn up the old road from there to Tomdoun.

There is a locked gate across this road near Cluanie Lodge, but it is quite possible, as an alternative to walking, to cycle up the road to its highest point. Eastwards from there the going is very wet and boggy across gradually rising moorland. Higher up the ground becomes firmer, though still rough, and the walking easier up to the stark round trig point of Druim nan Cnamh, the highest point of the long Beinn Loinne ridge. (From Cluanie Inn: 9km; 570m; 3h).

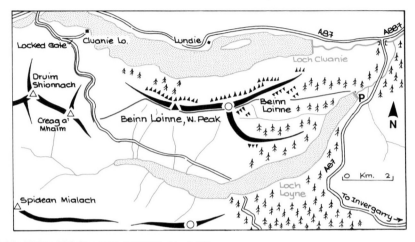

Meall Dubh; 788m; (OS Sheet 34; 245078); *black hill*

Meall Dubh stands in an isolated position, the highest point of an extensive area of high moorland between Loch Garry and Glen Moriston. However, its position makes it a good viewpoint for the mountains of Lochaber and the western Highlands.

The easiest ascent is from the A87 road, starting due west of the summit of the hill. At that point there is a car park near the Loch Loyne dam. From there head E up the very rough hillside on the S side of the Garbh Dhoire forest. The going is hard through deep heather, but higher up the Allt Bealach Odhair may be a useful feature to follow. The summit of Meall Dubh is marked by a small cairn with a bigger one not far away. (4½km; 560m; 2h).

A traverse of this extensive area of moorland can be made by continuing from Meall Dubh, first SE then ENE along the rocky crest marked by old fenceposts to the col between Meall Dubh and Mam a'Chroisg. From there descend ESE across easy terrain to reach the Allt Lundie, and go down this stream on its E bank past a series of waterfalls in a fine gorge and reach Loch Lundie. From there one can either follow a track NE down the Invervigar Burn, or S to Invergarry. The ascent of Meall Dubh by either of these routes is long, but enjoyable. (13km; 760m; 4h 20min).

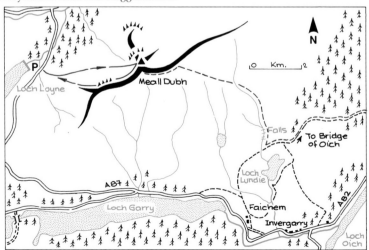

Looking down Strath Croe to the head of Loch Duich and Beinn Sgritheall   D.J. Bennet

Section 11

Glen Affric and Kintail

Looking west from Meall Fuar-mhonaidh to the Affric mountains   A. O'Brien

Meall Fuar-mhonaidh; 696m; (OS Sheets 26 and 34; 457223); *hill of the cold slopes*

Despite its relatively low height, Meall Fuar-mhonaidh (Mealfuarvonie) is a prominent feature of views up and down Loch Ness, for it is much higher than its neighbouring hills and rises directly above the loch on the north-west side of the Great Glen. It has the distinction of being the highest hill in the country made from rocks of the Old Red Sandstone system, although its summit rocks consist, not of sandstone proper, but of a very coarse conglomerate whose resistance to weathering has resulted in the hill's prominent outline. It is a long whale-backed ridge, flanked by cliffs on its north-west and south-east sides, and it is a favourite tourist ascent, notable for its views of Loch Ness and the Great Glen.

It is normally climbed from the NW, leaving the main A82 road at Lewiston, near Drumnadrochit, and driving up a minor road signposted to Bunloit. This road climbs very steeply, with awkward hairpin bends, to high moorland about 250m above Loch Ness. From there on the road is very narrow and confined between close fences, with an absence of places to park a car near Balbeg, so this is a problem.

At Balbeg the way to Meall Fuar-mhonaidh is marked first by a notice NO DOGS and NO PARKING, and further on by a notice TO THE HILL, which indicates a detour round farm buildings to gain an old track. From the end of this track open country can be reached and, bearing W at first, the long NE shoulder, flanked by crags on both sides, can be followed to the top. (4km; 500m; 1h 40min).

An altogether different route is from Alltsigh (Loch Ness Youth Hostel, on OS Sheet 34) on the A82 road 4km NE of Invermoriston. Opposite the hostel a forestry road leads steeply up the S side of the Allt Saigh for almost 2km to a height of 240m to cross the burn by a bridge. A few metres beyond the bridge a gate gives access to the open moor and so to the SW ridge of the hill. This route may be restricted due to timber operations, so enquiries should be made locally (6km; 650m; 2h 30min).

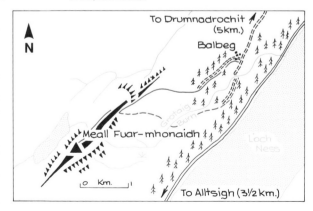

Looking north from Loch a'Choinich to Carn a'Choire Ghairbh and the Affric mountains   R. Wood

Carn a'Choire Ghairbh; 863m; (OS Sheets 25 and 34; 137189); *cairn of the rough corrie*
Aonach Shasuinn; 889m; (OS Sheets 25 and 34; 173180); *height of the saxon (sassenach)*

These two mountains lie to the south of Glen Affric, a valley well known for its beauty. It is one of Scotland's longest glens, and has one of the best preserved remains of the old Caledonian pine forest to set off the backdrop of mountain and loch. The colour changes in autumn make this the best time for a visit, but as this is also the stalking season, one has to be content with valley access. It is a grand place at any time.

To climb these two mountains from Glen Affric start from the Forestry Commission car park at the end of the public road 1½km E of Affric Lodge. Cross the bridge just W of the car park and follow the forestry road W through the Pollan Buidhe forest, where large sections of the native pinewood have been fenced off and the regeneration of young trees has been very successful. Just before reaching the Allt Garbh a white cottage is passed; it was once available as a bothy, but this is no longer the case. Follow a rather muddy footpath up the W bank of the Allt Garbh through lanky heather, and climb the steep slopes and crags of Na Cnapain, which is a superb viewpoint of the woodlands and lochs to E and W. Continue WSW to Carn Glas Iochdarach (771m), and slightly down along a broad ridge to a col at 707m, before climbing gradually to Carn a'Choire Ghairbh, where there are two tops about 200 metres apart, the

N one being the 863m point. (8½km; 690m; 3h).

Descend SW down a broad slope, keeping clear of the steep hillside to the W overlooking Gleann na Ciche, to reach the col called the Cadha Riabhach (664m). From the col climb SE up the broad ridge of Carn a'Choire Ghuirm to reach flatter ground near Loch a'Choinich. From the loch bear NE across a little plateau, crossing a bump (863m) and descending the narrowing ridge of An Elric to the Bealach an Amais (652m). Climb due E for 1km to the 875m W top of Aonach Shasuinn, and finally go ESE for ¾km to the summit. (15km; 1140m; 5h 20min).

To avoid the steep headwall of Coire Gorm, it is best to return to the W top and descend N then NE from there down the broad ridge of Ceann Aonach Shasuinn to reach the Allt Garbh near Loch an Sguid. Cross the burn and continue down its NW side to rejoin the ascent route near the tree line.

Aonach Shasuinn can also be climbed from Ceannacroc in Glen Moriston by a long, but easy and scenically attractive route along the private road up the River Doe. This road is very rough and would be hard going for mountain bicycles. From the end of the road in Coire Dho climb steeply N up to the broad ridge of Carn a'Choire Bhuidhe and continue NW to Aonach Shasuinn.

The west top of Aonach Shasuinn   R. Wood

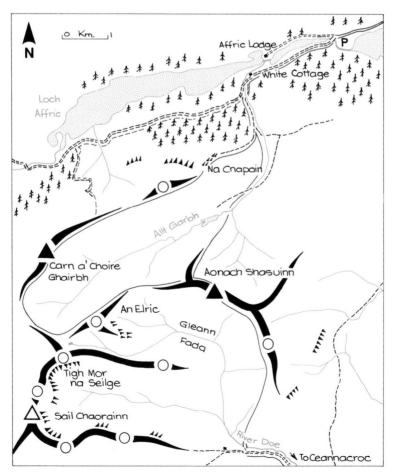

Am Bathach from Strath Cluanie   *H.M. Brown*

Am Bathach; 798m; (OS Sheet 33; 073144); *the byre*

Am Bathach is most often climbed during the ascent or descent of Ciste Dhubh, but it also gives an excellent half day's hillwalking on its own. Its undulating, narrow, grassy ridge is well-defined, and provides an airy highway from which, especially in winter, its Munro neighbours can be appreciated properly.

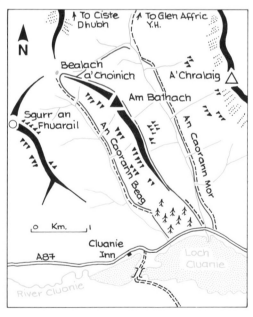

Start from the A87 road about 1½km E of Cluanie Inn. From a gate just to the W of the bridge over the Allt a'Chaorainn Mhoir an old and rather overgrown stalker's path leads for a few hundred metres up the SE ridge of the hill beside a small wood. Beyond it a way can be made easily up the steepening crest to the first top, 732m. Continue along the very narrow grassy ridge, to which the name Am Bathach refers, for about 1km to the summit at its NW end. (3km; 620m; 1h 50min).

To descend, continue down the ridge NW to the Bealach a'Choinich (567m). From there either go E down to the An Caorann Mor path, which is the main route from Strath Cluanie to Glen Affric youth hostel, or (to avoid a river crossing) go S from the bealach to the head of An Caorann Beag. Continue along a poorly-defined, but pleasant path down the E side of the Allt a'Chaorainn Bhig to return to the road.

Sgurr an Airgid; 841m; (OS Sheet 33; 940227); *peak of silver*

This hill rises very prominently and steeply at the head of Loch Duich, directly above the north end of the causeway which takes the A87 road across the head of the loch. Its ascent is very short, suitable for an afternoon's exercise, but the reward on a good day is a fine view of the higher peaks of Kintail in one direction, and the western lochs and Skye in the other.

Start from any convenient point on the minor road on the N side of Strath Croe. There is a stalker's path marked on the map, but its lower part is hard to find. Higher up its line upwards across the steep hillside is clear. Follow the path almost to the col E of Sgurr an Airgid, and then climb W up the rocky double crest to the summit. (3½km; 830m; 2h 10min).

Sgurr Gaorsaic from A'Ghlas-bheinn   *C. Peart*

Sgurr Gaorsaic; 839m; (OS Sheet 33; 036218); *peak of thrill (or horror)*

This hill is in a very remote situation at the watershed between the eastward flowing streams along Glen Affric and westward flowing waters which plunge down the Falls of Glomach to Glen Elchaig. It is surrounded by higher mountains, in particular its near neighbour, the mighty Sgurr nan Ceathreamhnan, and many hillwalkers approaching this mountain from the west are quite likely to traverse Sgurr Gaorsaic on their way to it.

There are three ways to Sgurr Gaorsaic, two of them very long. The shortest route is from Strath Croe at the head of Loch Duich. One can either start at the car park at the end of the public road near Dorusduain, or at Morvich on the opposite side of the strath. Both routes converge at the foot of Gleann Choinneachain and follow the fine path up that glen under the impressively steep northern spurs of Beinn

Fhada. The path leads to the Bealach an Sgairne, a splendid pass that gives access from the west coast to the head of Glen Affric. Descend from the pass along the path which goes round the S end of Loch a'Bhealaich, and once past the loch climb NE directly up the steep slopes of Sgurr Gaorsaic to the flat summit, with a lochan at its W edge. (7½km; 950m; 3h 20min. 1½km further from Morvich).

Of the two other possible routes, that from the E up Glen Affric and its upper part Gleann Gniomhaidh is a long walk unless one is staying at Alltbeithe youth hostel, which is only 5km from Sgurr Gaorsaic. The longest approach is up Glen Elchaig, and is only feasible if one cycles as far as Loch na Leitreach and then climbs up the superb gorge of the Allt a'Ghlomaich past the Falls of Glomach to reach the broad, flat glen N of Sgurr Gaorsaic.

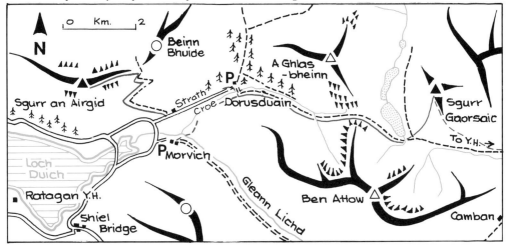

Meallan nan Uan and Sgurr a'Mhuilinn from Strathconon   H.M. Brown

SECTION 12

Glen Cannich to Glen Carron

Looking up Glen Elchaig from Carnach to Aonach Buidhe   *D.J. Bennet*

Aonach Buidhe; 899m; (OS Sheet 25; 058324); *yellow ridge*

Aonach Buidhe occupies an isolated position at the head of Glen Elchaig, in the centre of the great wilderness that extends from Glen Cannich to Glen Carron. Despite a lack of stature relative to the encircling Munros, the hill is finely shaped, with distinctive spurs on all sides, and it is separated from its neighbours by deep passes to the west and south-east. These passes carry the stalker's path from Glen Elchaig to Maol-bhuidhe, and the right of way to Pait Lodge on the shore of Loch Monar.

Unless the ascent is included in a camping or bothying expedition, only Glen Elchaig offers a feasible approach to Aonach Buidhe for the day walker. The private road up the glen is a right of way, but access to cars is barred by a locked gate at Killilan. As a result, a 13km walk up the glen is necessary just to reach the foot of the hill near Iron Lodge, and this of course must be reversed at the end of the day. The use of bicycles for the approach is therefore strongly recommended, and will shorten the duration of the expedition by some 3 hours. The cycle run up Glen Elchaig is very pleasant, and the return run down the glen even more so.

From the road end at Iron Lodge a good track continues up the N side of the Allt na Doire Ghairbh for 300 metres, and then splits into two paths which go through the hill's bounding passes, as described above. Follow the right-hand path for a very short distance until after it crosses An Crom-allt the foot of the S ridge of Aonach Buidhe is gained. After a steep start, this ridge gives an easy and undistinguished climb direct to the summit. (From Iron Lodge: 3½km; 770m; 2h 10min).

The best feature of the hill is its NE ridge, which narrows pleasingly below the subsidiary top of An Creachal Beag (870m). This ridge is the obvious route if one is climbing the hill from Maol-bhuidhe to its N, but it may also be reached from Iron Lodge by continuing across the pass at Loch Mhoicean. Although very circuitous, this route enables the hill to be traversed and its remote northern side to be explored.

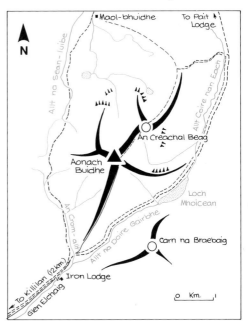

Ben Killilan and Sguman Coinntich from Loch Long   *D.J. Bennet*

Sguman Coinntich; 879m; (OS Sheet 25; 977304); *mossy peak*
Faochaig; 868m; (OS Sheet 25; 022317); *the whelk*

These two summits are the culminating points of the broad tract of hill country which bounds Glen Elchaig to the north, and forms the heart of the Killilan Forest. Sguman Coinntich makes a picturesque back-cloth on the drive up Loch Long from Dornie, and it is readily accessible from the public road near Killilan. By contrast, Faochaig lies in the remote interior 5km to the north-east of its neighbour, and hides its virtues (the chief of which is a finely scalloped eastern corrie) from all except the most dedicated of hillwalkers. The two tops are linked by a long undulating ridge, and can advantageously be combined in a grand day's tramp of some 22km from Killilan.

Cars are best parked just before the bridge over the River Ling at (937304). From Killilan, which is 1km further up the glen, a good path climbs on the N bank of the Allt a'Choire Mhoir, starting up the right-hand edge of a hillside plantation. At a height of 450m the angle eases and the stream valley broadens into the Coire Mor which divides Sguman Coinntich from its lower northern outlier, Ben Killilan. By crossing the stream there and striking up rough but uncompli-cated slopes to the SE, the summit ridge of Sguman Coinntich is gained and the top reached in a further 100m of climbing. (4½km; 870m; 2h 30min).

If time or energies do not permit the onward tra-verse to Faochaig, then in clear weather Ben Killilan should be traversed on the return journey in order to enjoy the superb westward vista to Skye. However, this traverse involves a steep scramble down through the crags guarding the Bealach Mhic Bheathain.

Alternatively, the southern flanks of Sguman Coinntich can be descended to reach a stalker's path in the Ghlas-choire which leads down to the right of way in Glen Elchaig.

The crossing from Sguman Coinntich to Faochaig is an enjoyable high-level walk of 6km, with 360m of ascent over many little knolls, mainly on short-cropped grass save for a rougher patch over the intermediate top of Sron na Gaoithe, which may be tricky in mist. There are fine exposures to the N over Coire Shlat, and excellent views to the SE towards Sgurr nan Ceathreamhnan throughout the walk to Faochaig. (10½km; 1250m; 4h 30min).

The summit of Faochaig stands on a boulder out-crop at the SW end of a broad plateau. Long easy slopes to its S lead into the catchment valley of the Allt Domhain, a favourite haunt of deer. As the valley deepens, a stalker's path can be picked up on the E side of the stream, and this leads steeply down to Car-nach in upper Glen Elchaig.

There remains an 11km hike along the right of way down the glen to Killilan, during which any soreness of the feet should be alleviated by the pleasant envi-rons of the glen and the many glimpses up into the clefts and gorges on its S side, of which the Glomach chasm is one.

Faochaig can also be ascended from Maol-bhuidhe bothy to its NE, following the path up the Allt na Sean-luibe almost to the pass at its head and then the stalker's path which climbs steeply W to a height of 750m on the hill's NE spur.

Sguman Coinntich from Faochaig   *J. Renny*

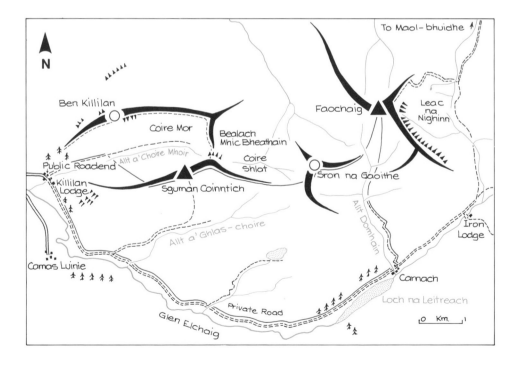

Beinn Tharsuinn from the north-east, with Bidein a'Choire Sheasgaich beyond   D.J. Bennet

Beinn Tharsuinn; 863m; (OS Sheet 25; 055433); *transverse hill*
Sgurr na Feartaig; 862m; (OS Sheet 25; 055454); *peak of the sea-pink (thrift)*

These two hills lie to the south-east of Achnashellach in Glen Carron, and suffer from the proximity of higher and more popular mountains round the head of Loch Monar and above Achnashellach. Beinn Tharsuinn has little interest itself, but as it lies on the most direct route to Bidein a' Choire Sheasgaich and Lurg Mhor, it is commonly traversed *en route* to those mountains. Sgurr na Feartaig, however, is an attractive hill, forming a long level ridge with steep corries on its NW side overlooking Glen Carron. It provides a grand circuit , with fine views of the mountains round Coire Lair and the Torridonian giants beyond.

Both hills are easily climbed from Craig in Glen Carron, 3½km E of Achnashellach station. There is limited roadside parking on the A890 road, and the gate at the railway level crossing is locked, so there is no car access up the private road along the Allt a' Chonais.

To reach Beinn Tharsuinn follow this road for 5km from Craig to a footbridge at (074466), and climb up a stalker's path SW to the Bealach Bhearnais. From the bealach go S for a short distance almost to the Bealach Crudhain, and then climb steeply SW towards Beinn Tharsuinn. Once above this steep section, continue along the broad grassy ridge to the summit. (10km; 810m; 3h 30min).

Sgurr na Feartaig can also be approached by the private road up the Allt a' Chonais as far as a footbridge over the river at (070482). From there a stalker's path con-

tinues right up the hill and along its summit ridge, passing a short distance W of the summit cairn. (7km; 810m; 2h 50min).

The two hills can easily be combined in a single traverse. After climbing Beinn Tharsuinn return to the Bealach Bhearnais and climb NW for 270m up a steep slope of grass and boulders to the summit of Sgurr na Feartaig.

Alternatively, an easier but less direct ascent can be

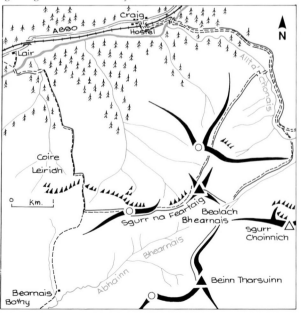

made by following an unmapped stalker's path from the bealach on a gradually rising traverse W to reach the ridge of Sgurr na Feartaig a few hundred metres WSW of the summit. (13½km; 1080m; 4h 50min). Descend NE to the Allt a' Chonais by the stalker's path mentioned in the preceding paragraph to complete the traverse.

To make an alternative descent from Sgurr na Feartaig, follow the path WSW from the summit along the ridge for almost 3km to the flat col to the W of the hill. Descend N by the path down Coire Leiridh to the River Carron which, if it cannot be waded, can be crossed by a wire bridge a short distance downstream.

Beinn Dronaig from the Bealach Alltan Ruairidh   *M. Moran*

Beinn Dronaig; 797m; (0S Sheet 25; 037382); *hill of the knoll or ragged hill*

Lonely Beinn Dronaig sits squat and neglected in the outback of the Attadale Forest to the east of Loch Carron, remote of access and lacking any distinctive features. From either Attadale by Loch Carron or Achintee in Strathcarron, its ascent necessitates a round trip of at least 25km, and involves a long walk just to reach Bendronaig Lodge at its foot. This lodge lies in the valley of the Black Water which flows S into Glen Ling and thence to Loch Long.

The route from Attadale to Bendronaig Lodge follows an estate Landrover track and may be made easier by the use of an all-terrain bicycle. The Achintee approach takes a fine stalker's path over loch-strewn moorland, crossing the Bealach Alltan Ruairidh to join the Attadale track W of the lodge, which lies directly beneath the hill at a height of 270m.

Beinn Dronaig is climbed by the steep slopes to the SE of the lodge to reach the undulating summit ridge, which is followed ENE to the top. (From Attadale: 14km; 880m; 4h 40min).

The crowning trig point is well sited, for it affords a magnificent survey of the encircling wilderness, particularly SE across the Killilan Forest to the Cannich hills. Save for a glimpse of Lochcarron, no public road or settlement disturbs the solitude.

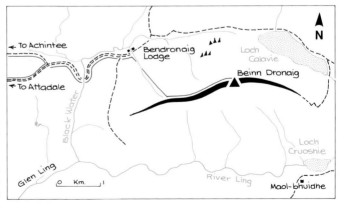

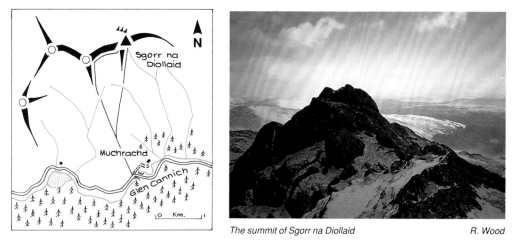

The summit of Sgorr na Diollaid   R. Wood

Sgorr na Diollaid; 818m; (OS Sheet 25; 282362); *peak of the saddle*

This fine little rocky peak lies between the lower reaches of Glen Cannich and Strathfarrar. It provides an excellent short day with particularly good views of the Strathfarrar, Mullardoch and Glen Affric hills, worth saving for a fine day.

The hill is inclined to be wet, rough and heathery, but on the higher southern slopes the terrain is more slabby. Two prominent rocky knolls mark the summit, from which the northern slopes drop steeply into Strathfarrar.

The best approach to Sgorr na Diollaid is from the south. Park at the bridge in Glen Cannich where the road crosses to the N side of the river near Muchrachd. Ascend by a line slightly E of N, seeking the easiest going up the quite steep hillside. Bearing to the right of a prominent knoll, easier ground is soon reached and slabs provide pleasant walking. Finally, the rocky comb of the summit gives interesting scrambling over a series of knolls. (3km; 660m; 1h 50min).

A lower 775m top lying 1km SW of Sgorr na Diollaid may be traversed before descending SSE over rough ground to return to Muchrachd.

Beinn a' Bha'ach Ard; 862m; (OS Sheet 26; 361435); *hill of the high byre*

This triple-topped hill stands on the north side of Glen Strathfarrar near its junction with Strath Glass at Struy. It is the highest point of a large area of rolling heathery upland between Glen Orrin and Strathfarrar, and is a very prominent hill, well seen from points to the east such as the Kessock Bridge over the mouth of the Beauly Firth. Being so isolated, it commands splendid views all round.

Beinn a' Bha'ach Ard is best approached from Glen Strathfarrar, starting from Inchmore where there is a locked gate across the road. Walk up the glen for 2km to the power station at Culligran, and from there follow a track WSW then W for 2km through pleasant birch woods and alongside the Neaty Burn until a small dam is reached. Continue up the E side of this burn following vehicle tracks for 2km to the Allt Doire Bhuig, a small stream which flows down from the NE. Ascend the NW side of this stream directly to the summit of Beinn a' Bha'ach Ard. (7½km; 810m; 3h 10min).

Continue N along the broad ridge over Pt 834m, then NE to the flat summit of Sgurr a' Phollain. Descend steeply SE to reach the end of a stalker's path which is followed down to a col and up a slight rise for ½km

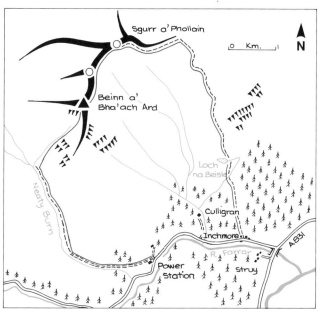

to Carn na Gabhalach. From there descend SSE over rough moorland, the path shown on the 1:50000 map being almost non-existent for much of the way, and reach Loch na Beiste. A good path, becoming a track in due course, leads downhill through attractive birch woods to Inchmore.

An Sidhean; 814m; (OS Sheet 25; 171454); *the fairy hill*

An Sidhean is a rounded heathy hill with few marked features, and it has a feeling of remoteness, standing as it does in the tract of wilderness north of Loch Monar and at the very head of Strathconon. Above 650m the hill has an extensive undulating plateau which provides good summer grazing for deer and pleasant going for hillwalkers.

There is a choice of approaches to this hill, from the north or the south, but the southern approach, starting from the Loch Monar Dam, is recommended as being the more scenic and following better paths. The road up Glen Strathfarrar above Inchmore near its foot is private, but access by car is permitted during the summer except on Tuesdays and Sunday mornings before 1.30p.m. Application to drive past the locked gate should be made at the cottage beside the gate. (For access during the winter months it is advisable to telephone 046 376 260 to make enquiries).

It is possible to drive as far as the Loch Monar dam and park near there. Continue on foot along the road for 1km to Monar Lodge, and thereafter follow the well-maintained stalker's path crossing several attractive deep-cut ravines along the N side of Loch Monar. After 4km take the well-graded path up the hillside W of the Allt na Cois. Leave it at about 500m and continue N up the shoulder of Mullach a' Gharbh-leathaid. This broad ridge is steep at first, but opens out onto a wide plateau and the prominent summit cairn is reached 2½km after leaving the path. (7½km; 600m; 2h 40min).

To vary the return route, descend 2km SE to the col (c590m) at the head of the Allt na Cois and contour E round the N side of Meall Dubh na Caoidhe into the steep-sided glen of the Allt a' Choire Dhomhain. Follow the stalker's path down this glen to Loch Monar and so back to Monar Lodge and the dam.

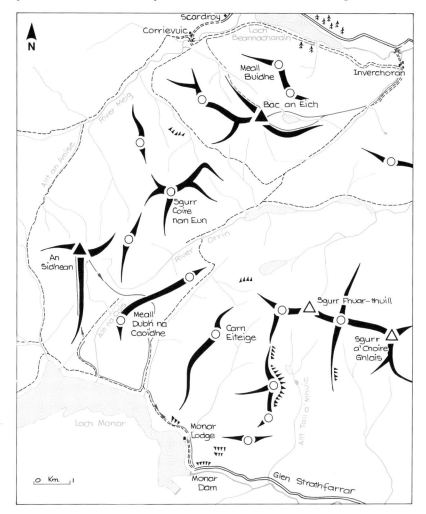

Bac an Eich from the north ridge of Maoile Lunndaidh   H.M. Brown

Bac an Eich; 849m; (OS Sheet 25;222489); *bank of the horse*

This is a bold hill with steep slopes to the north-east, and it is very prominent in views up Strathconon from Milltown. It rises above the deer farm at Inverchoran, and is in the heart of stalking country, with stalker's paths right round it.

The shortest route to Bac an Eich starts at Inverchoran. Follow the Landrover track which climbs quite steeply S from the farm and goes SW up Gleann Chorainn for 2km. Then take a path going down to the burn, which is crossed most easily just beyond the Scots pines on the NW bank. (In wet weather it may be preferable to follow the NW side of the burn from Inverchoran to avoid a possibly difficult river crossing).

Make a rising traverse WSW to cross the stream which flows from Loch Toll Lochain high up above its lower rocky ravine. Continue up the shoulder which forms the S wall of Coire an Lochain, climbing steeply between rocks to reach the more level ridge above the corrie. Finally go along this ridge over peat hags, bearing WNW up the final gentle slope to the summit. (5km; 700m; 2h 20min).

To make a circular walk one can descend very steeply duc N to reach the head of the burn flowing SE into Loch Toll Lochain, and go down it and along the N shore of the loch to eventually regain the route of ascent. Alternatively, descend the NW ridge of Bac an Eich quite steeply to Corriefeol and follow the path along the river and very pleasantly round the S side of Loch Beannacharain, rising above the loch and going through the forest back to Inverchoran.

Map on page 171.

Meallan nan Uan; 840m; (OS Sheet 25; 264545); *little hill of the lambs*
Sgurr a'Mhuilinn; 879m; (OS Sheet 25; 265558); *peak of the mill*

This small group of attractive hills lies due west of Milltown in Strathconon. They look particularly interesting when viewed from the Black Isle or across Strath Bran.

There are six well-defined summits in the group. Sgurr a'Mhuilinn and Meallan nan Uan lie in the centre, 2km apart and separated by a col at 700m with the small Loch Coire a'Mhuilinn nestling in a stony corrie at 600m between them. About 2½km to the northwest of Sgurr a'Mhuilinn, and very prominent in views from Strath Bran, lie the attractive twin tops of Sgurr a'Ghlas Leathaid (844m) and Sgurr a'Choire Rainich (847m) (not named on the 1:50,000 map). Creag Ruadh (740m) is the termination of the fine undulating south-east ridge of Meallan nan Uan. The sixth top, Creag Ghlas (685m) overlooks Gleann Meanich, but being a rather low outlier separated from the other tops by some very rough ground, it is seldom climbed. Gleann Meinich to its south is a fine example of a U-shaped valley.

A clockwise circuit of the tops is suggested. Park at Strathanmore and ascend by the S bank of the Allt an t-Srathain Mhoir, steeply at first up grass and bracken covered slopes, then turning SW to the prominent summit of Creag Ruadh. From there a very pleasant walk leads NW for 1½km along a narrow ridge with aerial views down into Gleann Meinich, over an intermediate knoll to the final steeper 120m climb to Meallan nan Uan. (3½km; 800m; 2h 10min).

Descend NW along a broad ridge for 1km over an-

Meallan nan Uan from Creag Ruadh   *R. Wood*

other knoll to reach the col at 700m which is at the centre of the group. The summit of Sgurr a'Mhuilinn is only 1km NE, but the addition of the two western summits is recommended first. Contour across the slopes of Sgurr a'Mhuilinn NW to another col, also at 700m, at (249565) and from it ascend in turn the cones of Sgurr a'Ghlas Leathaid and Sgurr a'Choire Rainich. Return ESE for 2km to Sgurr a'Mhuilinn along a broad ridge of pleasant springy grass. (9½km; 1230m; 4h 10min).

To return to Strathanmore follow the ridge which drops steeply ESE from the summit of Sgurr a'Mhuilinn. Lower down, where the ridge merges into more level peaty slopes, bear SE and cross the Allt an t-Srathain Mhoir to make the final descent to the road in the glen down its S side.

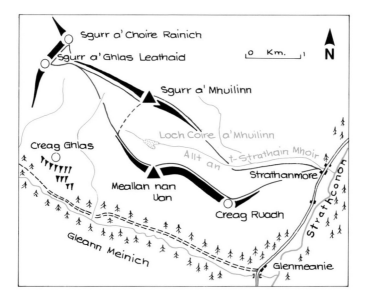

Sgurr a'Chaorachain from the head of Loch Kishorn   D.J. Bennet

SECTION 13

Applecross, Coulin and Torridon

Sgurr a'Chaorachain; 792m;
(OS Sheet 24; 797417); *peak of the little field of berries*

Sgurr a' Chaorachain may not be the highest of the Applecross hills, but it certainly appears the most impressive when seen across Loch Kishorn from Achintraid. From that viewpoint one looks directly into Coire nan Arr *(the giants' corrie)*, and its great cliffs and buttresses are a spectacular example of Torridonian mountain architecture, terraces and walls of sandstone rising almost vertically from the corrie floor.

The crest of Sgurr a'Chaorachain forms a horse-shoe ridge facing east above this corrie, the summit at its south-east end. Near the middle of the horse-shoe is the lower top (776m), which has a radio mast on its summit and a rough track leading to it from the nearest point on the Bealach na Ba road 1km to the west.

Three routes to the summit are possible. The easiest is from the Bealach na Ba road, starting just N of the highest hairpin bend near a little lochan at the roadside. Bear E on a rising traverse across the bouldery hillside to reach the summit ridge near its lowest point at a grassy col. Continue E over (or round) a typically Torridonian tower of terraced sandstone to reach easy grassy slopes leading to the summit. (2km; 200m; 1h). However, this route is unworthy of such a fine little mountain, and better ones are available for those prepared for some easy scrambling.

A very fine, but longer, route which will reveal the grandeur of Coire nan Arr starts from the bridge which takes the Applecross road over the Russel Burn (814413). Follow the rough path up the E side of the burn and along the shore of Loch Coire nan Arr to its head. Climb due W, quite steeply at first below the great tower of A'Chioch, and continue up the stream towards the head of the little corrie enclosed by Sgurr a'Chaorachain's horse-shoe. There is another tiny lochan high up in the heart of this corrie, whose headwall is a vertical sandstone cliff. To the left (S) of this cliff a steep slope of grass and boulders leads to the grassy col on the summit ridge, and the previous

A'Chioch of Sgurr a'Chaorachain   D.J. Bennet

route is joined there, less than 1km from the summit. (4½km; 690m; 2h 10min).

To return to the starting point by the most direct route, descend ESE along the broad crest of the ridge, which becomes steeper and is broken by small cliffs and terraces. Provided one stays on the crest of the ridge on a bearing SE as it steepens, there are no serious obstacles. Scramble down a series of short easy walls with grassy ledges between them until the angle eases and a walk E across the rough lower slopes leads to the road near the Russel Burn.

Map on page 176

The eastern corries of Beinn Bhan   *D.J. Broadhead*

Beinn Bhan; 896m; (OS Sheet 24;804450); *white hill*

The highest and most imposing mountain in Applecross is Beinn Bhan, a great ridge 8km long whose eastern face forms a grand series of five corries, typically Torridonian in their architecture of terraced cliffs and dark gullies.

The best view of the mountain and its corries is from the A896 road a few kilometres north of Loch Kishorn on the way to Shieldaig. The western side of the mountain is less steep, a long slope of grass, scree and low terraced cliffs. The summit is near the south end of the long narrow plateau formed between these east and west facing slopes.

The most convenient point of approach to Beinn Bhan is the bridge over the River Kishorn (834423) just west of the A896 road at Tornapress. From there the slopes dropping from the south end of the mountain look dull and featureless, and the ascent of these slopes is similar in character, although it gives the shortest route to the summit.

The most interesting route, and one that everyone seeking to discover the true character of Beinn Bhan should follow, is to visit Coire na Poite, the grandest of the five corries, and make the ascent to the summit from there. Take the path from the River Kishorn bridge N for 2½km to its crossing of the streams flowing from Coire na Poite and then climb up to Lochan Coire na Poite, set in a

superb position at the mouth of the corrie between the high spurs of A'Chioch and A'Poite.

For those with a good head for heights and some scrambling ability, the best route of ascent is up the ridge over A'Chioch. Start ½km S of Lochan Coire na Poite and scramble easily up the ridge to A'Chioch. From there the crest becomes narrower and drops slightly to cross an intermediate minor top before reaching the foot of the final steep climb to the plateau. This is quite exposed, up a few short rock steps, but there are traces of a path and the plateau is reached ½km SE of the summit. (6½km; 950m; 3h 20min).

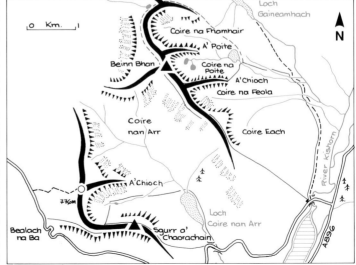

Looking east from the A'Chioch ridge to Beinn Damh and the Coulin peaks   *D.J. Bennet*

If the A'Chioch ridge seems too steep and narrow, the alternative ascent from Lochan Coire na Poite goes NW below A'Poite and Coire na Fhamhair and up the spur forming the N side of this corrie. The climb involves only the very mildest of scrambling and leads to the plateau near tiny Loch na Beinne Baine, from where a walk S along the edge of the corries leads to the summit. (7½km; 900m; 3h 10min).

The descent goes SE down the narrowing plateau, past Coire na Feola and Coire Each and on down the wide slopes above the tidal flats at the head of Loch Kishorn to reach the River Kishorn bridge.

Coire na Feola and the summit of Beinn Bhan from the south   *J. Cleare/Mountain Camera*

An Ruadh-stac; 892m; (OS Sheet 25; 922481); *the red conical hill*

The quartzite cone of An Ruadh-stac boldly crowns the tangled moorland to the north of Strathcarron. With its northern precipice in profile, the mountain is also well seen from Loch Coultrie on the Kishorn to Shieldaig road to the west. Although the summit lies in the midst of some of the roughest country imaginable and is 4km distant from the nearest road, the ascent is greatly facilitated by a stalker's path leading up to the Bealach a'Choire Ghairbh at a height of 580m on its NE side. Using this approach, the ascent of An Ruadh-stac can be conveniently combined with that of Maol Chean-dearg, 2km to the north.

The starting point is at Coulags bridge (958451) on the A890 road 7km NW of Lochcarron village. There is ample parking space in a disused gravel pit on the S side of the road. The right of way to Annat starts across the road and skirts left round a new shooting lodge to follow the E side of the Fionn-abhainn, climbing gradually towards Coire Fionnaraich. After 2½km the stream is crossed by a bridge, and shortly after one passes Coire Fionnarach bothy and Clach nan Con-fionn *(the stone of Fingal's dogs)*, to which the legendary Fingal is said to have tied his hunting dogs. In another ½km the path divides; taking the left fork, the boggy floor of the corrie is soon left and the path climbs under the craggy nose of Meall nam Ceapairean to the triple-sided bealach.

An Ruadh-stac from Maol Chean-dearg   D.J. Bennet

At that point the great north face of An Ruadh-stac comes into view, a magnificent sight with its cliffs harbouring four lochans, each one at a different level. Leave the bealach and go S,then SW along a knobbled rocky ridge above two of these lochans to gain the steep final ramparts of the peak. These give a rough 340m climb with some bits of scrambling to the summit. There are two eminences on the top, the southerly one being the higher. (7½km; 900m; 3h 10min).

An interestinng return to Strathcarron can be made by descending due S over the moors, although clear weather is recommended to appreciate the beauty as well as to navigate over this bewildering trackless terrain. Quartzite ridges and outcrops hide a series of jewel-like lochans, which are revealed in a glorious succession as far as the final eminence of Torr na h-Iolaire, from which easy slopes lead down to the Strathcarron road.

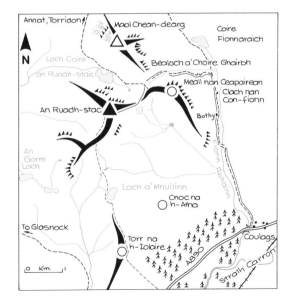

Fuar Tholl and Sgorr Ruadh from Glen Carron   D.J. Bennet

Fuar Tholl; 907m; (OS Sheet 25; 975489); *cold hole*

Rising at the head of Strathcarron is Fuar Tholl, its triple-topped profile as seen from Loch Carron giving rise to the local name 'Wellington's Nose', a reference to the tip of the Mainreachan Buttress which can just be seen over the skyline of the mountain. The most interesting approach to Fuar Tholl is not from Coulags on the Strathcarron side, but from Achnashellach, several kilometres further up Glen Carron where its great sweeps of red Torridonian sandstone tower over the tiny railway station.

Parking of cars is possible at the side of the A890 road near the access track to the station. Take this track to the station and cross the railway directly to enter the forest, where 100 metres further there is a junction in the forest road. Turn left and follow a road for 600 metres until a small path leads down left just beyond a small stream (cairn). In 50 metres this path joins the original stalker's path up Coire Lair which here goes close alongside the River Lair. The path climbs steadily out of the forest and through magnificent scenery, the river cascading down a deep and narrow gorge on the left with pine trees clinging to its inaccessible ledges.

At an elevation of 370m, with Coire Lair opening out ahead, the gradient eases and the path divides. Take the left (W) fork and cross the River Lair. In spate this can be difficult, and if in doubt a lengthy detour round Loch Coire Lair is necessary to rejoin the path higher up.

Continue heading W along the path to a height of 630m, then bear off S into Coire Mainnrichean and climb towards the foot of the stupendous Mainreachan Buttress. Whatever one's experience, it will be agreed that this is as impressive a mountain setting as can be found anywhere in Scotland. Keeping the buttress on one's right, climb steeply up grass,

then stones and scree to a col on the summit ridge, the crowning trig point and shelter being 50m higher and 200 metres to the NE. (6km; 870m; 2h 50min).

The descent may be varied by going W along the ridge over the mountain's other two tops, the first one being on the giddy brink of the Mainreachan Buttress and the second one giving a dramatic view of its sheer 250m cliff in profile. From there a steep descent NW down a rocky ridge leads to flatter ground among several small lochans where the path leading to Coire Lair is joined and followed E down the corrie to the River Lair and Achnashellach.

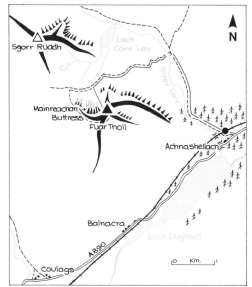

The summit of Beinn Damh from the north-west   A. O'Brien

Beinn Damh; 902m; (OS Sheets 24 and 25; 893502); *hill of the stag*

Beinn Damh is the most prominent of the mountains situated immediately on the south side of Loch Torridon. It stands in splendid isolation, rising steeply from the southern shore of the loch to the craggy top of Sgurr na Bana Mhoraire (687m), then sweeping gracefully south-eastwards over two subsidiary summits to the highest peak, Spidean Coir'an Laoigh, which is dramatically buttressed on its east side.

The classic route of approach starts near the Loch Torridon Hotel on the A896 road, about 100 metres to the west of the bridge over the Allt Coire Roill. At that point follow a well made stalker's path uphill through the forest of rhododendron, native pines and some more recent fir plantings, with the Allt Coire Roill roaring down on the left in its gorge. At the head of this gorge the river makes a spectacular 30m plunge over a sandstone cliff which may be glimpsed from the path.

Just beyond the waterfall, where the forest thins, the path divides. Take the right fork and climb SW into the corrie of Toll Ban. The path becomes less distinct as it mounts the steep upper slopes of the corrie to gain the broad col which separates Sgurr na Bana Mhoraire from the main mass of Beinn Damh. At this point a detour NW to this outlier is recommended as giving superb views of Loch Torridon, but this might be better done during the descent.

From the col easy slopes lead up SE to the first of the subsidiary tops, which may be bypassed on its W side. Traverse quartzite boulders across a slight dip to the next top, from which a narrow ridge leads up to the main summit. (6km; 900m; 2h 50min). The crowning cairn is perched on the brink of the very steep east-facing corrie, and commands a fine panorama SE to the Achnashellach hills, and N to the

Torridonian giants.

The NE ridge of Beinn Damh called Stuc Toll nam Biast is an alternative route of ascent which gives a good scramble from the Drochaid Coire Roill. The left fork of the normal approach path is taken and followed for a further 2½km to this pass, giving grand views of the gullied NE cliffs of the mountain. From the pass climb a rocky ridge SW then more steeply W up a buttress to reach the short NE ridge of Beinn Damh. Any difficulties on the buttress can be avoided on the left.

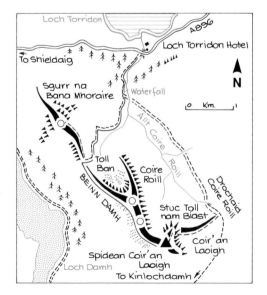

Beinn Dearg from the south, Baosbheinn to the left   H.M. Brown

Beinn Dearg; 914m; (OS Sheets 19,24 and 25; 895608); *red hill*

This hill is left by many for their last Torridonian peak, as its surrounding kin are better known and more accessible; but its very centrality makes it ideal to climb first for the excellent and unusual views it gives of its prominent neighbours. Even without its fine surroundings, Beinn Dearg is a gem of a hill, and if the narrowest of the towers along its crest are taken direct, a steady hand and a good head for heights are required. There are, however, no difficulties that cannot be avoided.

The most popular start at is the Coire Mhic Nobuil car park (869576). Follow the path up the corrie and shortly after crossing the Abhainn Coire Mhic Nobuil take the left branch that goes close under the imposing Horns of Alligin towards the Bealach a' Chomhla. Go almost as far as the wide,flat bealach and then climb the W spur of Stuc Loch na Cabhaig (888m). The ascent is steep and craggy and needs some route-finding ability. An airy ridge with some easy scrambling on the narrowing rocky crest leads to the flat top of Beinn Dearg. (7km; 960m; 3h 10min).

Continue the traverse SE at first down an easy ridge. In 200 metres the main ridge turns E and a short steep descent leads to a col. Beyond it the ridge rises again for a short distance and becomes narrow and rocky, giving a pleasant easy scramble along the crest which is quite exposed on its N side above Loch a'Choire Mhoir. Descend two or three short rock steps to reach the broad and easy continuation of the ridge eastwards. (The scramble along the crest can be avoided by traversing ledges on the S side of the ridge).

The traverse along the E ridge to its end at Carn na Feola (761m) is very easy.The descent from there is

best made by going S, aiming to reach the path beside the Abhainn Coire Mhic Nobuil about ½km W of Loch Grobaig. The S side of the E ridge of Beinn Dearg is steep and rocky for much of its length, with typically Torridonian terraced cliffs, and care is needed descending it. If one does not go to Carn na Feola, but wishes to descend further W, a possible route is beside a little stream which flows down the steep hillside at (906604).

The south side of Beinn Dearg is in National Trust for Scotland territory, and there is no restriction on climbing the mountain by the route described above during the stalking season.

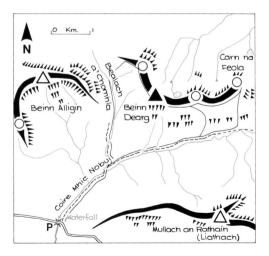

Ruadh-stac Beag from the north-east   J. Renny

Ruadh-stac Beag; 896m; (OS Sheet19; 973614); *small red conical hill.*
Meall a' Ghiubhais; 886m; (OS Sheet 19; 976634); *hill of the fir tree.*

The drive west into Glen Docherty is always a moment to be savoured. Loch Maree, the surrounding mountains and the Outer Isles all conspire to hit the eye at the same breath-catching moment. The descent to Kinlochewe slowly unfolds more of the majestic Torridonian peaks, and amongst the first to reveal themselves are the two that we seek here.

The most satisfying way to climb these hills is to combine them in a single fine tour. The Pony Track which starts near the Aultroy Visitor Centre of the

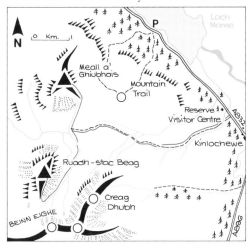

Beinn Eighe National Nature Reserve, 1km NW of Kinlochewe, gives access to both hills. The ascent of this path slowly reveals more of the inner Torridonian grandeur, with Creag Dubh, the NE peak of Beinn Eighe, dominating the view southwards.

At the highest point of the path strike NW to the small summit plateau of Meall a' Ghiubhais. There are two tops, the higher one being at the SW end of the plateau. (5½km; 850m; 2h 40min). In descent take an ESE line to avoid the unstable SE boulder field.

Once the Pony Track is regained, the next objective is to drop down SW to the Allt Toll a' Ghiubhais and then follow this stream up between Ruadh-stac Beag and the main ridge of Beinn Eighe. Ruadh-stac Beag is well defended by cliffs and scree, and the only easy ascent is from the south. The unstable flanking scree are best avoided by following the burn upwards until it is possible to bear W to gain the SSW spur of the hill above a lochan nestling in the col. From there the way is clear to the top, although the large boulder scree requires care. (10km; 1300m; 4h 40min). Return by the outward route and the Pony Track (18km; 7h).

Meall a' Ghiubhais and Ruadh-stac Beag are in the Beinn Eighe National Nature Reserve, and access is restricted during the stalking season. However, the estate has indicated that access via the Pony Track is usually acceptable all year. Access to Meall a' Ghiubhais by the Mountain Trail (shown on the 1:50,000 map) is at present discouraged due to erosion of the path.

Sgurr Dubh from the ridge to Sgorr nan Lochan Uaine   *J. Renny*

Sgorr nan Lochan Uaine; 873m; (OS Sheet 25; 969532); *peak of the little green loch*
Sgurr Dubh; 782m; (OS Sheet 25; 979558); *black peak*

These two hills occupy a large part of the Coulin Forest, the wild and open country lying between lochs Clair and Coulin to the north-east and the Coire Lair peaks to the south. They are well seen, but rarely identified by travellers on the Achnasheen to Kinlochewe road, who naturally look for the more famous Torridonian peaks on the western skyline. However, whilst they lack the height and grandeur of their neighbours on the opposite side of Glen Torridon, their ascent is recommended as giving an appreciation of Torridonian scenery unequalled anywhere else in the district.

The round trip taking in both summits may conveniently be started from the car park near the foot of Coire Dubh on the A896 road in Glen Torridon. A path leaves the road 100 metres E of the car park, and goes S past Lochan an Iasgair and the Ling Hut. The path continues SW close to the Allt Frianach, passing a fine waterfall and entering Coire a'Cheud-chnoic *(corrie of a hundred hillocks)*. This remarkable valley is filled with innumerable moraine mounds of perfectly regular proportions.

The path steers a course through this maze of hillocks, and is followed for about 2km until Sgorr an Lochan Uaine is passed and one is below the col on its SW side. Continue SE up heathery slopes towards this col in which the Lochan Uaine is cradled, and is revealed with sudden splendour, a perfect oval 400 metres across and girt by cliffs. A second and larger lochan lies a short distance SE. From this delectable spot a steep scramble of 230m to the NE leads to the conical summit of Sgorr an Lochan Uaine. (6½km; 800m; 2h 50min).

A broad and contorted ridge 2½km long and dropping as low as 510m links this peak to Sgurr Dubh. Miniature lochans abound, and the views are magnif-

icent. In particular, the terraced flanks of Liathach loom massively across Glen Torridon to the NW. Although this is a superb walk on a fine day, it would be a navigational nightmare in mist.

From the quartzite summit boulderfields of Sgurr Dubh a rough descent can be made to the WNW down to the Ling Hut, moving left initially to outflank a sandstone cliff, then weaving through quartzite outcrops to easier lower slopes.

An easier but much longer descent can be made by returning SW along the ridge for 800 metres and then dropping SE to reach a stalker's path in Coire an Lethuillt which leads down to Coulin Lodge. From there a path leads along the beautiful W shore of Loch Clair and the A896 road is reached 3km E of the Coire Dubh car park.

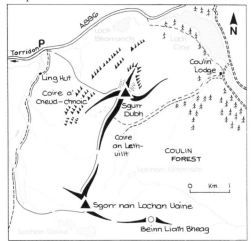

Baosbheinn (left) and Beinn an Eoin from the south-east   *I. Brown*

Baosbheinn; 875m; (OS Sheet 19; 871654); *wizard's hill.*
Beinn an Eoin; 855m; (OS Sheet 19; 905646); *hill of the bird.*

The two ridges on opposite sides of Loch na h-Oidhche radiate like spokes north-west from the central Torridon group. They are wild and lonely hills set amongst grand scenery, where paths are few and visitors rare. They present no scrambling difficulties, but nevertheless have an air of seriousness due to their length and remoteness when compared with the more frequented Torridon peaks. The route described below traverses both mountains in a long circuit from the A832 road to their north.

Start at a shed (known locally as the Red Barn) at (857721) on the A832 road and cross the footbridge over the outflow of Am Feur-loch. Follow the track SE for 5km to the crossing of the Abhainn Loch na h-Oidhche (886677). Once across this stream bear SE up the NW spur of Beinn an Eoin, and follow the ridge over three minor tops to its final steepening and a very airy traverse to the high point. (9km; 820m; 3h 30min).

Descend the S ridge to Gorm Loch na Beinne and cross the flat ground W to reach the SE end of the fine Baosbheinn ridge. Two minor tops of 707m and 806m are passed on the way to the steep final ascent of the main top, Sgorr Dubh. (15km; 1480m; 5h 50min).

Most of the climbing is now over, although you are only half way along the long ridge of Baosbheinn. It is possible to descend by the NE ridge to An Reidh-choire and regain the track near the N end of Loch na h-Oidhche (provided the straem flowing out of the loch is not in spate), but this is to miss much of the interest of this mountain.

To complete the traverse, follow the ridge over three minor tops to its end at Creag an Fhithich. The very steep NW face below this point dominates Gairloch, and was caused by a massive landslide in post-glacial times. Descend the NE flank, easier the further right you go, to reach more level moorland and 2km further down the Abhainn a' Gharbh Choire. As an alternative to crossing this stream to regain the track on its N side, continue down the left bank to its outfall into Loch Bad an Sgalaig, where there is a foot-bridge.

The E shores of this loch hold oddly shaped secrets that bring a final and unexpected reward at the end of a memorable day.

Baosbheinn from Beinn an Eoin   J. Renny

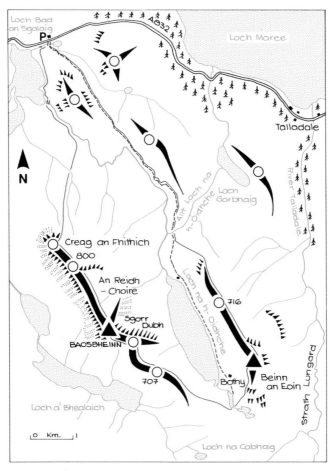

Looking north from Slioch to the Letterewe mountains   *D.J. Bennet*

SECTION 14

Loch Maree to Loch Broom

Looking across Loch Maree to Beinn Airigh Charr   *J. Renny*

Five of the hills described in this and the following pages are in the Letterewe and Fisherfield forests to the north of Loch Maree. This is one of the finest wilderness areas in the Highlands, combining some magnificent mountains in a very remote and inaccessible setting. Distances from the perimeter into the heart of this area are long, and accommodation within it is very limited.

Only the bothy at Shenavall in Strath na Sealga is habitable, the barn at Carnmore now being in a very dilapidated condition and giving shelter of the most spartan kind.

Access to the three southerly Corbetts is best made from Poolewe. With permission it may be possible to drive for 3km along the private road to Inveran, and start walking there. If all-terrain bicycles are used, it is possible to cycle a few kilometres further to the start of the Allt na Creige path.

These two deer forests are prime stalking country and should be avoided for six weeks following 1st September. After that date enquiries should be made from the keeper at Kernsary. See the booklet *HEADING FOR THE SCOTTISH HILLS* published by the Scottish Mountaineering Trust for the Scottish Landowners Federation and the Mountaineering Council of Scotland.

Beinn Airigh Charr; 791m; (OS Sheet 19; 930762); *hill of the rough shieling*

This is a very prominent hill at the western edge of the Letterewe Forest; it is well seen across Loch Maree and from the low-lying coastal area round Loch Ewe. A characteristic feature is the steep tower on the north face named Martha's Peak after a legendary shepherdess who fell to her death on the cliffs of the tower while tending her flock.

Being at the west end of the Letterewe Forest, Beinn Airigh Charr has the easiest access of all the chain of hills along the north side of Loch Maree. The approach is along the road from Poolewe past Inveran to Kernsary. Shortly after passing Loch an Doire Ghairbh take an unmarked path which goes SW and in 1km joins the path from Kernsary to Ardlair. Continue along this path S towards Loch Maree until an old stone sheep fold can be seen about 100 metres left of the path at (894768). From it an excellent path goes

E, contouring round the valley to a stream and continuing uphill beside it.

The path continues uphill for about 3km and eventually reaches the col between Spidean nan Clach and Meall Chnaimhean. To the south the whole range of Torridon mountains is suddenly and superbly revealed, while the objective of Beinn Airigh Charr is easily gained by ascending the right flank of the large bowl between it and Spidean nan Clach. (From Inveran: 7½km; 780m; 3h).

The summit of Spidean nan Clach is the conical top that has beckoned all the way up the lower path, so it is fitting to complete the traverse by going NW to its sharp rocky summit. From there descend S and then SW to reach the col and the end of the path back to Inveran.

Map on page 189.

The north-east face of Beinn Lair from the east   *I. Brown*

Beinn Lair; 860m; (OS Sheet 19, 982732); *hill of the mare*

Beinn Lair is a hill of two very contrasting aspects. On the south-west side it has long slopes of grass and heather dropping at a fairly gentle angle from the summit ridge towards Letterewe Lodge and the wooded shore of Loch Maree. The impression given is of a hill of no great character of interest. On the north-east side, however, there is a continuous line of cliffs 5km long dropping precipitously from the summit to Gleann Tulacha and Lochan Fada. It is one of the finest, and probably the longest, mountain wall in the Highlands, and is given added character by being in such a remote setting. Between these two sides the broad summit ridge extends for 5km, with the highest point near its middle, and the slightly lower top of Sgurr Dubh 1km to its south-east.

Bein Lair is almost equidistant from Poolewe and Kinlochewe, a long way from both villages. The Poolewe approach is a bit shorter if one starts by driving to Inveran or cycling to Kernsary. Go past Kernsary and along the track leading E to a fork by a plantation. Go right through the plantation for 1km to a distinct left turn (small cairns), and there go down right to follow the path on the N side of the Allt na Creige. This is a notoriously muddy path, but the alternative through trackless bog is no better. The way is not clear in places, but if the path is lost it can be regained by Loch Doire Crionaich, which lies below the cliffs of Martha's Peak.

Continue along the path SE to the foot of Srathan Buidhe and cross the stream in this narrow glen to follow the path as it drops below the NE face of Meall Mheinnidh towards Fionn Loch. Not far from the loch turn right up another path which comes over the Bealach Mheinnidh from Letterewe and climb for 1½km up to this bealach, which is between Beinn Lair and Meall Mheinnidh. From there climb the ridge of Beinn Lair, NE at first for 1½km then SE, all the way along the edge of the stupendous cliffs overlooking Fionn Loch and Gleann Tulacha. At about 800m there is a very fine promontory which juts out over the north face and gives dramatic views of the cliffs and lochs below. The summit itself is a wide and rather flat dome which might require some accurate navigation in mist, but the huge summit cairn is unmistakable. (From Inveran: 15km; 900m; 5h).

On the return to Poolewe a good alternative route from the Bealach Mheinnidh is to climb Meall Mheinnidh, a 230m ascent up the SE ridge past a little lochan just above mid-height. Descend by the NW ridge, which has some short slabby cliffs low down which are easily avoided. Towards the foot of the ridge drop into Srathan Buidhe and cross the stream to regain the path which leads back past Kernsary to Inveran. This is a very long day's hillwalking, the total distance being about 30km, and the time 10 hours, excluding stops.

Beinn a'Chaisgein Mor; 857m; (OS Sheet 19; 983785); *big forbidding hill*

This great flat-topped hill stands on the border between the Letterewe and Fisherfield forests on the north side of Fionn Loch, one of the most inaccessible of the mountains in the area between Loch Maree and

Little Loch Broom. To its west and north-west it has no high neighbours, only a vast tract of low-lying land covered by a myriad of lochs and lochans stretches to the sea at Loch Ewe and Gruinard Bay. On the south

Looking north-west from A'Mhaighdean to Beinn Airigh Charr (left), Fionn Loch and   G.S. Johnstone
Beinn a'Chaisgein Mor (right)

side of the hill, overlooking the lodge at Carnmore, are two huge crags - Carn Mor and Sgurr na Laocainn. Although much admired by rock climbers, they are features that hillwalkers have to circumvent.

The route to Beinn a'Chaisgein Mor from Inveran is the same as that for Beinn Lair as far as the junction of paths near Fionn Loch. At that point continue NE along the path which goes round the head of the loch and across the causeway between it and Dubh Loch.

It is not necessary to go right to the lodge at Carnmore, but follow the excellent path which makes a rising traverse E below the cliffs of Sgurr na Laocainn, then NE up the Allt Bruthach an Easain to Lochan Feith Mhic'-illean. From there climb WNW for just over 2km up an open hillside with no features except for a tiny lochan halfway up to the summit. (19km; 900m; 6h). The only feasible return to Inveran is by the same route.

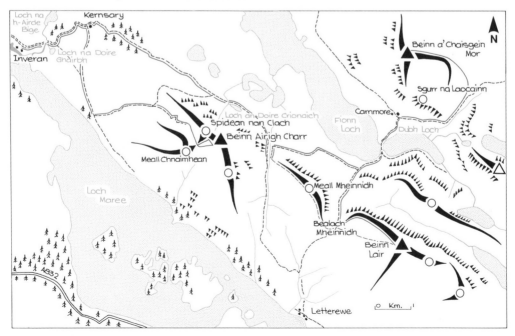

Beinn Dearg Mor and Beinn Dearg Bheag from the path above Shenavall   *J. Renny*

Beinn Dearg Mor; 910m; (OS Sheet 19; 0327990; *big red hill*
Beinn Dearg Bheag; 820m; (OS Sheet 19; 020811); *little red hill*

These two hills, rising grandly on the south-west side of Strath na Sealga, are just as remote as the Corbetts in the Letterewe Forest, but unlike them they are best approached from the north, leaving the A832 road at Corrie Hallie 4km up Strath Beag from the head of Little Loch Broom. Beinn Dearg Mor, in particular, is a magnificent mountain, comparable with An Teallach on the opposite side of Loch na Sealga. It may not have the height or complex structure of An Teallach, but it has the same narrow ridges, deep corries and steep sandstone cliffs, and it is a peak to be treated with great respect.

Leaving the A832 road at Corrie Hallie, follow a track S for 3km until near its highest point on bare moorland to the W of Loch Coire Chaorachain. Here a path leads off to the right, going level for 1½km across the end of the An Teallach range and then dropping to Shenavall bothy in Strath na Sealga. This bothy is preferred by many for climbing Beinn Dearg Mor and Bheag, but it is popular and liable to be crowded.

From the bothy cross the Abhainn Strath na Sealga, then a kilometre of very wet bog and finally the Abhainn Gleann na Muice to reach Larachantivore. This will usually be possible in reasonably dry weather, but difficult and even dangerous in or after

wet weather, when this expedition may be impossible. From Larachantivore go S along the path for a short distance and then make a rising traverse SW up a rather steep slope to reach a little hanging corrie SE of Beinn Dearg Mor. Climb NW up the centre of this corrie, trending N at its head to reach the summit of Beinn Dearg Mor. A more interesting route can be made by climbing the narrow rocky ridge which bounds the corrie on its SW side. (11½km; 1180m; 4h 40min).

Descend SW from the summit of Beinn Dearg Mor, soon turning NW down the ridge to Beinn Dearg Bheag. This goes along the rim of the Toll an Lochain, a classic example of a circular corrie with its little loch lying in a hollow scooped out by ancient glaciers. Finally the ridge rises to the airy summit of Beinn Dearg Bheag. (14km; 1400m; 5h 30min).

The very long return to Corrie Hallie can be shortened slightly by descending, with due care, the steep slope on the NE side of the col at the head of the Toll an Lochain. This descent leads down to the path on the S side of Loch na Sealga and one has to cross the combined streams flowing into the loch, which may be more difficult than the crossing of the streams separately on the outward route.

Creag Rainich; 807m; (OS Sheets 19 and 20; 096751); *bracken crag*

'The Destitution Road' is the name given to the A832 as it sweeps over the bare moorland from Braemore Junction to Dundonnell. The derelict house at its side, Fain, was a staging post in the days of the famine-relief scheme that built the road. The huge moors to the south-west swell upwards to the unob-

trusive Corbett Creag Rainich, a fine viewpoint, but a long slow ascent over the bogs and braes from Fain.

A better route to this hill starts 4km south-east of Fain at the point on the A832 where a private road branches off to Loch a'Bhraoin. It may be no shorter, but for most of its length one can follow first a track

Creag Rainich from the track to Strath na Sealga   *G.S. Johnstone*

and then a fairly good path. Walk down to the NE end of the loch and follow the path along its N shore which leads pleasantly to the cottage of Lochivraon, now used occasionally by estate stalkers and shepherds, and providing hillwalkers with a good bothy. From there climb NW up open grassy slopes over a knoll at 749m to the summit ¾km beyond. (8½km; 600m; 3h).

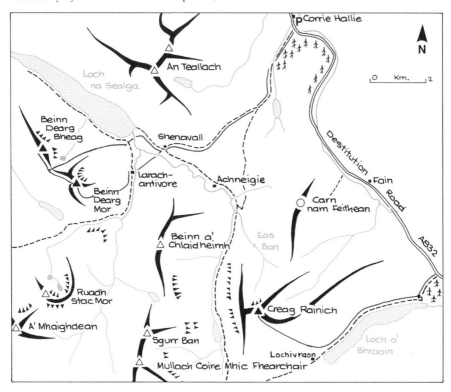

Beinn Liath Mhor a'Ghiubhais Li from Loch Droma   *G.S. Johnstone*

Beinn Liath Mhor a'Ghiubhais Li; 766m; (OS Sheet 20; 281713); *big grey hill of the coloured pines*

This hill, the only Corbett in the Fannaichs, is an outlier of the main group standing between it and Loch Glascarnoch. It is a rather featureless dome, rough grass and heather characteristic of the Fannaichs, but very accessible from the A835 road unlike the rest of these hills, all of which are quite a long way from the road.

The car park at the bridge over the Abhainn an Torrain Duibh is a good starting point, and there is a rough path up this stream which leads rather indirectly towards the hill before one has to leave it and climb the NW ridge to the summit. (4km; 510m; 1h 50min). The view from there is remarkably fine, for on one side is the whole length of the Fannaich chain, and north across the glen the Beinn Dearg group. The descent can be varied by going NE over the outlying top of Meall Diamh *(hill of the stags)* and N down to the road.

There are no pines visible on this hill nowadays, but the summit has some of the finest examples of solifluction boulder ramparts to be found in Scotland. They may be the relics of a time when the upper reaches of the hill protruded from glacier ice.

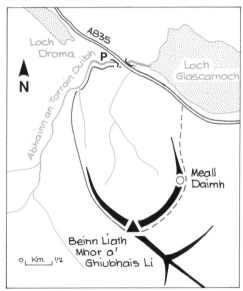

Sail Mhor; 767m; (OS Sheet 19; 033887); *big heel*

Sail Mhor lives up to its name, being a big lump of a hill rising from the elevated moorland several kilometres north-west of An Teallach. Its north side drops steeply to Little Loch Broom, and it is from that side that the ascent is made, starting at the foot of the Allt Airdeasaidh, the Ardessie burn.

The path up the burn is on its E side, but if there is a spate, a possibly difficult crossing higher up can be avoided by climbing up its W side. The splendid falls and cascades of the Ardessie Falls are the first point

of interest on the climb; they can be seen better from the W than the E side of the burn. Once in the flatter upper valley, cross to the W side of the burn and follow a smaller stream up into the corrie between Sail Mhor and Ruigh Mheallain for 1km before bearing N and climbing steeply to the SE end of Sail Mhor's curving crest. The walk round the rim to the cairn gives superb views of the sea and far islands. (4½km; 750m; 2h 20min).

Descend S along the edge of the steep W face to

Beinn Ghobhlach from Laide   H.M. Brown

reach the col below Ruigh Mheallain, and either climb that top or else go more directly down the corrie E to

return to the Allt Airdeasaidh and the uphill route.

Beinn Ghobhlach; 635m; (OS Sheet 19; 055943); *forked hill*

Beinn Ghobhlach is a prominent little hill which occupies a strategic position at the tip of the peninsula between Little Loch Broom and Loch Broom. From this point it commands a superb view in all directions, the high mountains of An Teallach, Beinn Dearg and the Coigach in an eastward arc, and the sea-lochs, The Minch and their islands to the west.

The approach to the south side of the hill is along the narrow road to the tiny village of Badrallach. There is very limited space to park a car at the end of this road. Start walking along the fine footpath which leads to Scoraig and after about 1km make a rising

traverse NW up the hillside to the little col near Pt.336m.

From there bear NNE between Loch na h-Uidhe and Loch na Coireig and continue up the SW flank of Beinn Ghobhlach to reach the W ridge a short distance from the summit. The final walk up this bare sandstone ridge leads to the spectacular summit panorama. (3½km; 640m; 2h 10min).

A slight diversion may be made on the descent to go round the W end of Loch na h-Uidhe and look down the cliffs where the outflow from the loch makes a spectacular waterfall.

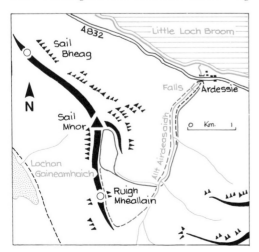

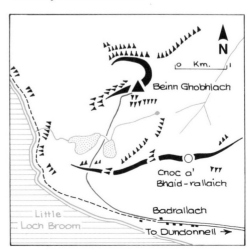

Looking south-east from Beinn Enaiglair to Loch Glascarnoch   M. Marshall

SECTION 15

Loch Broom to Easter Ross

Beinn Enaiglair; 889m; (OS Sheet 20; 225805); *hill of timid birds*

Beinn Enaiglair is an outlier of the Beinn Dearg group of hills, and is situated about 4km north of Braemore Junction on the A835 road from Dingwall to Ullapool. Although not as high as the principal members of the Beinn Dearg group or the nearby Fannaichs, it is an obvious feature to travellers approaching Braemore Junction from either Garve, Ullapool or Gairloch, and it gives extensive views of the Ross-shire hills. The south and west slopes are generally grassy, but the north facing flanks are steeper and quite rocky, and should be avoided.

The ascent of Beinn Enaiglair can conveniently be combined with that of Beinn Dearg across the intervening summit of Iorguill (872m), and this is a very good way to Beinn Dearg. The route starts from the A835 road at Braemore Junction. Follow the forest road NW from the gates of the house for about 1½km to a disused estate building. At that point take a stalker's path NE past the Home Loch to a junction in a further 1½km, from which two paths lead onwards to encircle Beinn Enaiglair. The shortest route is to take the right-hand path E to the bealach between Beinn Enaiglair and Meall Doire Faid (730m) and from there climb N to the broad and mainly grassy summit plateau. (5½km; 710m; 2h 30min).

For a more interesting and varied ascent, take the left-hand branch of the path which skirts round the NW end of Beinn Enaiglair and steadily ascends beside the Allt na h-Ighine towards the bealach between Beinn Enaiglair and Iorguill. Follow the path which climbs above this bealach by zig-zags and traverses into the small grassy corrie from which springs the west source of the Allt Mhucarnaich. Follow a path (unmarked on the 1:50,000 map) firstly W up the floor of this little corrie, then SW up a steep slope onto the summit plateau of Beinn Enaiglair. (9km; 610m; 3h 10min).

The descent can be made by either of the two ascent routes described, and the combination of them makes a good circuit of the hill.

Alternatively, if appropriate transport arrangements can be made, a longer descent can be made to Loch Droma some 7km E of Braemore Junction. Descend the SE ridge of Beinn Enaiglair to the junction of stalker's paths near Loch Feith nan Cleireach. The continuation SE of this path goes for a further 3km along an undulating ridge, with good views of the SW side of Beinn Dearg, to reach a col N of Lochdrum. From there either descend the path S to the A835 road at the W end of Loch Droma, or continue over a few more undulations of the ridge to reach an unmapped path which descends to the E end of Loch Droma.

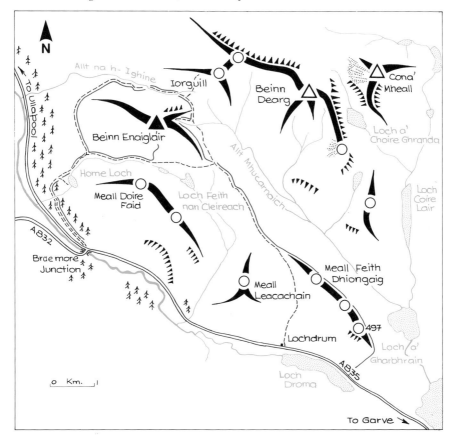

Meall a'Ghrianain with Beinn a'Chaisteil to its left, from Strath Vaich   G.S. Johnstone

Beinn a'Chaisteil; 787m; (OS Sheet 20; 370801); *castle hill*

This mountain lies 9km north of the A835 road from Dingwall to Ullapool, and forms the highest point of a ridge on the east side of Loch Vaich. It is at the north end of this ridge, and is separated from Meall a'Ghrianain (772m) at the south end by 2½km and a col at 650m. Both hills have uniform steep heathery slopes on all sides, but a stony plateau above 650m gives easy walking.

Beinn a'Chaisteil is best approached from the south along the private estate road up Strath Vaich, as for Carn Ban (see page 198). Park at Black Bridge 2½km east of Aultguish Inn and follow the estate road for 4km. Just before the road crosses the Abhainn Srath a'Bhathaich near Lubriach a rough track takes off through a locked gate, keeping to the east of the river. Continue up this well-made but stony track for a further 5km until Lubachlaggan with its rusty red-roofed bothies, now inhabited only by sheep, is reached. This point can be reached by bicycle, thus saving some time.

The burn flowing down from Beinn a'Chaisteil is followed on its N bank, remnants of an old stalker's path making the ascent a little easier. Its end is marked by a small cairn at 500m, and from there another 2km of fairly easy climbing NE bring one to the summit. (10½km; 580m; 3h 20min). On a clear day there are fine views of Seana Bhraigh to the NW, and through one of its cols an unusual angle of Suilven may be glimpsed.

To include Meall a'Ghrianain go S along the undulating ridge for less than 1km, then descend SSW for 1km to the 650m col, from where there is a climb of just over 1km to the top. There is a choice of descent routes. A short and steep return may be made to Lubachlaggan, avoiding steep ground immediately W of Meall a'Ghrianain and heading NW to follow the S side of the burn down to the bothy. Alternatively, descend the broad ridge S from the top, reaching a track in 3km near Meallan Donn. From there a path leads SW down to Lubriach and the road back to Black Bridge.

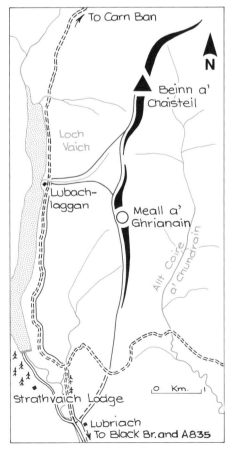

Little Wyvis from the south-west   *H.M. Brown*

Little Wyvis; 764m; (OS Sheet 20; 430635); *little awesome hill*

Little Wyvis forms a fairly insignificant outlier to the south-west of the dominant massif of Ben Wyvis. The hill is extensively planted with young conifers on its west and south-west sides and several tracks create ugly scars across the hillside, on which a deer-rearing programme is being carried out, so that hillwalkers are not welcome on that side of the hill at any time of the year.

The least contentious access is by the path along the north bank of the Allt a'Bhealaich Mhoir, starting from the A835 road just south of Garbat. Follow the rather muddy path to the edge of the forest and continue alongside the stream to a stile over a new fence round more recent afforestation. Once over this, cross the stream and follow the outside of the fence uphill, at first along a tenuous path, then through heather to the col between Tom na Caillich and Little Wyvis.

An alternative route continues up the Allt a'Bhealaich Mhoir by a very wet path to the Bealach Mor, and then steeply W to Tom na Caillich. There are fence posts and Argocat tracks along the ridge and over an intermediate knoll between that top and the summit of Little Wyvis. (5km; 520m; 2h 10min).

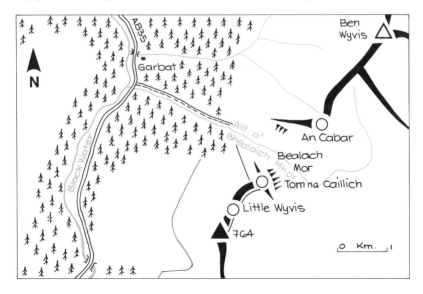

The north-west shoulder of Carn Ban above Loch a'Choire Mhoir   *D.J. Bennet*

Carn Ban; 845m; (OS Sheet 20; 338875); *white cairn*

This great dome-shaped hill is situated in the heart of some of the most remote hill country in Scotland in the Freevater Forest at the centre of Ross-shire. It forms a continuation eastwards of the Seana Bhraigh plateau, from which it is separated by Coire Mor. Being so remote, there is a very long walk from any

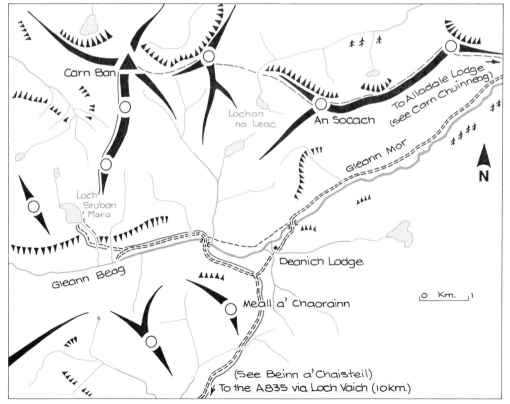

possible starting point to reach this hill, and the use of a bicycle is a considerable advantage along the roads that lead far into the glens surrounding it.

Four approaches are possible, all more or less equally long: from the head of Loch Broom in the west: from Corriemulzie Lodge in the north: from Strathcarron in the east: and from Strath Vaich in the south. The Strath Vaich route will be chosen; the first part of this way has been described on page 196 for Beinn a'Chaisteil.

Continue along the track on the E side of Loch Vaich to its head and on up the glen to pass round the E side of Meall a'Chaorainn and follow the NW branch of the track slightly downhill into Gleann Beag. Cross the river by a bridge and go up the glen for a further 1½km almost to a second bridge. This point, 16km from the start, can be reached by bicycle.

A stalker's path, starting at a small quarried area, goes up the hillside below the crags of Cail Mhor, making a rising traverse towards waterfalls and the burn coming down from Loch Sruban Mora. In wet weather it may be difficult to cross this burn, in which case it is necessary to climb steeply up beside it to the loch. From there follow a faint path then head NNE onto the shoulder of Carn Ban over peat hags and bogs and past occasional cairns. Once on the long S ridge continue over three undulating tops, the ground becoming better, typical plateau country of moss and fine scree, and reach the summit. (21½km; 650m; 5h 50min).

The logical return is by the same route unless one is equipped for a major traverse, in which case the descent E either down the Alladale River or Gleann Mor might be considered.

Carn Chuinneag; 838m; (OS Sheet 20;484833); *hill of the churn (bucket)*

Carn Chuinneag, with its distinctive twin tops, enjoys an isolated position amongst the rolling hills and deer forests of Easter Ross. It is best approached from Ardgay at the head of the Dornoch Firth, taking the public road up Strathcarron to The Craigs, then turning south to Glencalvie Lodge. Cars should be left just before the bridge near the lodge as the road up Glen Calvie is private.

Go through the gates and keep to the left of the lodge along the road past the keeper's house towards the river. Continue up the private road in Glen Calvie leading pleasantly through birch woods which end just before the junction at Diebidale Lodge. There take the well-defined stalker's path up the W shoulder of Carn Chuinneag to a cairn marking the junction of two paths. From there one can continue S along the path for a short distance further, climb the SW ridge of the W top of Carn Chuinneag and then continue along the ridge to the E top which is the true summit and has a trig point. Alternatively, one can follow the path NE from the cairn for 1km and climb to the summit via the col between the two tops. (9km; 750m; 3h 20min).

The return can be made by retracing the ascent along the stalker's paths. Alternatively, a descent from the summit can be made NE down fine scree to Cairn Maire and N past the head of Loch Chuinneag through very rough deep heather to the track leading back to Glen Calvie.

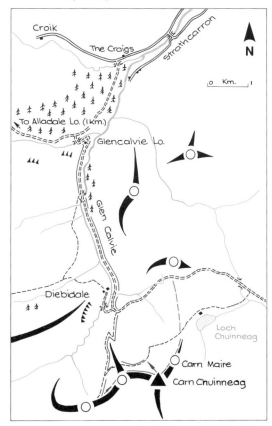

The peaks of Ben Mor Coigach from the north-west   D.J. Bennet

SECTION 16

Coigach to the Pentland Firth

Ben Mor Coigach; 743m; (OS Sheet 15; 094043); *big hill of Goigach*

Seen from the main A835 road from Ullapool to Inchnadamph, Ben Mor Coigach appears as a rather massive wall-sided mountain, apparently with little to recommend it except that, almost uniquely on the Scottish mainland, its western end plunges steeply and directly down to end in sea-cliffs. This appearance conceals the fact that the top of the wall is a fine narrow ridge behind which the mountain massif is a grand complex of shapely peaks and deep cliff-backed corries. This array of peaks is best seen from the minor road which branches off to Achiltibuie round the north side of the mountain. These fine peaks and corries, and the prospect over sea and islands from them, make the traverse of Ben Mor Coigach one of the most attractive in the northwest Highlands; one from which the hillwalker will be reluctant to descend until the sun is well down to the western horizon.

The hill is easily climbed from Achiltibuie, making a circular traverse over as many peaks as one wishes. These include Cairn Conmheall, Beinn nan Caorach, Sgurr an Fhidhleir (whose celebrated prow is the finest feature of the whole mountain) and Garbh Choireachan, a curious name for such a salient point. To reach Achiltibuie, however, involves a 26km circuit of Coigach from the A835 road at Drumrunie, and for those seeking a more direct approach, the hill can be climbed attractively and more directly from the Ullapool side.

From the bridge at Strath Kanaird on the A835 road a branch leads to Blughasary, where there is a car park. From there a hill road, not shown on the 1:50,000 map, leads N then W to Loch Eadar dha Bheinn. From the E end of this loch a short steep ascent leads to the

E shoulder, almost a shelf, of Speicin Coinnich. When reached, this will be found to become a huge, gently-inclined pavement of Torridonian sandstone slabs which provide easy walking to the steep, narrowing final part of the ridge. Despite its appearance, there is no difficulty in reaching the finely-situated rocky top. A short descent leads to a last easy climb to Ben Mor along a wind-blasted ridge. The actual summit is slightly to one side of the crest of this ridge and could be bypassed in mist - if one were foolish enough to climb this fine mountain on a day when the glorious views are obscured. There is a massive shelter-cairn on top. (6km; 740m; 2h 40min).

The easiest descent is by the ascent route, though it is worthwhile going out to Garbh Choireachan for the view before returning.

For the strong walker a fairly demanding alternative return route may be considered. From the summit of Ben Mor Coigach traverse the fine airy ridge to Garbh Choireachan, and before it plunges down towards the sea descend the NW side of the ridge down disintegrating scree which would be toilsome to ascend. The coastal path is reached about 1km SE of Culnacraig and from there to Blughasary there is 7km of exceptionally hard going which could take 3 hours or more. Despite the indication on the map, no real path exists and the way is in places quite spectacular. The route over boulder-fall, crag and gully is marked by yellow-topped stakes and small red paint marks on the rocks, but notwithstanding these, one can easily go astray, so careful route-finding is essential. Over the last 1½km to Blughasary do not enter the sheep-grazing pastures, but keep on the uphill side of the fence.

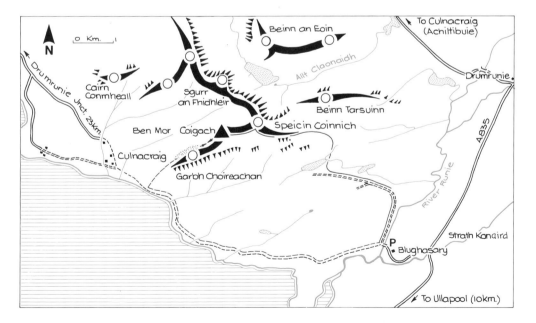

Cul Beag and Stac Pollaidh from the east   *J. Renny*

Cul Beag; 769m; (OS Sheet 15; 140088); *small back*
Cul Mor; 849m; (OS Sheet 15; 162119); *big back*

Cul Beag rises immediately above the narrow single track road on the north side of Loch Lurgainn, and the approaches to it are short and steep. As with its neighbour Cul Mor, care should be taken to avoid the bands of sandstone cliffs which are on the upper part of the hill facing west and north.

Rather than ascend and descend by the same route, a traverse is suggested which, though short in terms of distance and time, is a more attractive variation. Start from the single track road ½km E of Linneraineach where a good stalker's path ascends N through a small group of Scots pines. Follow the path to just beyond Lochan Fhionnlaidh, from which point climb steep slopes ESE to reach a shallow col immediately S of a shoulder on the N ridge of Cul Beag. Continue steeply S up this ridge, taking care to avoid the sandstone crags of the W face, to reach the summit. (2½km; 700m; 1h 50min).

The continuation of the route to complete the traverse is straightforward. Start by descending SSE for 1km, then SSW for a further 1km to reach the road at the head of Loch Lurgainn 2km SE of the starting point.

Cul Mor is the highest of the Assynt Corbetts, and has very steep flanks on three sides: south, west and north. Only the east side is easy-angled, and the ascent up it is straightforward and poses no problems. When combined with Cul Beag in a continuous traverse, it provides a magnificent day's hillwalking.

Start at a gate in the fence on the west side of the A835 road ½km north of Knockanrock. A footpath, which is often wet, crosses

boggy ground and continues N diagonally up the hillside to reach the rather ill-defined E ridge of the mountain. Continue on the path, which soon disappears, WNW up the broad ridge to reach Meallan Diomhain. Turn NNW along the ridge, descending 20m, and cross the side of a shallow corrie to a tiny lochan. From there the route goes first W then SW up the steep ridge which is bounded on the NW by the precipitous Coire Gorm, and ends abruptly at the summit. (6km; 620m; 2h 30min). If a traverse is not intended, return by the same route.

Cul Beag from Stac Pollaidh   *D.J. Bennet*

Cul Mor from Stac Pollaidh   A. O'Brien

The traverse of both these mountains is much more attractive than climbing each one on its own, but the terrain between them is rough, and the time required may be more than the mere distance suggests.

From the summit of Cul Mor descend steeply W for 50m, then turn S to reach a bare gravel col at 750m below Creag nan Calman. From the col descend E for ½km before curving round S and then W to a rough animal track which steadily loses height under a sandstone cliff which is generally black and wet. Lochan Dearg a'Chuil Mhoir lies below, but the outflow from it is a precipitous waterslide and is avoided by making a descending traverse to its S to cross the Allt an Loin Duibh either just above or below Lochan Dearg. From the outflow of the lochan ascend SW to reach the shallow col on the N ridge of Cul Beag and climb that ridge to the summit.

From the summit of Cul Beag descend E for 170m to a col with a lochan from where there is a short ascent over the top of Meall Dearg. Continue descending E and follow the crest of Creag Dhubh to reach a good stalker's path which starts just S of Loch nan Ealachan and leads to the A835 road ½km S of Knockanrock. (14km; 1350m; 5h 30min).

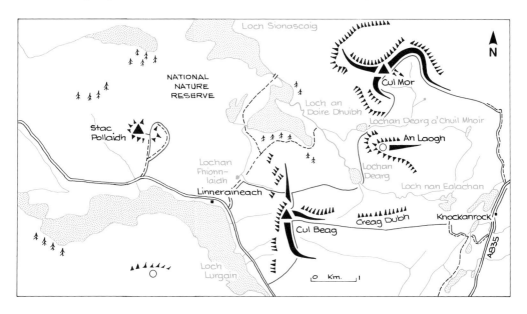

Cul Mor and Stac Pollaidh from the north-west   *A. Watson*

Stac Pollaidh; 613m; (OS Sheet 15; 107106); *peak of the peat moss*

Stac Pollaidh (Polly) is a unique little hill which shows to an extreme extent the results of the weathering action of rain, frost and wind on Torridonian sandstone. Horizontal strata of varying resistance to these effects have been etched out into ridges and pinnacles of bizarre shape along the flanks of the narrow crest which is about ½km long and terminates at both ends in steep rounded buttresses. Geologically and scenically outstanding, the hill well justifies its place in the Inverpolly National Nature Reserve, in which it lies.

Unfortunately, the low height and ease of access to this hill has resulted in its becoming a tourist attraction, accentuated by the car park at its foot. The summit ridge of the hill can be reached without much difficulty by paths up several gullies, and these paths have become so eroded as to resemble trenches in the boggy ground. In places the peat has been eroded down to the bed-rock. This disfigurement of the hill is hardly compatible with its status as part of a Nature Reserve, but the solution to the problem is not easy.

The route is so obvious as hardly to need description. A path from the car park goes directly up towards a col on the summit ridge just E of its midpoint. The path branches, one branch going directly up a crumbling gully on the S side of this col, the other going round the E end of the hill to mount the NE side in zig-zags to reach the same col. From there the traverse of the summit ridge westwards is the best part of the climb, making the slog up the lower eroded slopes worthwhile. A well-marked path, with occasional easy scrambling leads to the top of a gully near the W end. The climb out of this gully is exposed and quite awkward for a few metres, as the rock is loose in places and the holds are sloping. Once up this little pitch, the summit is only a short distance away. (1½km; 550m; 1h 20min).

The best time to climb this little peak is out of season, possibly in mid-winter when the lower slopes are frozen and the summit ridge is encased in snow, but in such conditions the last pitch would be rather hard.

Map on page 203.

Suilven (Caisteal Liath); 731m; (OS Sheet 15; 154184); *the pillar* (Norse), *the grey castle*

It may come as a surprise to many hillwalkers that such a spectacular and dominating mountain as Suilven fails by a fair margin to reach Corbett height. Nevertheless, by any mountaineer's standard it yields nothing to any of the higher Scottish hills. An 'Inselberg', or 'Island Mountain' of Torridonian sandstone, surrounded by a sea of Lewisian gneiss from which the softer rocks have been stripped, the Grey Castle when viewed from the west stands as a rather forbidding bastion defying the ravages of wind and

weather. In fact this appearance, and also its pinnacle form when seen from the east, is rather misleading, as the mountain is actually a narrow serrated ridge with three main summits, presenting no great difficulty to the ascent of its highest (western) top by way of the Bealach Mor.

The two commonly used approach routes are very similar as regards length and quality. Both are long, but until near the base of the mountain itself both follow good paths.

Suilven from the Inverkirkaig path   *T.J. Ransley*

The route from Inverkirkaig leaves the road at (085193) and follows the pleasant wooded glen of the River Kirkaig, whose 20m falls are an attraction in themselves. This is probably a more aesthetic route than that which follows the road from Lochinver past Glencanisp Lodge. From the Kirkaig path the mountain itself is hidden from view for several kilometres, but comes as a dramatic sight when first seen close-to. Beyond the Falls, at a small cairn, make sure to take the path which shortcuts the peninsula at the NW end of Fionn Loch. This path is boggy, but the route round the loch-side is longer and rougher.

Although various cairns may suggest diversions from the path marked on the 1:50,000 map, it is best to continue on it along the NE shore of the Fionn Loch until the stream from the Bealach Mor is reached at (143168). A boggy stretch up the burn leads to a heather-clad debris fan leading very steeply up to the Bealach Mor. The path is eroding and the steepness may seem rather intimidating to some. The bealach is reached near an incredibly well built wall, and through a gap in it the way continues easily WNW along the narrow and rather exposed ridge to the rounded summit of Caisteal Liath. (10½km; 730m; 4h).

From Lochinver follow the road to Glencanisp Lodge and the path from there to the bridge at the outflow from Loch na Gainimh. The ground leading SW towards the Bealach Mor is rather boggy in places, and the slopes below the bealach itself are more broken than those on the opposite SW side, so that climbers dislodging stones can cause a hazard. (10½km; 730m; 4h).

The middle peak of Suilven, Meall Mheadhonach, can be reached from the Bealach Mor by some easy but exposed scrambling. However, the continuation of the traverse to the south-east peak, Meall Bheag, involves some more serious scrambling and is for experienced climbers only.

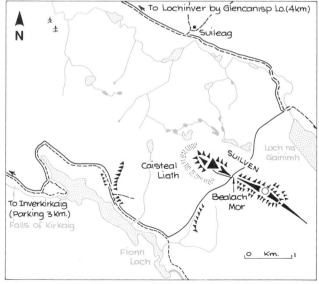

Canisp from the north-east, with Cul Mor far to the south   J. Renny

Canisp; 846m; (OS Sheet 15; 203187); *white hill*

Canisp, like its near neighbour Suilven, rises abruptly from a tableland of Lewisian gneiss, but although higher by 115m, it lacks the steepness and sharply serrated spine of Suilven that makes the latter such an outstanding peak, and so popular with hillwalkers. Nevertheless, because of its isolation, Canisp is well worth climbing for the excellent views of the other Assynt hills.

The hill itself is a steep-sided ridge running from south-east to north-west, and it may be approached from either end. The walk from the north-west, starting at Lochinver or Little Assynt, is much longer than the south-eastern approach, so the latter is recommended.

Four kilometres N of Ledmore the River Loanan flows out of the N end of Loch Awe where there is a footbridge to simplify an otherwise difficult crossing. Follow the path from the footbridge to Loch na Gruagaich, and continue along the line of the Allt Mhic Mhurchaidh Gheir up to a lochan under the N flank of Meall Diamhain. The hillside becomes progressively more stony, and several cairns should be ignored as they have no significance. From the lochan climb SW to the col immediately W of Meall Diamhain, and from there continue W

then NW up the rounded ridge of Canisp, or if the not infrequent strong SW wind is blowing, up the shallow corrie on its N side. These two routes join at 750m and a further 100m of climbing on a bearing NNW bring one to the summit. (6km; 690m; 2h 30min).

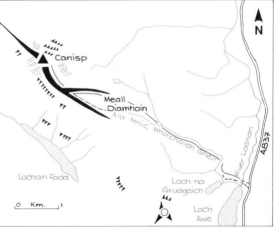

Breabag; 815m; (OS Sheet 15; 287158); *little back*

Breabag forms a high tableland between the upper reaches of the River Oykell to the east and the A837 road from Ledmore to Inchnadamph to the west. The highest point of this plateau is at its south end, and is un-named apart from the name Creag Liath which

applies to the crags to the south-west of the top. Although the mountain itself is composed of quartzite which forms the broken cliffs of its eastern corries, the approach from the west traverses glens where Durness limestone predominates.

Creag Liath, Breabag from the south   H.M. Brown

The most interesting approach starts from the A837 road 5km N of Ledmore at a salmon hatchery. The route follows the glen of the Allt nan Uamh. One kilometre from the road the river wells up from a spring in the floor of the glen, and from there on the riverbed is dry. Further up the glen there are several caves in which bones of long-extinct mammals have provided evidence of the presence of early man. The glen becomes much narrower and the entrance to a deep cave is passed on the left just before a rock step.

At that point climb the slopes to the E which are initially steep, but soon ease into a more gently sloping hillside. One kilometre ahead there is a break in the escarpment just N of a prominent quartzite slab. Climb through this break onto the more gently sloping upper part of the mountain. The summit lies 1km to the S with 200m of ascent. (5km; 680m; 2h 20min).

Rather than return to the A837 by the same route, it is more pleasant to traverse Breabag northwards and descend Gleann Dubh. From the summit head NNE initially down gently sloping ground to the col at 630m. From there the terrain changes to quartzite slabs, very slippery if wet, which are followed to the N top (715m). Continue NNE to the deep and narrow pass between Breabag and Conival, and then go NW down the Allt a'Bhealaich which soon disappears down a limestone pot.

Thereafter follow the dry bed of the stream to meet the path from Loch Mhaolach-coire. Soon after joining this path it is worth making a short detour to the right to view the caves through which the stream may be seen rushing. Continue down Gleann Dubh to the A837 road at Inchnadamph, 4km N of the salmon hatchery.

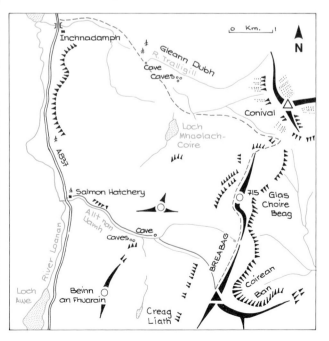

Sail Gharbh (left) and Sail Gorm from the east   *J. Renny*

Quinag, Spidean Coinich; 764m; (OS Sheet 15; 205278); *mossy peak*
Quinag, Sail Gharbh; 808m; (OS Sheet 15; 209292); *rough heel*
Quinag, Sail Gorm; 776m; (OS Sheet 15; 198304); *blue heel*
(Quinag is probably derived from Cuinneag, meaning milk bucket or water stoup)

Quinag is an eye-catching mountain from any direction, being one of the great peaks of the North West, and it presents a formidable array of rocky features. The walker may be relieved to know that its three main summits can be climbed relatively easily. The most dramatic view of Quinag is from the north; the rock prows of Sail Gharbh and Sail Gorm tower above the sea at Kylesku. From the west the hill appears as a long wall of cliffs. Only to the south-east does it relent, and it is from that side that walkers will almost invariably climb it. There are other possible routes on the mountain, but they are best left for those with exploratory or climbing experience.

The start is from the A894 road between Loch Assynt and Kylesku at (233274), where there is the beginning of a stalker's path and a large parking area. From there the broad ridge of Spidean Coinich faces one, with its northern edge clearly marked by crags. The ascent goes up this ridge, whose angle is determined by the tilt of the quartzite strata, and much of the way is up bare rock, in places littered with boulders. A rocky bump is crossed before the cone of Spidean Coinich is reached. From afar it appears to be cliff-girt, but the crags all face NE and there are no problems for the walker. (3½km; 550m; 1h 50min).

The biggest surprise when one sees Quinag close at hand is that it is such a green mountain. The areas of rock are less extensive than expected, and are well demarcated, offering the walker ground that is either easy (though steep) or obviously impossible. The long traverse N takes one over the airy crest of Pt.713m and along the twisting path down to the Bealach

a'Chornaidh (c 555m), where one should study the line of the path descending the eastern corrie, the route off the mountain.

The path zig-zags up to Pt.745m and then drops to a more knobbly col (c 555m) and the ridge out to the spectacular prow of Sail Gorm, the northernmost spur of the mountain. This route is reversed to return to the knobbly col, but the ascent to Pt. 745m can be avoided by a traverse across its N side to reach the ridge leading to Sail Gharbh. This peak is the highest point of Quinag; at it the grey quartzite just overlaps the sandstone, and the summit is the high point on a ridge which extends nearly 1km further NNE to end above the great cliffs which are the finest feature of the mountain.

Return along this ridge to its lowest point and again avoid an ascent of Pt.745m by a descending traverse SE to the Bealach a'Chornaidh, below which one reaches the start of a path which leads down to the N of Lochan Bealach Cornaidh. This path joins the stalker's path back to the starting point on the A894 road.

It is also possible to drop down SW from the Bealach a'Chornaidh. A narrow path makes a descending traverse S of barring cliffs to easier, but still steep, ground above the Bealach Leireag. From the top of this pass descend 2km SW along the path to Tumore on the A837 road by Loch Assynt, a long way from the day's starting point. An even longer end to the day can be made by walking NW from the Bealach Leireag down Gleann Leireag to the B869 road near Nedd.

Looking north from Spidean Coinich to the distant dome of Sail Gorm   D.J. Broadhead

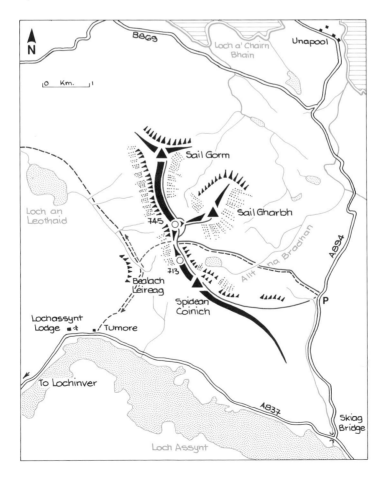

Glas Bheinn from Pt. 713m on Quinag; Spidean Coinich on the right,
Ben More Assynt and Conival in the distance

A. O'Brien

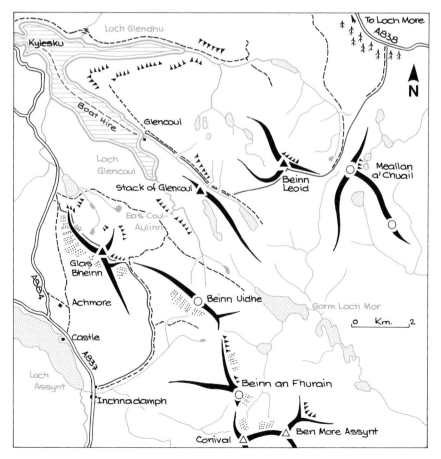

Beinn Leoid from Meallan a'Chuail   *J. Renny*

Glas Bheinn; 776m; (OS Sheet 15; 255265); *grey hill*

This is a rather neglected hill, being surrounded by such a host of grand peaks as Quinag, Suilven and Ben More Assynt, but the discerning will quickly realise what fine views such a summit must have. Glas Bheinn is also the start of one of the great high-level walks in the northern Highlands, southwards to Conival and Breabag. There is plenty of rough rocky ground on the hill,but it is easily avoided.

The start, which is not too obvious, is just N of the highest point of the A894 road between Loch Assynt and Kylesku at (238284). From there start E on the path which goes round the S end of Loch na Gainmhich, but soon leave it to climb up the grassy edge of the crags on the NW ridge of the hill. This ridge is followed, and after several steps and more level sections it leads onto the broad, mossy summit plateau. (3km; 550m; 1h 40min).

The route can be reversed on the descent, or a steep way taken SW to return to the start by the path which goes from Achmore round the foot of the hill. The best continuation goes SE then E down a narrow ridge to the col between Glas Bheinn and Beinn Uidhe. A stalker's path crosses this col and is followed for 6km past Loch Fleodach Coire down to Inchnadamph. Although this leads back to the road several kilometres from the day's starting point, it is a very fine traverse in grand surroundings.

Beinn Leoid; 792m; (OS Sheet 15; 320295); *sloping hill*

Beinn Leoid is not a tame mountain. It is remote and if one approaches it from the west there is some wild country to be crossed. From the east, however, the ascent can be made quite easily starting from the A838 road between Lairg and Laxford Bridge and following stalker's paths to reach the hill. The landscape between Beinn Leoid and Glas Bheinn is an amazing chaos of bare rock, deep glens, and a proliferation of lochs and bogs; it is a magnificent wilderness enhanced by the starkly prominent peak of the Stack of Glencoul and the cascade of Britain's highest waterfall, the Eas a'Chuil Aluinn. For the strong walker these are the approaches to explore, but the easy route is described first.

The best starting point on the A838 road is 2km SE of the SE end of Loch More at (357334). From there a stalker's path climbs steeply S between forest plantings to end after 2km on a broad saddle on the N ridge of Meallan a'Chuail. From there make a descending traverse SW to join another much longer stalker's path from Lochmore Side which leads to the col between Meallan a'Chuail and Beinn Leoid, whose E ridge leads directly to the summit. (7km; 760m; 2h 50min). As a varaint on the return, it is possible to traverse over Meallan a'Chuail with little more extra climbing than is involved by following the outward route.

The easiest approach from the west is by sea. In recent years it has been possible to hire a boat at Unapool to be taken up Loch Glencoul to Glencoul. Local enquiries should be made to ascertain the present situation. From Glencoul a good path goes up the glen below the dramatic Stack to end just beyond Loch an Eircill. From there Beinn Leoid is 2km NNE. (7km; 800m; 3h).

The return can be made down the NW ridge for 1km then N to join a path leading down to Glen Dubh, and out along the N shore of Loch Glendhu to Kylestrome. As an approach route, this is the easiest one entirely on foot from the west, but it is long. (13km; 850m; 4h 50min).

Ben Stack and Loch Stack from the east   T.J. Ransley

Ben Stack; 721m; (OS Sheet 9; 269424); *steep hill*

Standing to the west of and close to Loch Stack on the A838 road from Lairg to Laxford Bridge, this elegant little mountain is worthy of attention in spite of its modest height and the short distances involved in its ascent. Moreover, it is a superb viewpoint for its immediate surroundings. The symmetry, if not the character, of Ben Stack's conical shape is reminiscent of Schiehallion in Perthshire. Seen from the south-east, when approaching along the shore of Loch More, the mountain dominates the view.

The south-eastern approach to Ben Stack starts from the A838 at the entrance to the private road to Lone, about mid-way between the village of Achfary and the south end of Loch Stack. Follow a fairly obvious rib up the broad SE ridge of Ben Stack, named Leathad na Stioma on the 1:50,000 map. At first this is mainly heather and grass, but higher up rocks can be chosen as a pleasant staircase. A minor eminence at 540m followed by a short level stretch lead to the summit cone of steeper grass. The top is split by a landslip into two nearly level ribs, the trig point at 718m being on the southern one, and the cairn about 100 metres further on at the western end of the northern one. (3½km; 680m; 2h).

Looking westwards from the summit, the eye is drawn down to the low ground that extends to the distant and much-indented coastline; it is a landscape in which water seems to predominate over rock in intricate mixture.

An alternative route starts from the ruined cottage on the roadside at (265437) near Lochstack Lodge. Follow the stalker's path that climbs W until a small burn is reached at about 230m. Then strike SE up steeper broken slopes direct to the top. With conveniently placed cars, or a willingness to walk 5km along the road beside Loch Stack, a pleasant traverse of the hill can be made by the two routes described.

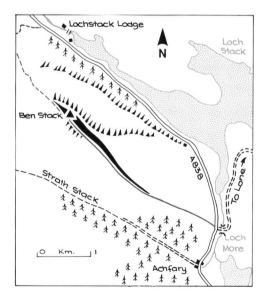

Foinaven from Arkle   *I.A. Robertson*

Foinaven (Ganu Mor); 911m; (OS Sheet 9; 317507); *white hill (big wedge)*
Arkle; 787m; (OS Sheet 9; 303462); *hill of the level top*
Meall Horn; 777m; (OS Sheet 9; 353449); *hill of the eagle*

This group of mountains lies at the heart of the Reay Forest in the angle of the A838 road east of Laxford Bridge, and holds some of the greatest climbing interest to be found in north-west Sutherland.

Foinaven is only little short of Munro height, and can be considered an outstanding mountain in any context. Its long narrow crest bearing many summits, the sweep of quartzite screes on its south-west flank, and the grandeur of its corries and spurs on the north-east flank all contribute to its superb mountain architecture. Arkle is composed of the same sharp angular quartzite as Foinaven, and is of a similar character, although a much smaller mountain covering only about half the extent. The walking on both these mountains is generally rough, and care is required on their summit ridges, particularly when the rocks are wet. Neither mountain is recommended for inexperienced hillwalkers in adverse weather or winter conditions.

Meall Horn, together with its adjacent hills, is much less impressive than Foinaven or Arkle. There are some very steep rock faces on its north-east side, but seen from the south-west it is rounded and lacking in any special character. It can be climbed as an extension to a day on either of the other two, but is only a short day's climb by itself.

The easiest approach to this group of hills is from Lone (309422) at the eastern end of Loch Stack. This remote cottage is reached by a private road which starts less than 1km north of the village of Achfary on the A838, and permission to drive along it is usually granted on enquiry at the estate office in Achfary. From Lone an excellent stalker's path that turns sharp left after a few metres (small cairn) leads in ½km through a gate between two remarkable boulders to a small pine plantation. Beyond it the path zig-zags up the steep hillside and then continues at an easy gradient beside the Allt Horn. The three mountains can be climbed from different points on this path.

For Foinaven take the path to its highest point at 510m (340460), then strike due N to Creag Dionard (778m) over grass, boulders and bare rock. The upper part tends to be featureless, in contrast to the rest of the mountain, and careful navigation is required in mist. The pink flowers of thrift and moss campion abound in June.

From Creag Dionard the broad stony ridge leads to Pt.806m, which is the start of the summit ridge proper. From there descend steeply to the next col, Cadha na Beucaich, over loose rocks and unstable scree, keeping close to the crest. Continue up the ridge, which is steep and narrow, or along its W flank to Pt.867m. From there the route continues NW over a minor top and along a much broader, but still quite rough, ridge with no obstacles to reach the highest point, Ganu Mor. There are two cairns about 100 metres apart. (From Lone: 11½km; 1110m; 4h 30min). One more top on the main Foinaven ridge can be added if desired; this is Ceann Garbh (901m), which is about 1km N along a mainly grassy ridge.

An alternative starting point for the ascent of Foinaven is the track which leaves the A838 road

Arkle from the north   *T.J. Ransley*

about ½km N of Gualin House (310570). Follow this track up Strath Dionard to its end and then aim for Cnoc a'Mhadaidh (589m). From there continue up steep broken ground to reach Ceann Garbh and the start of the main ridge. Given suitable transport arrangements, the two routes just described can be combined to give a splendid traverse of the mountain.

For the ascent of Arkle, leave the stalker's path

1½km beyond Lone at (321432) and strike N up mixed heather and stony slopes between two small burns until the flat top of Meall Aonghais is reached. Open stony slopes lead on to the start of the summit ridge at Pt.757m. The true summit is 1km further on at the end of a magnificent curving ridge, which is narrow and rough going for one short stretch along a natural pavement of quartzite. Any alternative to the

Meall Horn   *I. Waller*

route on the crest at the narrow section is on the W side. (From Lone: 5½km; 820m; 2h 40min).

The route to Meall Horn goes up the stalker's path to about 400m at (336453). From there bear E through a gap in a line of incipient crags, then NE up steep grass, ablaze with thrift in June, to the col on the broad summit ridge. From there the top is about ½km SE up easy ground. (From Lone: 6km; 740m; 2h 40min). The return route may be varied by descending the SW spur over Creachan Thormaid.

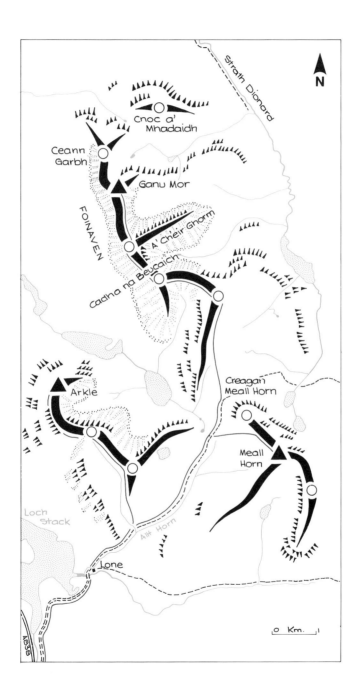

Meallan Liath Coire Mhic Dhughaill from Loch Stack   *J. Cleare/Mountain Camera*

Meallan Liath Coire Mhic Dhughaill; 801m; (OS Sheets 9,15 and 16; 357392); *grey hill of MacDougall's corrie*

This hill with its several radiating spurs and ridges lies to the north-west of Loch More, from where its summit appears as a broad dome. It is in the centre of the Reay Forest, and so is a good vantage point for appreciating the surrounding country. Although its northern corries are crag-lined, the southern slopes are more easy-angled and the walking everywhere is easy and pleasant, particularly on the summit ridge.

The best starting point is near Kinloch at the SE end of Loch More. Follow a private road to Aultanrynie, but just before reaching the house take a stalker's path up the hillside on the right. Ignore the left-hand branch and continue uphill by a series of easy zig-zags. The path bears right and ends at a small cairn at about 430m.

From there a broad undulating ridge gives easy walking over Meallan Liath Beag and up to the sum-mit ridge a short distance WSW of Carn Dearg (796m), which can be easily included in the traverse. Return along the summit ridge W, then NW and finally SW up the final slope where slabby stones make a pleas-ant staircase to the top of Meallan Liath Coire Mhic Dhughaill. (9½km; 850m; 3h 40min).

Leave the summit due S, bearing slightly left to avoid incipient crags and rough scree, and descend to the E of the flat peaty knoll of Meall Reinidh. From there cross the Allt an Reinidh at a convenient point to rejoin the stalker's path above the zig-zags. Con-tinue down the path to return to Kinloch.

An alternative approach to this hill can be made from Lone at the east end of Loch Stack. Follow the stalker's path E up the Abhainn an Loin and either climb the Sail Rac ridge or continue up to the Bealach na Feithe and climb S to Meall Garbh (752m). Both these routes lead quite directly to the summit of Meallan Liath Coire Mhic Dhughaill, and a pleasant traverse can be made by combining them.

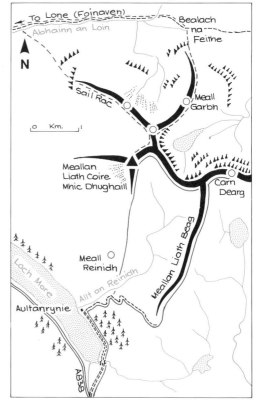

Ben Hee from Mudale   H.M. Brown

Ben Hee; 873m; (OS Sheet 16; 426339); *fairy hill*

Ben Hee lies on the eastern edge of the high ground in the Reay Forest, and when seen from the road in Glen Mudale to the west of Altnaharra it rises prominently above a moorland wilderness. From most viewpoints it appears as a rounded hill, and except for steeper ground in its east-facing corries, Ben Hee has mostly gentle gradients which give easy walking.

The most convenient approach is from the SW, leaving the A838 road at West Merkland. The private road leading N from there towards Ben Hee is usually barred by a locked gate, so walking must start from the A838. Follow the private road for 1½km to a stalker's path , marked by a small cairn, which leads off to the right about 50 metres before a wooden bridge. This path leads easily uphill on the S bank of the Allt a'Chruiteir into the corrie enclosed by the W slopes of Ben Hee. Continue, bearing more to the S, up to a col at 630m (416334), and from there NE up

the rock-strewn ridge to the summit. There is a small cairn with a trig point 20 metres SE of it. (5½km; 830m; 2h 40min).

The simplest return is by the route of ascent. Alternatively one can go W along the broad ridge leading to Sail Garbh and descend SW from there to rejoin the outward route, but the going is rather rough.

A traverse of the hill over its unnamed NE top can be made by continuing along the private road to the historic Bealach nam Meirleach *(robbers' pass)*. A path, shown on the 1:50,000 map, branches off SE between Loch an t-Seilg and Loch an Aslaird. Follow it and climb the NW flank of Ben Hee, passing N of a small hidden lochan, to reach the 850m NE top. From there traverse SW along a well-defined ridge, passing an obvious area of old landslips on the E flank, to reach the summit. Descend by the route of ascent described above.

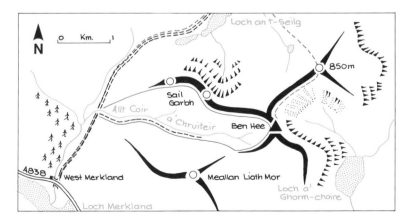

Cranstackie and Beinn Spionnaidh from Loch Eriboll   H.M. Brown

Cranstackie; 800m; (OS Sheet 9; 351556); *rugged hill*
Beinn Spionnaidh; 772m; (OS Sheet 9; 362573); *hill of strength*

These twins, rising east of the A838 road from Rhiconich to Durness, and west of Loch Eriboll, lie in the northern reaches of the Reay Forest. Not only is Beinn Spionnaidh the most northerly Corbett, but the two hills together form the most northerly high ground of any consequence in Britain. From the shores of Loch Eriboll they rise in interminably long and featureless slopes, which are afforested at lower levels. The southerly extension of Cranstackie falls in very steep, rocky slopes into Strath Dionard, thus leaving the western flank as that of most interest for the hillwalker.

The walking on these two hills is pleasant and undemanding, while in common with all the isolated mountains of Sutherland the views are extensive. In favourable conditions Orkney can be seen to the north-east across the Pentland Firth.

Start the ascent from Carbreck on the A838 road (333593), and proceed for 2km along the private road to the shepherd's house at Rhigolter. From there bear SE up steep grassy slopes into the high corrie between the two hills, and reach the col between them at 550m. Cranstackie can be climbed directly up its well-defined NE ridge from this col. (5½km; 750m; 2h 30min).

Return to the col and continue up the broader SW ridge of Beinn Spionnaidh, where the trig point stands at the N end of the short summit ridge. (7½km; 970m; 3h 20min). Descend by the WNW ridge and leave it at a convenient point before incipient crags are reached to drop down steep slopes back to Rhigolter.

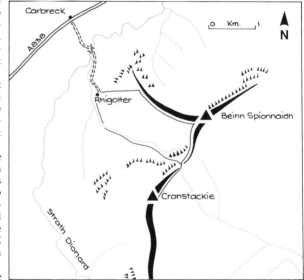

Ben Loyal seen across the Kyle of Tongue   H.M. Brown

Ben Loyal; 764m; (OS Sheet 10; 578489); *elm tree hill*

Ben Loyal lies about 7km south of the village of Tongue and 4km west of Loch Loyal. The fame of this mountain as one of the finest in Scotland is well-deserved. Its isolated position and striking appearance more than compensate for its lack of height, which is only just sufficient to justify its Corbett status. The striking outline of its four granite peaks is best seen across the Kyle of Tongue, but the formidable appearance of these peaks belies their difficulty, and the traverse of the mountain is a delightfully easy walk.

Ben Loyal is almost invariably climbed from the north, for that route shows the best of the mountain. The alternative approach from the east (starting from Loch Loyal) is dull by comparison and the ground on that side is often boggy and wet.

Leave Tongue by the minor road which goes S to the farm of Ribigill (583538), where a car can be left. A track, wide at first then narrowing to a footpath, continues due S to the deserted shepherd's cottage of Cunside. Head towards Sgor Chaonasaid and bear leftwards to climb steep grass and heather slopes to the E of the rocky prow of this peak. From the bold, well-rounded summit rocks of Sgor Chaonasaid (708m) the broad ridge continues due S to the main summit, An Caisteal, in 1km. The rocks of the intervening Sgor a'Bhatain (700m) are easily bypassed on their E side, and the granite tor of An Caisteal should be ascended and descended on the W side. (6km; 710m; 2h 40min).

To complete the traverse continue due S from An Caisteal over Pt.741m by a well-defined but easy grass ridge. The spur which juts out NW from this point to Sgor a'Chleirich (642m) is not a suitable route of descent, for the W prow of that peak is very steep and rocky. Continue S to Carn an Tionail (714m) and from there descend grassy slopes W towards the prominent conical Pt.568m, which is the right-hand summit

of Ben Loyal as seen from the Kyle of Tongue. Go down the Allt Fhionnaich to about 400m and then go N round the W flank of Pt.568m, traversing along convenient deer tracks and gradually descending to about 350m until a little stream can be followed down to the Coille na Cuile. Descend through this wood and once clear of the trees, at a height of about 100m, walk back to Cunside below the NW slopes of Ben Loyal.

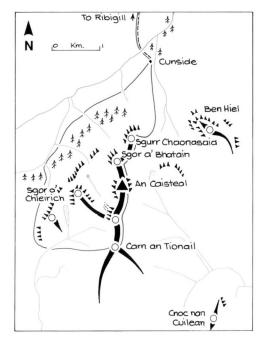

Ben Griam Mor and Ben Griam Beg from the Kinbrace road   *H.M. Brown*

Ben Griam Mor; 592m; (OS Sheets 10 and 17; 806389); *big dark hill*
Ben Griam Beg; 580m; (OS Sheets 10 and 17; 832412); *little dark hill*

These rounded sandstone hills stand 3½km apart among the headwaters of the River Helmsdale and the Halladale River, some 10km north-west of Kinbrace. Ben Griam Beg is noted for having on its summit the remains of the highest hill fort in Scotland, consisting of a thick stone wall enclosing an area of about 150 metres by 60 metres. On the south flank there are also the remains of other walls and walled enclosures which suggest that the fort may have been part of a larger occupied area.

Although an approach to these hills can be made by leaving the A897 road near Balloch Cottage and following the private road to Greamachary and onwards NW over boggy ground to Ben Griam Beg, a better route starts from the B871 road at a small quarry (786397) about 5km north of Badanloch Lodge.

Start along an angler's path heading N towards Loch Coire nam Mang across the moorland below the W flank of Ben Griam Mor. In about 1km leave the path and choose the best line E to reach the crest of the NW shoulder of Ben Griam Mor below the prominent tier of sandstone which extends SE below the upper slopes. Continue up the crest of the NW ridge where the sandstone outcrop presents no difficulty and onwards over stony ground to the summit. (3km; 430m; 1h 30min).

Descend the NE ridge of Ben Griam Mor, keeping to the crest to avoid sandstone outcrops on its NW flank. Cross flat boggy ground near the S end of Loch Druim a'Chliabhain and climb NE up the broad grassy slopes of Ben Griam Beg, keeping above the sandstone outcrops overlooking the loch. Steeper rocky heath-clad slopes lead to the summit past the hill fort and other remains. (6½km; 780m; 2h 50min).

Return by descending to the S end of Loch Druim a'Chliabhain and then go W below the N side of Ben Griam Mor to reach Loch Coire nam Mang and the angler's path back to the B871 road.

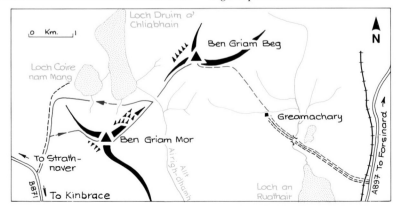

Morven   *H.M. Brown*

Morven; 706m; (OS Sheet 17; 005286); *big hill*
Scaraben; 626m; (OS Sheet 17; 067268); *divided hill*

Morven is the highest hill in Caithness, and it is easily seen from as far away as the south side of the Moray Firth, its isolated position and steep conical shape being very distinctive.

The best route to Morven starts at Braemore, reached by road from the A9 at Dunbeath. Park at the bridge (073304) and continue past Braeval and W along a track below Maiden Pap (484m) to reach Corrichoich. Continue up the river for ½km to a grassy knoll on which is sited the remains of an ancient wheelhouse. From there head SW over rough moorland to the saddle E of Morven. A steep and rough ascent of 400m over heather and scree, passing S of a rocky bluff, leads to the summit. (7km; 560m; 2h 30min). On a clear day the views extend as far as Orkney, where the Old Man of Hoy can just be seen. The best return is by the same route, although the very

fit might elect to traverse the rough intervening hills and moorland to Scaraben. The ascent of this hill is, however, better done as a separate walk from Braemore.

Scaraben is a long quartzite ridge with three very distinctive whitish stony summits. The starting point for this hill is also at Braemore. Cross the bridge and follow a track SE. After about 1km leave the track and head S over rough moorland towards East Scaraben (590m), which is reached in 3km over gradually steepening ground. Continue WSW along the ridge to reach the main summit. (5km; 630m; 2h 10min). Finally, West Scaraben (600m) can be reached in a further 1½km. From there descend NE over the moors to return to Braemore, or head N over rough boggy ground to climb Maiden Pap and drop down to the track on its N side.

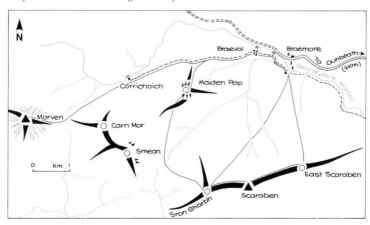

In the Rhum Cuillin, looking down Glen Dibidil to Eigg with Ainshval on the right   J. Cleare/Mountain Camera

SECTION 17

The Islands

Goatfell from Brodick pier   *G.S. Johnstone*

Goatfell; 874m; (OS Sheet 69; 991415); *hill of wind*

This splendid hill, Arran's highest and one of the best-known in Scotland, lies 6½km NNW of Brodick pier, and it contributes much of the famous silhouette of Arran seen from the mainland. From its summit three ridges radiate: the south ridge is about 1km long and rather attractive, but merges with the lower bouldery hillside; the east ridge is well-defined, its upper part being the line of the Tourist Route to the summit; the finest ridge runs north to North Goatfell and beyond to the superb little peak of Cioch na h-Oighe before dropping to Glen Sannox.

The Tourist Route, by which the ascent is most commonly made, begins at Cladach, 3½km from Brodick pier and a short distance SW of Brodick Castle. A private road starts from there, going first left, then right, passing through the castle grounds and a forested area. After 1km this road ends and a path leads NNW to reach the open hillside in ½km. It continues uphill and bears N up the SE corrie of Goatfell to reach the E ridge and the path which comes up from Corrie. The last ½km of this ridge is much steeper and quite rocky; a little scrambling is possible, but can be easily avoided by staying on the path. The summit has a trig point and a mountain indicator. (From Cladach: 4km; 870m; 2h 20min). The descent should be made by the same route unless a traverse is intended.

The route described above is by no means the most attractive, and two good alternatives may be mentioned. The ascent from Corrie follows a good path which leaves the A841 road just N of the bridge over the Corrie Burn and goes up this burn to about 400m before crossing it to reach the E ridge and join the Tourist Route.

The best route, but one which is much longer and involves some scrambling, is the complete traverse of the N ridge, starting at Sannox and traversing Cioch na h-Oighe, Mullach Buidhe and North Goatfell.

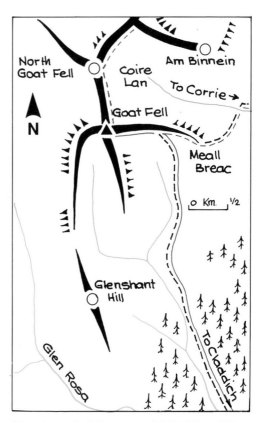

There is a path all the way, and if it is followed there are no undue difficulties, but this is only a route for experienced hillwalkers.

Beinn Tarsuinn; 826m; (OS Sheet 69; 959412); *transverse hill*
Cir Mhor; 799m (OS Sheet 69; 973432); *big comb*
Caisteal Abhail; 859m; (OS Sheet 69; 969444); *ptarmigan stronghold*

These three fine hills form, with the A'Chir ridge and the Witch's Step, most of the great central ridge of the Arran hills which extends from Beinn Nuis in the south to Suidhe Fhearghas in the north - 8km from top to top. The traverse of this ridge is recognised as a classic, considered by many to be the finest climb of its kind outwith Skye. It is assumed here that most climbers will want to do the ridge in its entirety, and the traverse is described accordingly. However, the individual hills may be climbed separately. The traverse is more usually done from south to north, starting at Brodick and returning there by bus from Sannox.

From Brodick follow the main road N through the village and 1½km further take the road to Black-waterfoot for a short distance, then the narrow road up Glen Rosa. Follow this to its end and continue past Glenrosa farm for almost 2km until a prominent path is seen on the hillside on the left, climbing diagonally upwards towards the Garbh Allt. Follow this path

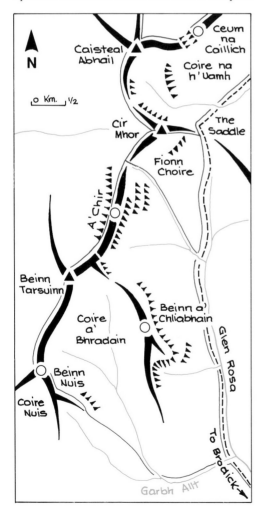

and cross the burn by the dam at a small reservoir to continue up a path, rather muddy in places, on the N side of the burn. A few hundred metres further on cross to the W side of the tributary which comes down from Coire a'Bhradain and in ½km a cairn is reached marking the start of the path up Beinn Nuis. The views at this point are very fine, with the Nuis precipice on the left, the great Meadow face of Beinn Tarsuinn dominating the centre and Beinn a'Chliabhain on the right. The path, faint but definite, crosses the corrie to reach the SE shoulder of Beinn Nuis, and zig-zags steeply upwards to reach the summit in little over 1km. (9km; 800m; 3h 20min).

The hardest work of the day is over, and the path continues N along the ridge to Beinn Tarsuinn. (10½km; 910m; 4h). The descent from this peak is straightforward in good weather, but requires care in mist. The ground is steep and craggy and the path, mainly on the W side of the ridge, twists and turns between the crags and boulders on its way down to the Bealach an Fhir-bhogha *(pass of the bowmen)*.

Just beyond this pass the path divides. Take the lower path, which makes a gradual descent on the W side of the A'Chir ridge below its slabby face, and with no great loss of height traverse N along this path to regain the ridge at the col between A'Chir and Cir Mhor. The higher path leads along the crest of the ridge to the summit of A'Chir and from there down to the col by a narrow rocky ridge which involves some difficult scrambling and one or two short passages of rock-climbing. This is the famous A'Chir Ridge, but its traverse is only for those with rock climbing ability.

From the col the magnificent views of the great Rosa Pinnacle on the south face of Cir Mhor compensate for the rather tedious climb up the SW ridge to the craggy summit of this hill. (13km; 1200m; 5h). The continuation to Caisteal Abhail goes along the Hunters' Ridge overlooking the magnificent Coire na h-Uamh at the head of Glen Sannox, possibly the finest corrie in Arran. Not far below the summit of Caisteal Abhail the famous springs (cairned) are passed, and a cluster of granite tors form the summit itself, the second one reached from the S being the highest. (14½km; 1400m; 5h 40min).

With this ascent the third of the day's Corbetts has been climbed, but the best way to Sannox is to continue along the ridge on the N side of Glen Sannox over two more minor summits. The path leads E for 1km down to the narrow gap below Ceum na Caillich *(the witch's step)*. To avoid a direct climb up the rocks ahead, descend the gully on the N side of the gap for about 15m to an obvious path on the right. Follow this round to rejoin the ridge beyond the steep summit rocks of Ceum na Caillich. Continue NE along the broad ridge over the top of Suidhe Fhearghas and for a further 1km to the end of the ridge. Just short of this point an obvious path zig-zags steeply down the N side towards North Glen Sannox. It meets a horizontal path coming from the W, and this is followed E to its end near old barytes mine workings and the road to Sannox.

Cir Mhor from the south   *G.E. Little*

As mentioned previously, separate ascents of the three hills may be made. The following are brief notes of the recommended routes:-

Beinn Tarsuinn. Follow the route described above by Glen Rosa, the Garbh Allt, Coire a'Bhradain and Beinn Nuis.

Cir Mhor. Follow the route described above as far as the foot of the Garbh Allt. Continue up the path in Glen Rosa either to The Saddle or the A'Chir-Cir Mhor col, and climb the hill from either of these cols. Alternatively, from Sannox by the path up Glen Sannox to The Saddle.

Caisteal Abhail. Climb the NE ridge over Suidhe Fhearghas and past Ceum na Caillich, thus reversing the route described above. Alternatively and more easily, go up North Glen Sannox and climb the N ridge of Caisteal Abhail on the W side of Coire na Ceum.

Cir Mhor and Caisteal Abhail from Goatfell   *G.E. Little*

Beinn Bharrain from the west   *W.M.M. Wallace*

Beinn Bharrain; 721m; (OS Sheet 69; 902428); *barren hill*

This is the highest of the western group of Arran hills, and lies 3½km ESE of the Post Office in the centre of Pirnmill. The name Beinn Bharrain is given to the whole twin-topped hill, but its higher top is also known as Mullach Buidhe. The slightly lower southwest summit is 1km away. Both summits have well-defined parallel ridges running NNW which enclose a rather attractive secluded corrie, the Coire Roinn. While it cannot rival the craggy grandeur of the eastern hills, the discerning climber will consider Beinn Bharrain to be worth a visit. It has a quiet charm of its own and a splendid isolation, with fine views across the Kilbrannan Sound to Kintyre, Islay and Jura, and of course over Loch Tanna to the eastern hills of Arran.

At the starting point at the Post Office in Pirnmill parking space is usually available. Next door is an excellent little tea-room open all year. Immediately to its north a rough farm road leads up the hill past some houses. It soon bends left, then turns right and after about 100 metres turns sharp left again towards a farm. At that point leave the road, walk past a gate on the right and a rather muddy path will be seen ahead. It leads into a sparsely wooded area of hillside through which the Allt Gobhlach flows down from Beinn Bharrain. The path follows the N side of this burn past an attractive waterfall and higher up past a gorge. Cross the burn and head SSE along an indistinct path across rather boggy ground towards the foot of the ridge on the

W side of Coire Roinn. Once on this ridge, the path improves and leads easily to the south-west summit of Beinn Bharrain. From there continue NE for 1km to reach the highest point. (4½km; 740m; 2h 20min).

An alternative and more attractive route of ascent is up the ridge on the E side of Coire Roinn. It is narrower and more rocky than the ridge on the W side, and there is some unavoidable scrambling near the top similar to that encountered on other Arran ridges such as North Goatfell or Cioch na h-Oighe.

The descent may be made by the route of ascent. Alternatively, continue NE along the ridge round the head of Glas Choirein to Beinn Bhreac (711m) and descend its W slopes towards Pirnmill.

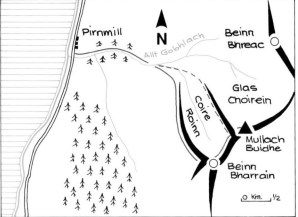

Beinn an Oir from Beinn Shiantaidh   *I.A. Robertson*

Beinn an Oir; 785m; (OS Sheet 61; 498749); *hill of gold*

Beinn an Oir is the central, highest and finest peak of the renowned Paps of Jura. These three hills are in the southern part of the island, the other two being Beinn Shiantaidh *(holy hill)* and Beinn a'Chaolais *(hill of the narrows)*. They are high domes separated by deep bealachs, and their island situation makes them prominent features of the western seaboard of Argyll. Access to Jura is by ferry from Kennacraig on the mainland, and bicycles are useful for transport on the island.

The best starting point for the ascent of Beinn an Oir, and the other two Paps, is on the A846 road near the bridge over the Corran River at (543720). Climb NW past a plantation and over a shoulder to reach the Corran River about 1km below Loch an t-Siob. Continue past the loch to reach steeper slopes to the SE of Beinn an Oir. The ascent of this hill goes up the E face along a diagonal grassy rake that rises from S to N, enabling much of the rough quartzite boulders and scree that are characteristic of these hills to be avoided. The rake leads to the NE ridge, and the final climb up this ridge leads past two dry stone enclosures and along a stone pathway constructed by the Ordnance Survey during their early triangulation work. (6km; 770m; 2h 40min).

The traverse of the three Paps is a much longer expedition, but a classic. Using the same approach to Loch an t-Siob, climb Beinn Shiantaidh by its SE shoulder and descend the W ridge to the col from which the route described above leads to Beinn an Oir. Descend its S ridge, which calls for care, and climb Beinn a'Chaolais by its NE shoulder on unstable scree and, higher up, more pleasant mossy ground. Descend E to the col at (495733) and then NE to Gleann an t-Siob.

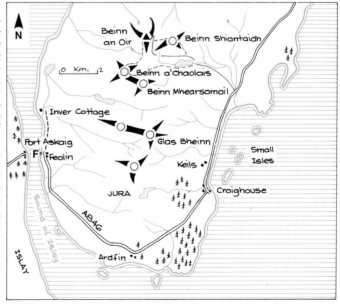

Mull hills from Duart Castle. Sgurr Dearg (left) and Dun da Ghaoithe   *J. Cleare/Mountain Camera*

Dun da Ghaoithe; 766m; (OS Sheet 49; 673362); *fort of the two winds*

This very attractive hill rises above Craignure on the island of Mull, and overlooks both the Sound of Mull and the Firth of Lorn. Access from the mainland is by the ferry from Oban to Craignure.

Direct access from the pier at Craignure to the open hillside above is restricted by trees, and the nearest open ground is about 2km north-west at Scallastle. From a point on the A849 road a few hundred metres beyond the bridge over the Scallastle River climb SW up the N side of the Allt an Dubh-choire. Continue up the broad ridge of Beinn Chreagach, gradually bearing S to reach the summit of Dun da Ghaoithe. (From Craignure pier: 6½km; 770m; 2h 50min). The views are possibly the best from any hill in Mull. The descent can be made by the E ridge which leads down to the upper edge of the forest. Go N along this edge

and cross the Allt an Dubh-choire to return to Scallastle.

An alternative descent route can be made by going along the level ridge SE to Mainnir nam Fiadh (754m) and then E along the ridge above Creag Dubh to the telecommunications mast on Maol nan Uan. From there follow the private access road down to the A849 road, which is reached about 2km S of Craignure pier.

It is possible to make a much longer traverse with the help of the bus service between Craignure and Tobermory. Leave the A849 road at Fishnish Bay and climb SW to Maol Buidhe, the NW point of the long ridge which extends for about 8km to Dun da Ghaoithe. This ridge proceeds over a series of progressively higher hills, with quite small drops between them, and gives a very fine high-level walk.

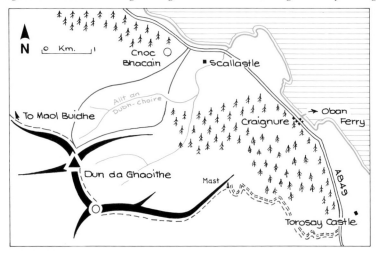

Beinn Talaidh from Glen Forsa   D. Green

Beinn Talaidh; 762m; (OS Sheet 49; 625347); *hill of happiness (* or *good pastures)*

The island of Mull has a complex volcanic history, with the centre of past activity situated in what is now hollow ground near Loch Ba. Beinn Talaidh forms part of the rim of hills surrounding this site. It is easily accessible from the A849 road from Craignure to Bunessan and the Iona ferry at the point where it passes the head of Glen Forsa. This point can be reached by bus from Craignure, there being services to Bunessan and Fionnphort which connect with the ferries between Craignure and Oban.

Leave the A849 road at (643329) and head NW towards the prominent col, the Mam Bhradhadail, or the shoulder of Maol nam Fiadh on the S ridge of Beinn Talaidh. From there climb NNW to the summit without difficulty. (2½km; 660m; 1h 40min).

An alternative approach to Beinn Talaidh is from the north, starting at Glenforsa airstrip 2km E of Salen. Go up the forestry road in Glen Forsa for 6km to Tomsleibhe and from there climb the long, easy-angled NNW ridge of the hill which leads directly to the summit. (9km; 760m; 3h 20min). A bicycle might be used with advantage up the long road in Glen Forsa to save over an hour's walking in each direction.

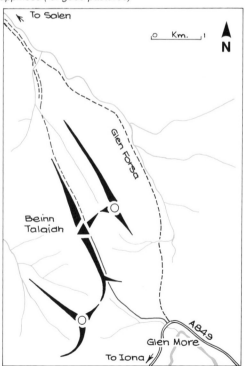

Askival from Ainshval   *J. Cleare/Mountain Camera*

Askival; 812m; (OS Sheet 39; 393952); *hill of ash trees*
Ainshval; 781m; (OS Sheet 39; 378944); possibly *hill of strongholds*

These two fine little mountains are the highest points of the Rhum Cuillin, a ridge of five very distinctive peaks that bear comparison with their larger and more celebrated neighbours across the Cuillin Sound in Skye. The Black Cuillin of Skye may be higher, more numerous and more starkly rocky, but the Rhum peaks have equal character and individuality. The traverse of these five peaks is comparable with the traverse of the Arran peaks described earlier in this section. Both are mountaineering expeditions of exceptional character and beauty.

The island of Rhum is a National Nature Reserve under the control of the Nature Conservancy Council, and climbing on the island can only be done with permission from the Council's Chief Warden who is resident there. (Address: The White House, Isle of Rhum. Telephone: 0687 2026). Access to Rhum from Mallaig is by Caledonian MacBrayne Passenger Ferry, four days per week. There are also sailings by Bruce Watt Cruises, Mallaig (Telephone: 0687 2233) and Arisaig Marine Ltd, Arisaig (Telephone: 06875 224). Accommodation in Rhum includes camping at Loch Scresort where the boat arrives, the bothy at Dibidil and self-catering and full board accommodation at Kinloch Castle and in one or two houses nearby.

Although Askival and Ainshval are but two of the five main peaks of the Rhum Cuillin, they can be climbed as part of a complete ridge traverse almost as easily as by separate ascents, and the traverse is such a fine expedition that it will be described. It can be shortened at one or two points. Kinloch (or the Loch Scresort camp site) is probably a more popular starting point than Dibidil bothy, although the latter has the advantage of being very close to the mountains.

From Loch Scresort go through the grounds of Kinloch Castle and take the path SW up Coire Dubh. At the head of the corrie this path goes up gravelly slopes to reach the broad Bealach Bairc-mheall. Go E then SE up the broad ridge to Hallival (723m), the upper part being quite steep and rocky. This is the first of the five main peaks on the ridge, and there is a splendid view towards Askival, the next one. Descend S, steeply at first down two or three short rock steps, then easily along a grassy ridge to the col. The N ridge of Askival is rocky and narrow, but quite easy until one reaches the Askival Pinnacle, a steep and narrow prow which can be climbed by a moderately difficult pitch on its W side. The Pinnacle can, however, be easily avoided by a traverse on the E side of the ridge to reach steep but easy rocks leading to the summit. (5½km; 940m; 2h 50min).

Descend the steep W ridge of Askival to the Bealach an Oir (450m). At this point there is a choice. The five-peak traverse goes up the E ridge of Trallval to its twin rocky summits (702m), and then makes a steep and rocky descent from there to the Bealach an Fhuarain (510m). This is a worthwhile diversion, for Trallval is a fine peak, but it is perfectly easy to avoid it by an almost horizontal traverse from the Bealach an Oir to the Bealach an Fhuarain across grassy slopes below the rocky SE face of Trallval.

From the Bealach an Fhuarain avoid the lower rocky buttress of Ainshval's N ridge by a rising traverse to the right (W) on scree and broken rocks to reach a level shoulder on the ridge. The upper part of the ridge is also rocky and rather narrow, and the scramble up the crest can be avoided on the E side by a narrow path which climbs upwards across the screes just below the rocky crest and emerges onto the

Sgurr nan Gillean (left) and Ainshval from the Dibidil path

D.J. Bennet

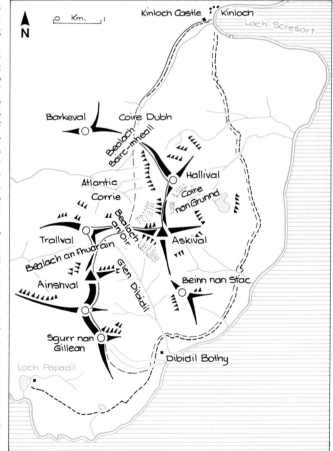

flat grassy summit close to the cairn of Ainshval. (Excluding Trallval: 7½km; 1220m; 3h 50min. Including Trallval: 8km; 1410m; 4h 10min).

At this point, having climbed Rhum's two Corbetts, the quickest way back to Kinloch is to return to the Bealach an Fhuarain by the N ridge of Ainshval, traverse to the Bealach an Oir and from there make a long traverse N across the head of the Atlantic Corrie, well below the steep rocky W face of Askival. This traverse leads easily across grassy slopes, with some descent and reascent, to the Bealach Bairc-mheall, from where the path leads down to Kinloch. The return from Ainshval takes about 2½ to 3 hours.

The fifth of the Rhum Peaks, Sgurr nan Gillean (764m), can be reached from Ainshval by an easy walk along a broad grassy ridge over an intervening peak. Sgurr nan Gillean is a superb summit, the remotest in Rhum, but a long way from Kinloch. The return may be made by Ainshval and the route described above, or by descending to Dibidil and walking back to Loch Scresort by the path above the eastern coastline. The latter route is no shorter, and involves first a steep descent S from Sgurr nan Gillean to avoid the very rocky slopes to the E of the summit.

Whichever route one choses, the long return to Kinloch will be a fine end to a memorable day.

Ainshval (left) and Trallval from the west ridge of Askival   A. O'Brien

Looking towards Eigg from the summit of Trallval   D.J. Bennet

The approach to An Sgurr from the east   G.E. Little

An Sgurr (Eigg); 393m; (OS Sheet 39; 463847); *the peak*

As seen from the Morar coastline, the Cuillin of Rhum and Skye compete to hold the eye, but fail; it is the striking form of Eigg that is the focus of attention. An Sgurr, at 393m, is not a hill but a mountain, yet thankfully it does not feature in any of those lists where height is the sole gauge of status. This massive cockscomb of primitive pitchstone, crowning one of the most beautiful islands in the Hebridean seas, is quite without equal, its summit a 100m high tower of Dolomitic steepness.

From the pier at Galmisdale it is An Sgurr that totally dominates the landscape. A road, track and then a path lead up through deep, wild garlic scented woods, over an open field, past a white house and finally out across the wide brown moor towards the great pillar. Necks crane in disbelief as one skirts to the north of the dark ramparts along a path worn in the softer basalts which have been eroded round the base of the monolith. At the first obvious break a diagonal path leads through a rocky gateway onto a grassy col. A switchback and short scramble give access to the spine of An Sgurr where pitchstone columns have been weathered into a cobblestone pavement. Walk across the rooftop and look out over the emerald wedge of Muck and across the sparkling sea to the high peaks of the mainland. The trig point is perched on the very edge of the summit, one of the truly magical places in the Western Isles.

The summit of An Sgurr   A. O'Brien

Garbh-bheinn, Clach Glas and Bla Bheinn from the west   G.S. Johnstone

Belig; 702m; (OS Sheet 32; 544240)
Garbh-bheinn; 806m; (OS Sheet 32; 531232); *rough hill*

Although the Isle of Skye is rightly renowned for The Cuillin, there are many other fine hills on the island, though they may be less starkly rocky and jagged than that celebrated range. This is very evident to anyone travelling along the road by Loch Ainort and looking towards the head of the loch; the hills which encircle it are an impressive sight with their contrasting dark gabbro cliffs and red screes. Belig, Garbh-bheinn, Marsco and Beinn Dearg all present a very obvious challenge to the hillwalker.

The traverse of Belig and Garbh-bheinn is a very pleasant short day which starts from the A850 road at the bridge over the Abhainn Ceann Loch Ainort. Go S across the rising grassy hillside aiming for the foot of the N ridge of Belig. A steeper rocky section of this ridge is best climbed on the left (E) and above it the climb continues up the narrow grassy crest to the sharply pointed summit of the hill. (2½km; 700m; 1h 40min).

Descend the WSW ridge which is steep and quite rocky, with rough bouldery scree and the remains of a well-built dry stone dyke. From the col at its foot, the Bealach na Beiste, start the long climb to Garbh-bheinn; this is easy going at first, then steeper scree and finally a pleasant narrow ridge ending right at the summit. (4km; 1050m; 2h 40min).

The return to Loch Ainort goes very easily down the N ridge, whose lower part below a grassy knoll (489m) is called the Druim Eadar Da Choire. There is a faint path in places, but the last kilometre is over rather rough peat and heather without much sign of a path.

Another very pleasant route to Garbh-bheinn is from the head of Loch Slapin up the SE ridge of Sgurr nan Each (716m). There is a good scramble along the rocky crest of this peak leading to the col at the foot of the SE ridge of Garbh-bheinn, which is also narrow and rocky, but quite easy.

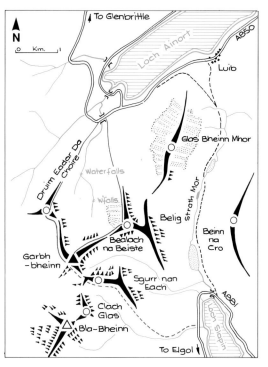

Glamaig from the west   H.M. Brown

Glamaig; 775m; (OS sheet 32; 514300); *greedy woman*

Glamaig is the highest of the Western Red Hills, or the Red Cuillin as they are also called to distinguish them from the Black Cuillin on the opposite side of Glen Sligachan. It rises as a great rounded cone directly above Loch Sligachan, its stark boldness both attractive and repulsive to those who would attempt its notorious screes. In 1899 Harkabir Thapa, a Gurkha soldier brought to Skye by the Himalayan explorer General Bruce, ran from Sligachan Hotel to the top in 37 minutes and down again in 18, a record not equalled since then.

There is no particular route up this hill which is best, but by taking care the worst of the screes can be avoided.

The most popular choice is to walk a short distance along the road from Sligachan towards Sconser and then climb the W shoulder of the hill. The highest point is called Sgurr Mhairi *(Mary's peak)*. (2½km; 780m; 2h).

As an alternative to descending by the route of ascent, one can traverse NE along the ridge to An Coileach (675m), enjoying the view of sea and mountain on the way, and descend NE then N to Sconser.

Glamaig can also be the starting or finishing point of a much longer traverse over the Red Cuillin. For example, having reached the summit one can descend SSE to the Bealach na Sgairde and climb steeply SE to reach the N end of the ridge leading to Beinn Dearg Mhor (732m). From there continue along the crest of the hills to Beinn Dearg Mheadhonach (652m) and return to Sligachan by the long, easy-angled ridge of Druim na Ruaige.

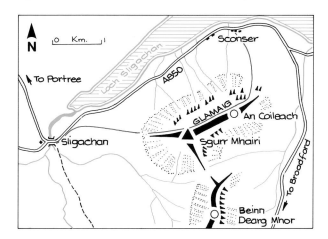

The rounded dome of Beinn na Caillich is prominent in this view of Skye from the mainland   D.J. Bennet

Beinn na Caillich; 732m; (OS Sheet 32; 601233); *hill of the old woman*
Beinn Dearg Mhor; *709m; (OS Sheet 32; 588228); big red hill*
Beinn Dearg Bheag; 584m; (OS Sheet 32; 593219); *little red hill*

The Eastern Red Hills are the the trio of steep hills which rise abruptly from low-lying moorland just west of Broadford. Being among the easternmost hills in Skye, they are prominent in views from the mainland, particularly from Kyle of Lochalsh, and they certainly dominate the view as one travels from there towards Broadford. Beinn na Caillich is the highest and dominant hill of the trio, more often admired than climbed, but its steep stony flanks are less arduous than one might expect from its appearance and the summit view is as fine as any in Skye. From it a pleasant horseshoe walk can be made round Coire Gorm over the other two hills in the group.

The usual starting point is at Coire-chat-achan, which can be reached by a path across the moor from the A881 road between Broadford and Torrin. The name commemorates the wild cats which may once have been there, but are now exterminated on Skye. Pennant in 1772 made the earliest recorded ascent of Beinn na Caillich from Coire-chat-achan; it was the first recorded ascent of any Skye peak. Dr Johnson, staying there, made a familiar-sounding remark: "The hill behind us we did not climb. The weather was rough and the height and steepness discouraged us".

Present-day hillwalkers should not be so easily discouraged. From the ruins of Coire-chat-achan head WNW up the steadily steepening hillside. Higher up large boulders lend themselves to a fast and easy ascent and one reaches the E shoulder of the hill not far from the grassy summit. It is reputed that a Norwegian princess is buried under the huge cairn. (3½km; 700m; 2h).

Continue W for the traverse round Coire Gorm over the tops of Beinn Dearg Mhor and Beinn Dearg Bheag. The former also has a large cairn and a grandstand view of Blaven's east face. A chaos of scree leads down to the Bealach Coire Sgreamhach between the two hills, and a twisting ridge continues to the substantial cairn on Beinn Dearg Bheag. From there the E ridge gives an easy descent, and when the Allt Beinn Deirge is reached it is less tedious to follow it to Coire-chat-achan than to strike directly across the rough heather to reach the road in Strath Suardal.

The circuit of the Eastern Red Hills is very much one to keep for a clear day, such as Pennant enjoyed, when he looked over the Black Cuillin and Red Cuillin and pictured them coloured by "the rage of fire".

Beinn na Caillich   *J. Crumley*

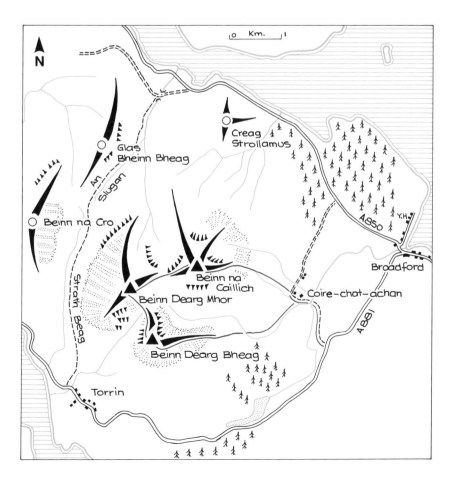

The Storr and The Old Man of Storr from Storr Lochs   *G.S. Johnstone*

Trotternish, the large north-eastern peninsula of Skye which reaches to the northernmost point of the island, has a backbone of hills which offers a long and classic traverse. The start and finish are at the two most interesting features of the area, The Storr in the south and The Quiraing in the north, and the walk from one to the other is in no way inferior to any day on the more famous Black Cuillin.

The twisting Trotternish escarpment in its entirety is nearly 30km long, constantly edged by sheer cliffs on the east , and rolling down in wind-swept grass slopes to the west. The complete walk from Portree to The Aird is a two-day venture. The following description is of a more feasible one-day journey which still entails 22km of walking, 1700m of climbing and may take 9 or 10 hours from end to end.

From Portree drive N on the A855 road, with its much photographed view of the Old Man of Storr beyond the Storr Lochs. Park at the end of Loch Leathan and walk up the edge of a forestry plantation to reach The Sanctuary of The Storr. A rising traverse from the corner of the plantation leads N to the famous Old Man of Storr and other strange pinnacles which are grouped below the vertical 200m cliffs of The Storr. The mountain flowers are a notable feature here and along the cliffs.

To reach the summit of The Storr, keep on traversing N until easy ground is reached and one can turn back along the cliff-top on the edge of Coire Scamadal to curve up to the 719m trig point, the highest summit of the walk. The views are fantastic and remain so throughout the day.

Drop NW to the Bealach a'Chuirn and

traverse the Norse-named Hartaval (668m) to the Bealach Hartaval. All the named passes on the ridge offer escape routes if need be. Many were regularly used by the population in centuries past. The walk, always edged by cliffs to the right (E) leads after 7km of dramatic bumps and dips to Beinn Edra (611m), the major peak of the middle section. A path and fence lead down to the Bealach Uige, once an important pass. There is a steep bluff to pull up to reach Bioda Buidhe where the landscape below suddenly takes on an element of the weird and wonderful, a landscape full of towers and lochans.

The Old Man of Storr   *D.J. Bennet*

The Quiraing   *D.J. Bennet*

The continuation N leads to the Bealach Ollasgairte, the only pass crossed by a road, the narrow one which links Staffin and Uig. From the top of the pass one can climb Meall na Suiramach (543m), the most northerly hill on the Trotternish ridge, but this bypasses the extraordinary, unique world of The Quiraing. This should on no account be missed, so walk down the road towards Staffin past the hairpins and follow the path leading NE gradually uphill towards the cliffs. The Quiraing means *fold* or *pen*, and imaginatively describes the towers, pinnacles, gullies and cliffs which enclose The Prison. The slender spire guarding the most obvious gully is The Needle, and scrambling upwards past it one comes to The Table, a perfectly horizontal platform of grass in the centre of The Prison. The Quiraing is certainly a place of atmosphere, a stark contrast to the view down to the comfortable crofting communities and turquoise waters of Staffin Bay.

The weird landscape of both The Storr and The Quiraing is due to land-slipping, and a descent from The Quiraing NE by Loch Fada and Loch Hasco towards Flodigarry takes one through country more reminiscent of Iceland than Scotland.

Those who feel that the long traverse described above is over-strenuous can savour the best of Trotternish by making separate visits to The Storr and The Quiraing.

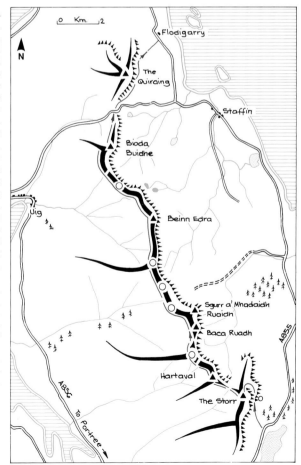

Mulla-fo-dheas and Clisham from the south   G.S. Johnstone

Clisham; 799m; (OS Sheet 14; 155073)

The central group of hills in North Harris, situated between Glen Meavaig and the A859 road from Tarbert to Stornoway, includes the highest peak of the Western Isles, Clisham. The massif of this mountain forms a prominent horseshoe ridge of summits enclosing Loch Vistern at the head of the Scaladale River. Seen from the south, Clisham is a finely shaped hill with the edge of the steep crag of Aonaig Mhor well defined on its north flank. Further west the shapely ridge that connects Clisham to Mulla-fo-dheas shows up clearly above the broken tiers of rock

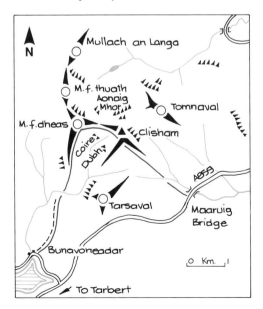

at the head of Coire Dubh.

The climb to the summit of Clisham is perfectly straightforward from almost any point on the A859 road which passes round the south and east sides of the hill, reaching a height of almost 200m. The nearest approach is from the bridge over the Maaruig River (173058). There is no clear path from there, but by following the river for ½km, skirting round the N side of Sron Carsaclett, the SE flank of Clisham and then its SE ridge are easily climbed. The final ridge is quite narrow, its width being almost fully taken up by the large cairn surrounding the trig point. (3km; 610m; 1h 50min).

The summit of Tomnaval (552m) can be easily reached from the same starting point and included in the ascent. From the grassy bealach between the two hills the slope to the summit of Clisham is steep and stony.

If suitable transport arrangements can be made, Clisham can be traversed over Mulla-fo-dheas (743m) to the long-since derelict whaling station at Bunavoneadar. The short summit ridge of Clisham runs from SE to NW, with a short rocky N ridge running out to Aonaig Mhor which calls for care in mist. From the NW end of the summit ridge a rounded stony slope drops steeply due W to a long grassy bealach, beyond which a short easy ascent leads to the eastern subsidiary summit of Mulla-fo-dheas, called An t-Isean on the 1:25,000 map. Beyond this small peak the ridge narrows again, dipping to a small green and bouldery col and then rising to the rocky main summit of Mulla-fo-dheas.

From there the descent goes down the S shoulder, Mo Buidhe, and across the Abhainn Horabray to join a path on the W side of Creag Ghreine-brigh leading down to Bunavoneadar.

Looking south-east from Ullaval to (l to r) Clisham, Mulla-fo-dheas and Uisgnaval Mor   D.J. Fabian

Uisgnaval Mor; 729m; (OS Sheets 13 and 14; 121086)
Teilesval; 697m; (OS Sheets 13 and 14; 125091)
Stulaval; 579m; (OS Sheets 13 and 14; 134124)

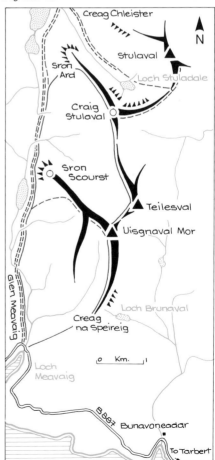

To the west of the Clisham horseshoe and the Abhainn Loch a'Sgail, in the centre of the North Harris hills, is a small group of which Uisgnaval Mor is the highest. It forms a twin summit with Teilesval, its close neighbour to the north-east. The pair show up well, appearing as one hill when seen from the south, and lying directly west of the deep glen formed by the Abhainn Loch a'Sgail and the Allt a'Sgail, the latter becoming the River Langavat which flows north into Loch Langavat.

The long SSW ridge of Uisgnaval Mor gives a very pleasant way of ascending this group of hills from the head of Loch Meavaig, heading for the shoulder above Creag na Speireig and keeping above the small line of bouldery crags to the N of Loch Brunaval. This ridge leads direct to Uisgnaval Mor (4km; 720m; 2h 10min). Teilesval is reached ½km further. The summits are stony, but pleasant grassy ridges run out NW from Uisgnaval Mor to the steep headland of Sron Scourst, and N from Teilesval round the head of Coire Sgurra-breac. An easy descent can be made SW from the col ½km SE of Sron Scourst to Loch Scourst in Glen Meavaig.

From the summit of Teilesval the grassy ridge above Coire Sgurra-breac leads NNW to Craig Stulaval and Sron Ard, from where a pleasant descent can be made SW to Glen Meavaig. Alternatively, from Craig Stulaval one can go along the grassy E ridge above the north-facing crags to reach the col at the head of Glen Stuladale. From there the ascent to Stulaval is easy, and the return should be made to the col from where the descent past Loch Stuladale is straightforward. From the foot of Glen Stuladale a track S through Glen Meavaig makes for an easy return to the B887 road at Loch Meavaig, the whole round trip from there taking 6 or 7 hours.

Oreval (left) and Sron Scourst from Glen Meavaig   *D. Scott*

Oreval; 662m; (OS Sheets 13 and 14; 084100)
Ullaval; 659m; (OS Sheets 13 and 14; 086114)
Tirga Mor; 679m; (OS Sheets 13 and 14; 055115)

The western hills in North Harris are grouped around Loch Chliostair, Oreval and Ullaval to its east and Tirga Mor to its west. It is quite possible to climb all three hills in a single day, but it may be more pleasant to do them in two separate walks.

Oreval and Ullaval are the two high points of a 7km ridge which extends north from West Loch Tarbert at Soay Sound to the great overhanging cliff of Sron Ulladale, which is the most awe-inspiring crag in the British Isles. The traverse of this ridge, including a visit to look at, but not climb, the great overhang of Sron Ulladale ranks second only to the traverse of the Clisham horseshoe in the Harris hills.

From the hamlet of Cliasmol on the B887 road climb Cleiseval (511m) by its SW shoulder, just to the W of the short low-lying crags of Mulla Cleiseval. This gives a pleasant line of ascent to the stony summit, which as might be expected is a fine viewpoint. Crags drop steeply to its N, as well as eastwards from the NE shoulder which is descended to reach a bouldery bealach. From there a stony and grassy ridge veers N to the grassy intermediate summit of Bidigi (500m). Apart from this short stony descent from Cleiseval, the rounded ridges and shallow bealachs of the group, extending N across Oreval, Ullaval and Muladal (454m) to the summit of Sron Ulladale (442m) give easy walking on grass, and the ascent from the road to Sron Ulladale takes only about 3 hours.

Descend by the E flank of Sron Ulladale and view its awe-inspiring cliff above Loch Ulladale. It is seen at its best from the western slopes of Mullach na Reidheachd to its NE, or from Tirga Mor to its SW. The return to the B887 road from Loch Ulladale can be made along the excellent path up Glen Ulladale

and over the pass to Loch Ashavat and Loch Chliostair. From the dam at the foot of Loch Chliostair a private road leads down to the B887 at Amhuinnsuidhe, 1½km from Cliasmol.

An alternative route of return from Loch Ulladale is to take the glen running SE from the loch, over the bealach N of Gormul Mor and descend from the small lochan there to Loch Voshimid and the private road down Glen Meavaig.

Tirga Mor is the highest and most rugged of the western group of North Harris hills. It towers above Loch Chliostair, but is awkward to ascend from there except by its relatively steep and slabby SE ridge which is approached from the dam at the S end of Loch Chliostair. Grassy gullies between slabs make this ridge straightforward. It forms the SW edge of the SE corrie of Tirga Mor in which is hidden Loch Maolaig.

The quickest ascent of Tirga Mor from the B887 road is to take the private road leading to Loch Chliostair as far as the bridge over the River Leosaid, then branch W onto the path up Glen Leosaid. After 1km strike due N up the steep but straightforward S flank of Tirga Mor. (4km; 680m; 2h 10min). In many ways, however, a more pleasant though longer route is to continue along the Glen Leosaid path for a further 1km as far as Gill Avay and climb the shallow glen there to the bealach between Tirga Mor and Ceartaval above the attractive Loch Braigh Bheagarais. From this bealach both hills can be easily reached.

If one wants to combine the ascent of Tirga Mor with Oreval and Ullaval in a single day, the connection is made at Loch Ashavat. Returning from Sron

Looking north across the sands at Luskentyre to (l to r) Tirga Mor, Oreval, Sron Scourst and Uisgnaval Mor   D. Scott

Ulladale, one comes to a fisherman's bothy at the N end of this loch. From there climb W up steep slopes to Tirga Beag and continue up the NE shoulder of Tirga Mor. Descend from there either by the SE ridge or down the S flank, reversing the routes described above.

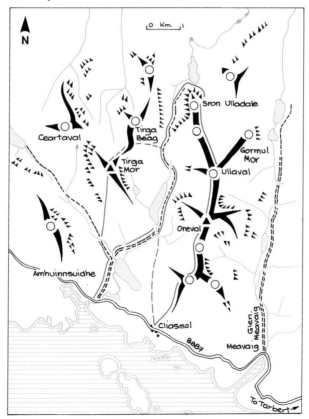

Hecla, Ben Corodale and Beinn Mhor from the west across the machair of South Uist   *G.E. Little*

Beinn Mhor; 620m; (OS Sheet 22; 809311); *big hill*
Hecla; 606m; (OS Sheet 22; 826345); *hooded or shrouded hill*
Ben Corodale; 527m; (OS Sheet 22;820329)

These three hills form a group lying from north to south along the east coast of South Uist. They are a shapely trio, especially when seen from the northwest, and they are by far the most important hills in the Outer Hebrides outwith Harris and Lewis.

The round of the three hills in either direction makes a fine excursion with about 1200m of climbing. If transport can be arranged, the traverse of the three summits from Loch Skipport to Loch Eynort makes an excellent and memorable day requiring 6 to 8 hours. Indeed, the most pleasing ascent of Hecla is by its long north-east shoulder, especially if a landing by boat can be arranged on the Ornish headland from one of the exquisite rocky bays, Caolas Mor or Caolas Beg, on the south shore of Loch Skipport.

However, for those without the assistance of a boat, the best place at which to start and finish the traverse of these three hills is the point on the A865 road where a peat-cutter's track heads south-east across the moor at Loch Dobhrain. From there the approach to Beinn Mhor is surprisingly dry. Aim for the NW shoulder, called Maola Breac, which leads first to a small subsidiary NW peak (608m) marked by a stone-circle cairn. From there a narrow but easy grassy and rocky ridge leads to the trig point of Beinn Mhor. The final section of the ridge has several bouldery outcrops which in mist produce the impression of a few false summits (5½km; 550m; 2h 10min).

To continue the traverse return to the 608m NW top and a short distance beyond it go down E on a shoulder leading to the Bealach Hellisdale. This shoulder is broken and rocky and the descent requires care in mist, especially on the section directly above the bealach where there are several short vertical steps.

From there the ascent of the S ridge of Ben Corodale is straightforward, with only a small loss of height at the almost level Feith-bealach.

Ben Corodale has a bouldery summit and a steep and rocky, though short, NW ridge. This ridge goes out towards the bealach at the heads of Glen Usinish and Glen Dorchay. and just below the summit it has a deep cleft dividing it into two moderately difficult buttresses. The descent from the summit requires care in mist to avoid these buttresses by seeking out a short scree gully which drops NE from the ridge some 50 metres E of the summit cairn. This gully leads to a sloping grassy shelf and thence to the bealach from where the ascent to Hecla is steep but otherwise straightforward. (11km; 1090m; 4h 20min). The summit of Hecla is grassy, but the N side is a mass of fractured rock, mostly Lewisian gneiss. The compass is unreliable there. The return to the road may be made by retracing one's steps to the col and descending the spur of Maoladh Creag nam Fitheach across Glen Dorchay to take a fairly direct line back to the starting point near Loch Dobhrain.

If Beinn Mhor alone is to be ascended, the quickest way is from Arinambane on the shore of Loch Eynort to its SW, but this is not a particularly rewarding climb. A good path (unmarked on the 1:50,000 map) passes S then E of Loch nam Faoileann for more than 1km to the NE corner of the loch. From there the going NE is boggy until the heathery slopes of the Bealach Crosgard are reached, from where the ridge to the summit is mostly grassy. This route provides an easy descent from Beinn Mhor following a traverse from Hecla or Ben Corodale.

An approach to the NE shoulder of Hecla can be

Hecla (left) and Ben Corodale from the north-west peak of Beinn Mhor   D.J. Fabian

made from the ruined shielings on the S side of Loch Skipport (833382), but there are no paths or tracks and the going is very rough across ground that is a mixture of rocky bluffs and knolls, peat and heather.

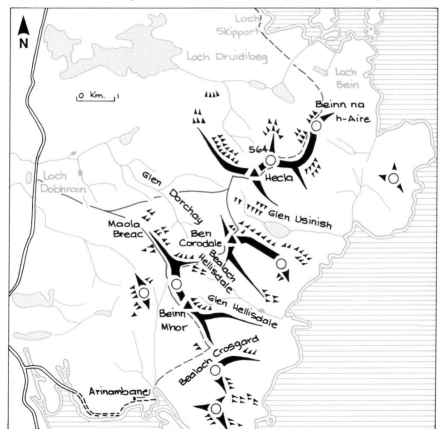

Looking across Uig Bay to Mealisval, with Cracaval on its left   R. Gollin

Mealisval; 574m; (OS Sheet 13; 022270)
Cracaval; 514m; (OS Sheet 13; 030253)

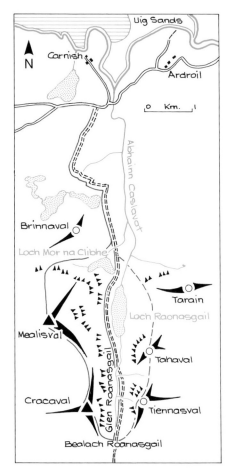

The Uig hills near the west coast of Lewis form a compact group of quite low, but remarkably rough and rocky hills which are well worth a visit. There are about a dozen of them of heights 400m and more, but it is their rugged nature and not their height that give them their individual character. Two ridges run from south to north, separated by Glen Raonasgail and Loch Raonasgail, but the cols between the hills are quite low so that there is a lot of climbing to be done if one wants to traverse them all.

The highest of the Uig hills, and the most prominent in views from the fine sandy bay to their north, is Mealisval on the west side of Loch Raonasgail, and the traverse of it to Cracaval and down to the Bealach Roanasgail is a good introduction to this area. Although it may seem to be a short expedition, the roughness of the terrain and the many crags and cliffs mean that it will probably take longer than expected.

There is a recently made private track starting near the road bridge over the Abhainn Caslavat on the south side of Uig Bay, and going south past Loch Brinnaval and up Glen Raonasgail. This gives quick walking access to Loch Mor na Clibhe at the foot of the north-east face of Mealisval. This face of the hill is very steep and rocky, with a prominent gully, the Palla Glas, in its centre. The broad slabby buttress to the left (E) of the Palla Glas gives a fine scramble on slabby rock, but it is not entirely easy, so the recommended route is to go W past Loch Mor na Clibhe and climb the NW shoulder of Mealisval. (6km; 570m; 2h 20min).

Continue SE along a broad bouldery ridge down to a col at 293m where there are two small lochans and climb the rocky ridge to Cracaval. From there descend easily SE to the Bealach Raonasgail, across which the track goes to Loch Tamanavay. The quickest return is along this track, but those wanting a longer day can traverse the hills on the E side of the glen, Teinnasval and Tahaval, with a descent across the slopes of Tarain above the N end of Loch Raonasgail.

Barra landscape   *G.S. Johnstone*

Heaval; 383m; (OS Sheet 31; 678994)

The island of Barra is quite hilly, as one can see looking north from the sharp summit of Heaval. The ascent of this, the highest and most prominent hill on the island, is easily made from Castlebay, walking up the road from the village NE until past the houses and then climbing directly up steep grassy slopes. The summit itself is rocky, and there is a scramble for those who want one. From Heaval the round of the Barra hills goes over Hartaval, Grianan (from where a short diversion should be made NW to look at the chambered cairn of Dun Bharpa), Ben Verrisey and Beinn Mhartainn. Descend from there to Borve and walk back to Castlebay along the road. This round involves about 15km, almost 1000m of climbing and takes about 5 or 6 hours.

Ben Tangaval in the south-west corner of the island is a pleasant short walk on its own, and the sea-cliffs to its west have some fine natural arches and caves.

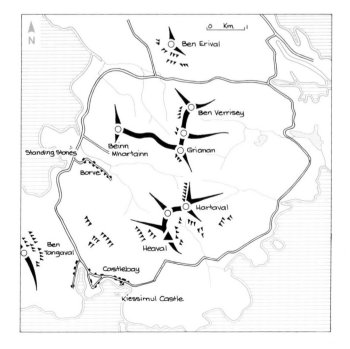

INDEX OF CORBETTS

INDEX OF OTHER HILLS